Pocket Folders p.21
Bulletin Bds. p.27
Put sub folder in dailyfolder (might put location of
sub folder on inside
of daily folder)

- location of
  sub folder
- class list
  w/ stud. #'s
  that match
  desks

p.39 Journal writing @ end of day
p.52 Sign-out sheet for leaving
     room : ex - bathrm
p.53 Practice "coming to order" upon signal
p.54 Turn & talk after presenting concepts
p.55 clipboard monitoring
p.76 Rd. Robin Writing
Written responses on note cds. limit amt. of response

Classrooms that SPARK!
Recharge and Revive Your Teaching

* p.88 Clear & Unclear Window Assessment ☺ + Mind Map Assessment +
     5 "I Learned" Statements (prioritized)

p.91 Portfolio Scale of 1-4 : Correct, Complete, Comprehensive

p.96 Rubric (Scoring Guide) Grading Scale

* p.97 2 grades for writing composition; one for content + one for mechanics

* p.97 Sample Writing Rubric ☺

→ p.100 * Modified Grading Scale *

p.112: Personal Vision Statement; Poem: Pretty Good by Charles Osgood
       State expectations + look each in eye

p.113: Rules - play Is/Is Not

p.115: Object Activity: draw item that you think of when you think of yourself

p.117: Have students do something to display the first day!

☺ p.122: M+M "warm-up" activity

p.127: "Star" Activity (to post)

p.126 Goal Setting: stud. set
       personal goals

Dyan M. Hershman
Emma S. McDonald, M.Ed.

p.128: Team Bldg.

p.143 3 parts of the brain + their function

Classrooms that SPARK!

Recharge and Revive Your Teaching

Emma S. McDonald, M.Ed.
Educator

Dyan M. Hershman
Educator

Inspiring Teachers Publishing, Inc. / Garland, Texas

Classrooms that SPARK!: Recharge and Revive Your Teaching
© 2005 by Emma S. McDonald and Dyan Hershman
ISBN#: 0-9667145-7-1

Library of Congress Cataloging Number: 2004114320

Publisher Cataloging-in-Publication Data

McDonald, Emma S., 1970-
    Classrooms that SPARK!: Recharge and Revive Your Teaching / Inspiring Teachers
Publishing, Inc / 2005
    p. cm.
Includes bibliographic references and index.
Language: English
ISBN 0-9667145-7-1
    1. Teaching - Handbooks, Manuals, etc.   I. Hershman, Dyan.   II. Title.

LB1048   2005
371.1

06 07 08 09 10   10 9 8 7 6 5 4 3 2 1

DEDICATION

This book is dedicated to our loving husbands, Sean and Matt, and our children, Joshua, James, Mason, and Kylie. Without their unfailing support and help this book would not have been possible!

In addition, we'd like to dedicate this book to our parents, Captain and Mrs. Charles O. Barker and Lt. Colonel and Mrs. Michael J. Ferguson. They have given us the drive and discipline to tackle any task with enthusiasm and determination. Without their love and support we would not be the teachers we are today!

We'd also like to dedicate this book to our beloved students who we have taught.

Lastly, we'd like to dedicate this book to our great friend and constant supporter, Rita Bukin. Although she is no longer with us, her constant sense of purpose and boundless energy continues to inspire and sustain us in our quest.

Acknowledgments

We would like to thank the following people for their contributions in terms of sharing experiences, ideas, or offering to review and provide feedback on Classrooms that Spark.

Erica Kruckenberg, Prosper, Texas

Carol Loper, Prosper, Texas

Juddson Smith, Plano, Texas

Tracy Paul, Australia

Connie Skipper, Garland, Texas

Angela Hall, North Ogden, Utah

Grace Yohannan, Orlando, Florida

Dahkine Lee, Hinesville, Georgia

Marci Davis, Davenport, Iowa

Alice Schnepf, Chandler, Arizona

Debbie Meadows, Stevenson Ranch, California

Shirley Ann Fukumoto, Kamuela, Hawaii

Terri Richards, Plano, Texas

Michelle Vaughn, Frisco, Texas

Tamora Mennenga, Mansfield, Texas

Alice McDuffy, Richardson, Texas

Karen Morris, Plan, Texas

Marie Fischer, Houston, Texas

Vicki Thompson, Mesquite, Texas

Nada Itani, Beirut, Lebanon

Suzanne Ryals, Marathon, Florida

Patti Hanlon, Scottsdale, Arizona

Trina Cochrane, Waco, Texas

Barb O'Brien, Ashland, Wisconsin

Table of Contents

1st 08 year seating, etc.

"A teacher affects eternity; he can never tell where his influence stops."
— Henry Adams

Dear Reader,

Fire, so primative and primeval, is at once both fearsome and friendly. It can offer security and warmth from a cold unfriendly night, and yet if it gets out of hand, can become a raging inferno that consumes everything in its path. Each of us looks at fire from a different persepective. We bring in our own memories of fire that color our attitude towards it.

While in college, my friends and I would gather down at the beach for a bonfire every month or so. It was the way we gathered together and became a community. Even though those days are long past, the memories of that fire are still so rich and vibrant in my mind. I can feel the heat of the fire against the cool ocean breeze and smell the sweetness of toasted marshmallows. I can feel the warmth of good friends surrounding me and the security of the bright orange light on the dark beach. Each of these are vivid memories which burn in my memory.

Fires can conjure up passionate and provoking thoughts for some, while providing peace and relaxation for others. *We can enjoy a cup of hot chocolate while resting by a fire on a cold snowy day. Forest fires blaze hot and heavy while putting homes and wildlife in danger. Fire fighters risk life and limb to extinguish this blazing roar of flames. Campers enjoy singing songs and telling stories around the evening campfire.*

A fire, so vast in its existence and ways it is used is such a perfect metaphor for teaching. Teaching is so complex and varied because we each bring to it our own experiences. We add new ideas and remove old ones, we have calm years and tumultuous years, and we feel the ebb and flow for the passion of learning in ourselves and our students. And yet, through everything, we continually fight to keep this fire of teaching burning in our hearts because we know that it makes a difference both in our lives and the lives of our students.

This book is broken into three sections that help build the analogy between teaching & learning and building a strong fire. The first section is "Preparing for the Fire," because as we all know, preparation is one of the keys to a successful classroom. Next, the second section offers ideas and strategies for "Lighting the Fire," helping us spark the love of learning in our students. Finally, the last section, "Fanning the Flames," offers a variety of strategies for maintaining that love of teaching within us and the love of learning within our students.

Whether you need to reignite that spark or simply fan the flames within your classroom, we hope that you will find the ideas and strategies described in this book to be helpful as you work towards rekindling the fire and excitement of learning within you and your students!

Emma and Dyan

Preparing for the Fire

" For the resolute and determined there is time and opportunity."

--- Ralph Waldo Emerson

"He who dares to teach must never cease to learn."

--- John Cotton Dana

Preparations:
Organization and More

Just as we need to find our firewood and stack it neatly to build a good fire, so we need to organize and prepare ourselves for each school year. Many of us begin the year just as harried and frazzled as new teachers because we've just spent a summer either working another job or relaxing and trying to forget about everything. It sometimes feels like we are starting all over. I, for one, just sit and stare at my pile of books, supplies, files, and notebooks for a while just trying to absorb everything that must be done. That doesn't even begin to describe the nightmare associated with anyone who has been forced to move their classroom to another or who has had to pack up everything while the school is under renovations. What to do? The obvious choice is to begin with organization.

Organize your files

The best place to start is by looking at each of your files. Are you still using that particular handout or resource? If so, hang on to it. If it is something that you are loathe to part with, then put it in a special pile of "keepers," but do not keep it in a separate file folder.

"Organization is the key to a successful year"

Do you have a million copies of the same handout? Will you remember that you have 50 copies of this handout? Most likely not. If you are honest with yourself, you'll admit that when it is time to use the handout, you'll have another class set copied. Keep one Master copy and throw the rest in the recycling bin. There is no need to take up precious filing space with extra copies.

Set up Binders

If you find that you have more files than you have room for, consider using a set of binders to hold your materials and "Masters" of handouts and/or transparencies.

Take that pile of "keepers" and separate them into categories by themes. Place your Masters into the appropriate section. Now you can easily find the handout you need.

- Subject areas
- Classroom management
- Assessment tools
- Thematic units
- Special needs strategies
- Gifted/talented strategies
- ESL
- Childhood development
- Learning/Thinking Centers
- Bulletin Boards
- Administrative (memos, policies, etc.)

Set up a Teacher Binder

An excellent way to organize yourself and your units is to create a binder for yourself. Within this binder you can keep your classroom information, lesson plans and handouts organized for each six weeks period. The binder should be organized with tab dividers and contain the following sections:

1. Student information section:

- Student list for your class(es)
- Seating chart
- Textbook records
- ESL and Special Ed lists and schedules
- Student locker and class job information

> *"Keep yourself organized with a three-ring binder."*

2. Calendars/ Schedules section:

- Library
- Counseling
- Computer lab
- Elective/ special areas
- Lunch schedules
- Daily classroom schedule
- A calendar with important district, school, grade level, and personal dates marked.
- Classroom management procedures

3. TEAM Planning section:

- Notes taken during team planning

- Detailed records help keep you safeguarded against problems in the future

4. Extra Forms section:

- Hardcopies of forms used frequently such as parent communication, bonus points, certificates, free homework coupons, etc.

5. Six Weeks Unit section:

- Planning calendar that shows an overview of the entire six weeks

- Six weeks lesson plans and daily handouts

- Keep everything in chronological order to make planning easier the following year

- Transparencies can be attached through hole-punched clear plastic covers – look for these in office supply stores

Set up Course Binders

- Keep one binder for each course you'll be planning (each prep).

- In the front of each should be a planning calendar that shows an overview of the entire grading period.

- Keep everything, including transparencies, in chronological order and utilize tabs for easy reference.

> **Idea Share**
>
> At the end of the six weeks or grading period, transport this section into another three ring binder and clearly label it for future reference with the name of the unit.
>
> If planning units in themes that last less than the grading period, move the "unit" into a new binder as soon as you have completed it.
>
> Many teachers like to plan at home rather than in the classroom. If you have a binder, this will cut down on the number of manila files you will have to take back and forth between school and home. It will also simplify your preparation for the next year.

- The more records you keep, the more you are safeguarded against problems in the future.

- The school's teacher manual is another great place to store memos, newsletters, or other paperwork you receive from the school. Create an additional tabbed section in the notebook if necessary.

"Prioritize your mail as high, moderate, or low priority as soon as you take it out of your box."

"File memos and other papers as soon as you read them."

Make a Substitute Folder

Taking the time to put together a folder for substitutes is an excellent way to stay organized when you are absent from school. We are each judged on how well our classroom runs even when we are not there. It is in our best interest to make things easier for a substitute who is a guest teacher in our school.

Across the nation there has been a huge shortage of substitute teachers available. The biggest reason for this deficit of "guest teachers" is the lack of respect and support from school staff and faculty. This includes a lack of prior preparation, communication, and acknowledgment.

One way you can ensure that substitutes will want to come to your classroom is to provide them with detailed plans, instructions, and classroom policies/procedures. If these necessary tools are readily accessible, the substitute teacher will be more comfortable and confident about leading your class through the day. This will more than likely result in a problem free day for both the substitute and the students!

When leaving instructions for guest teachers, be sure to offer detailed explanations of how your classroom management system works. When you determine your classroom procedures and motivational techniques, be sure to type and place them, not only in your teacher binder, but also in the substitute folder.

You also want to have alternative plans that can be used at any time during the year. Often grade levels, departments, or teams plan for special units or lessons that require everyone to have full participation. If you are absent, your team may decide to do different lessons on that day.

Also, the school may call for an assembly or another type of event may occur, disrupting your scheduled plans. If you have alternate plans which are easy to implement and follow, your substitute will have a much easier time of adapting to an unexpected situation.

Additionally, your substitute may not understand your plans and may not feel qualified to implement lessons or activities. Having alternate plans with hand-outs ready alleviates this potential frustration for the substitute and students.

"Returning to the classroom after an absence can be either a pleasure or a pain depending on how prepared you are for having a substitute teacher in your class."

Checklist for Substitute Folder

You may be able to get a Sub folder from a teacher store or your school secretary. However, if you cannot find a pre-made folder, it is very easy to make your own out of a manila or pocket folder. The following items should be included:

_____ **Seating chart**

_____ **Class schedule**

_____ **Easy stable lesson plans**
   -substitutes tend to work best with paper/pencil activities that can be easily monitored and explained.

_____ **Daily instructions**
   -classroom procedures explained in detail, lunch schedule for teacher and students, and students who are pulled out for special classes.

_____ **Class roll**

_____ **Sponge activities/ creative writing ideas**
   -just in case they finish lesson early

_____ **A form for them to report back to you**

_____ **Helpful students**

_____ **Names and room numbers of grade level/team members**

_____ **A copy of Emergency procedures (ex: Fire drill, lockdown, Hurricane, etc.)**

Idea Share

Type out your classroom procedures and other information that will not change too much over time. Save this file for future reference. Next year you can open the file, make the necessary changes, print it out, and you are ready to place the new information into your substitute folder.

Use a generic response form using Bloom's Taxonomy that can be used for any type of reading, both fiction and non-fiction. See the form in the back of the Reading/Writing chapter for reference. Have a class set of this form in your substitute folder ready for use. Be sure to replenish your supply when you return to school. See pages **148** and **195** for a description of Bloom's Taxonomy.

Substitute Report Form

DATE: _____

TODAY WE...

Use this space to report what was actually done during class. What activities did you do, how much of the lesson plans did you cover, what else did you do that was not on the original lesson plan, etc..

The following problems occurred:

Use this space to describe any serious misbehavior or other problems. Be specific and report the facts without emotion. Use the back of this page if necessary.

Problem: Action Taken:

Problem: Action Taken:

Problem: Action Taken:

Problem: Action Taken:

The following students were exceptionally good and/or helpful:

Dealing with Piles of Paperwork

Have you ever seen the cartoon drawing that shows a desk piled high with paperwork and a tiny hand waving above it as though someone were drowning? That's how I often feel when I get overwhelmed by the tons of papers put in my box throughout the year. The most important thing to do is to begin building positive habits that will keep this to a minimum. Here are our strategies for dealing with the paperwork issue:

1)   As soon as you check your mailbox, take 5-10 minutes to either file, respond, or trash each item. Go ahead and record the date(s) from memos, bulletins, etc. in your calendar along with any other pertinent information. Once this information is in your calendar, you can either file it or pitch it. If you are lucky enough to have a computer in your classroom, the Microsoft Outlook calendar is a wonderful tool to use. It can pop up the calendar and tasks (to do) items as soon as you turn on your computer.

> **Idea Share**
>
> Create a Classroom Resources section in your Teacher Binder (or a new file folder). In this section place any pages/order forms for items that you want to order for your classroom. This helps keep the catalogs from stacking up. Be sure that the contact information for the company is on the page. If it isn't, use a label or sticky tab to record the information before tossing the catalog.

If you get something that needs a response, go ahead and respond to it. When you put these things off till later, they never get done and just end up in a pile on your desk. If it requires a lengthy response, then schedule a time on your calendar to respond to it either during your planning time or after school. Put this item into a special folder so that you don't forget.

2)   Use your system for filing paperwork! Most of us have set up some sort of system for keeping files. Whether you use manila folders or a 3-ring binder with tabbed sections, go ahead and use it!

The most important thing to remember when dealing with paperwork is to get it taken care of as soon as possible. If you let it go, it will pile up on you and take forever to work through. Although it is hard to give 5-15 minutes away to responding to notes, memos, etc., it saves hours in the long run. Set aside time to do this either during your planning period or after school. Set aside a letter tray or plastic bin to hold your daily mail stack.

Website for staying organized

If you are someone who continually has issues with staying organized, we strongly recommend that you check out the website, FlyLady.com (www.flylady.com). This website is dedicated to helping people get and stay organized. Although it is mostly for the home, it does have many strategies that will help you in the classroom as well. Fly Lady stresses the importance of taking baby steps and building good habits. A few FlyLady-like tips from us would be:

*   Set a timer for 15 minutes each morning to work through your paperwork
*   Do today's mail before you do past mail
*   Do as much of the past mail in the 15 minutes that you can
*   When the timer goes off, stop and put all the past mail in a large tub (on the floor)
*   Repeat this same process in the afternoon

If you try to do too much at once, you'll get burned out. That is why baby steps are so important!

Getting Students Organized

Organization is an important life skill that should be taught and reinforced throughout a student's academic career. Spending time on training students in organizational skills through student binders, folders, lockers, and desks is time well spent. Use the beginning of the school year to make student organization a focus, not only during "homeroom" or advisory time, but also in your lessons.

Student Binder

It is important that students begin the year in an organized fashion. Teachers can help their students do this by requiring them to set up a binder. Here are a few tips on creating an organized binder:

√ Use tabbed sections. The best way is to organize them in the order you teach each subject.

√ Middle school students should order their sections according to their schedule.

√ Have students keep graded work in the appropriate subject area.

"Organization is a key element of Classroom Management "

√ An assignment calendar should be in the very front of the binder.

√ Class or school rules, procedures and syllabus should be placed behind the calendar.

It is important that you check the binders regularly (every six weeks will work). Sometimes it is helpful to take a grade for an organized binder. This will motivate students to continue using it correctly.

Teacher Talk

"One year I had an assistant principal who helped us keep the students accountable for their binders staying organized. She would dress up, every couple of weeks or so, as the "Binder Fairy" and do snap inspections on everyone's binder. You never knew what she would be dressed in - army fatigues, a ballerina tutu, a clown outfit, "biker" clothes, a poodle skirt - but always with a pair of fairy wings and a wand. For everyone who had a neat and organized binder, she would present them with a gift certificate of some sort. The kids loved it and it really kept many of them motivated to stay organized with their binder. I would often say to my kids, "I wonder if the Binder Fairy will come to class today," and they would all scramble to make sure their binder was in order."

Pocket Folders

In addition to the binder, it is helpful for students to keep and use separate pocket folders that STAY in the classroom. Color coding these folders will help with quick and easy access for each activity/subject area.

Writing Journal

Students place paper in the middle. Then they date and write their daily journal entry. In order not to waste paper, I encourage my students to use up an entire page before beginning a new one. There could be several entries on a page.

Writing Workshop Folder   (Nancic Atwell, 1992)

Students keep notes for Writing Workshop in the middle of the folder, Prewriting/Drafts in front pocket, Works in Progress in back pocket. Final copy will go in the Writing Portfolio. We will discuss Writing Workshop in greater detail in the Reading/Writing chapter.

Test Taking Skills Folder

Students place paper in the middle to keep notes on test taking strategies covered in class. Practice sheets, scan-trons, and answer keys should be kept in the pockets.

Reading Workshop Folder (Nancie Atwell, 1992)

Students keep a reading log that includes title, author, pages read and a short summary as well as a reading response. Students may also keep their book project work in this folder. We will discuss Reading Workshop in the Reading/Writing chapter.

Student Log

Students use this pocket folder to turn in any major projects. Any data collected and drafts should be placed in the front pocket to show the process of their work. The final copy of the project should be placed in the middle of the folder with any bulky or odd sized papers/products placed in the back pocket.

Teacher Talk

"A few years ago it was driving me crazy that my students kept losing their writing samples. In my Language Arts classes, we do several drafts on different topics throughout the semester. Towards the end of the grading period, I have the students to pick one draft to turn into a final copy. Half of my students could never find their previous work! Finally, I got smart and insisted that the students leave their writing in the classroom in a writing folder. Then all of my students were able to locate their drafts when it came time to choose. This made my life so much less frazzled!"

Manila Folders

Writing Portfolio

This manila folder is used to hold student writing pieces. Nancie Atwell, in her book In The Middle , describes an excellent way to set up a writing portfolio. This is a great way to track the progress of a student's writing skills throughout the year. A simple portfolio collects student work to be reviewed at the end of the year. Later in the book we will further discuss and give examples of the use of portfolios.

General Portfolio

This manila folder is used to hold student work of all kinds. Students should have some choice as to the works placed in this folder. Also, when students enter work into their portfolio, they should attach a 3x5 index card with comments about their product. These comments should tell the teacher whether the piece is the student's "best" work, a "work in progress," or a sample to show how they have improved over time (this can include their "worst" work also).

Thinking Folder

This manila folder is used as a place to hold enrichment work. Students who complete learning center activities on their own can place the products into their thinking folder to be graded for extra credit. In our Teaching Strategies Chapter we discuss how to set up learning centers for all age/grade levels.

Absent Folder

This manila folder is used to collect work and assignments for students who are absent. Have a student work as a "scribe" to copy down board assignments, homework, notes, and any other important information/activities done during class on a specific absent form that you use consistently all year. The student should place this form along with any handouts in the absent folder and place it on the absentee's desk. The teacher could be the "scribe" if necessary. This folder is a great way to help students get back on track when they return to school.

Student information

This manila folder is for teacher purposes. This is the perfect place to keep student and parent communication records.

> "Manila folders are of great
> value for teachers and students.
> They are economical and can
> be used in so many ways!"

Create Student Mailboxes

Each student should have a place to call their own in the classroom to keep folders, novels, papers, and personal supplies organized. This "mailbox" doesn't have to be a large tub or box. An inexpensive way to create mailboxes is to get plastic crates and hanging file folders with tabs. This works well for middle school teachers as well.

√ Mailboxes are handy for storing school supplies on the first day of school before students begin using them.

√ They work very nicely for handing out graded papers without taking up class time to do so.

√ When students are working on research or group projects, mailboxes are a good place to keep class work so it won't get lost.

> **Teacher Talk**
>
> *"For the longest time my classroom was in a constant state of chaos with papers and supplies floating around everywhere. I finally decided to get organized and set up mailboxes. I used hanging file folders and dedicated one for each student in my class. Students keep their journals, books, and unfinished folders in their mailbox. I also keep a folder labeled "graded work" in each. Once a day either I or my teacher helpers file graded student work into these folders. The students can then pull the work out of that folder and put it in their binder to take home. It has really kept the classroom less messy and I don't feel like I'm wasting class time every day to pass back student work!"*

Day of the Week folders

Day of the week folders are an invaluable tool for classroom organization. As teachers, we are faced with the challenge of staying organized on a day-to-day basis. Day of the week folders help us manage paperwork and materials in two main ways:

1. A place to hold materials

- During the week, as you plan for lessons later that week or the following week, you will begin to gather materials such as copies of handouts, etc.

    > *Example: Tuesday during your planning period you research information, gather materials, and make copies for Thursday's lesson. Immediately you place these materials in the Thursday folder so that they are ready to be used. Otherwise, they end up in piles on your desk, cause clutter, and often are lost when you need them!*

- If you have a special test or form for students to complete on Friday, stick these in your Friday folder

- If you have a field trip on Wednesday, then put all of the necessary information, forms, entrance tickets, etc., into the Wednesday folder.

2. Relieves Stress and Promotes Professional Appearance

Situation: You have a flat tire on the way to work Tuesday morning, and your principal must tend your class for an hour or so until you arrive, which would he/she appreciate more?

a)   A mass of papers are piled on the desk with your lesson plans somewhere in your room, but she doesn't know where they are.

b)   A Tuesday folder is placed neatly on your desk with lesson plans, warm-up activities, materials, copies, and a substitute folder inside, all ready to go.

Using Day of the Week folders not only gives you a more professional appearance, but you will actually feel more calm and prepared every morning when you follow these Day of the Week folder guidelines. It truly makes for a smooth start to every day. Try the following:

- Get everything ready for the next day BEFORE you leave the classroom. Set up your chalkboard with the date, agenda, objectives, and warm-up activity.

- Prepare your Day of the Week folder to be used the following day. Be sure your lesson plans and materials for the day are inside.

- Lay it flat on your desk so that it is the first thing you or anyone else sees when approaching your desk. Put the sub folder in last (on the bottom), just in case.

Idea Share

Use plastic shoe boxes with lids to store supplies such as scissors, crayons, tape, math manipulatives, etc..

These also make great storage places for supplies used by student groups. Label each box with the table number or name so that students can easily locate the supply box for their group.

Secondary Strategy

1) Create a different folder for each class you teach. For example, a teacher who has two sessions of English 101 and three sessions of American Lit will have two of each daily folder.

2) Be sure you label each folder with the title of the class for easy reference.

3) Folders not in use should stay in the filing cabinet in a hanging folder for each day. If you use hanging files with a gusset, you'll be able to make copies of handouts ahead of time and store them in the appropriate place.

Setting up the Day of the Week folders

Use manila folders and label each one with the day of the week (ie - Monday, Tuesday, etc.). Use different colored folders to color code each day of the week.

You need to:

- Laminate the folders so that they will last all year long.

- Put a stand-up file holder on your desk to hold the folders in an easily accessible place.

- Put all materials for each day's lesson in the folder. (ie - copies, lesson plans, newsletter, activities, etc.)

- Before you leave each day, place your substitute folder inside your day of the week folder in case you are absent.

Set up your Classroom

It is always a good idea to reflect on the effectiveness of your classroom setup each year. Look at the questions below to help you decide whether or not it is time to make a change.

- Make a sketch of your classroom as it is.

- Think about how the layout worked last year. Are there any changes that need to be made? What were the problems? What worked well?

- Make necessary changes to your sketch.

- Think about the flow of your room. Where do you want your students looking? Where is your overhead screen, presentation station, chalkboard, and bulletin board? How do you think your changes will affect these aspects?

- Try it out and see how it works.

Ask yourself:

- Is my current setup working? If not, should I change to rows or groups of desks?

- Should I use tables? Would they be more effective with my teaching style or subject area?

- How easily am I able to move between students?

- Can we all get out of the classroom quickly in an emergency?

- Do I have/want a writing center?

- Do I have/want a reading corner?

- Do I have/want learning centers?

- Do I have/want an arts area?

"Your room reflects your personality and teaching style. What does your room say about you as a teacher?"

- Do I have/want a time-out or conference area?

- Should I have a computer station? If I do, where will it go?

- How does my teacher area look?

  - Is my desk, filing cabinet, and/or shelves in the way of the flow?
  - Are my curriculum materials easily accessible?
  - Can I visually monitor students if at my desk?

The environment we create for our students is equally as important as the content we teach and the learning strategies we use. This applies to all teachers of all age groups from pre-school to graduate school. The environment includes the atmosphere, the traditions we set, the furniture arrangement, the centers or special areas within the room, and the decorations. All of these things add up to create either a positive or negative environment for students.

On the previous page we discussed classroom layout, furniture, and setting aside special areas for student use. Here we will discuss classroom traditions, attitudes, and decorations to help create a positive learner-centered environment.

1) Students should feel welcomed and inspired to learn from the moment they walk through your door.

- Decorate Your door with a theme or slogan. Some examples include:

-Welcome to a Beary Special Place   -Blasting off to Learning
-Come Explore Learning in Room 32   -Soar the Heights
-A class slogan such as:
    "Learning is Victory!" or "Learning=Success!" or
    "Using Our Minds to Conquer the World!"

- Greet students with a smile.

2) Create traditions within your classroom.
These are fun actions or events that students look forward to experiencing each day or week.

"What kind of traditions do you use in your classroom?"

- Every Friday we read from our *Acts of Kindness* box.
- Whenever we read a story, one student gets to introduce the reader.
- Mrs. M. always sings a silly song right before the end of class.

3) Classroom walls and bulletin boards are covered with thought provoking and stimulating material.

- Motivational posters
- Language rich
- Humorous posters
- Manners and Character Building posters

Remember:
Students will be more motivated to learn in an environment that is stimulating.

Blank Walls = Blank Minds

Bulletin Board Ideas

You may have some tried and true bulletin boards that you use each year, but it is always nice to do something different every now and then. Here are a few different ideas to add to your file. Also, think about different ways you can take the ideas below and get your students involved in locating information and creating their own bulletin boards. This encourages higher level thinking and creativity. Don't forget about using bulletin boards as mini "Thinking Centers" or "Learning Centers" with activities students can complete.

- Quotable Quotes

- What's New - to post classroom, school, community, and world events

- Birthday board - post student birthdays or a class birthday graph

- Centers - Use a board to post brain challenges or learning center activities for students to complete

- Miss Manners - posting manners posters or tips of etiquette

- Famous Authors - teacher can post information or have students research 1 author and post their findings on the board.

- Famous Mathematicians, Scientists, Artists, Musicians, Sports figures, People in History (same as above)

- Careers

- Highlight a concept being taught

- See What We're Doing - post student work

- Who's Who in Room___ (spotlight students & their work)

- Who Am I? - show a baby picture and offer clues. Students guess who that person is

- Classroom Expectations

- Class Slogan

- Theme - changes with each unit

- Creative writing/ journaling - post laminated calendar pictures showing landscapes and other types of images to help stimulate student writing.

Before School Checklist

_____ Laminate supplies

_____ Set up room
    _____ arrange desks/tables
    _____ set up reading corner
    _____ set up other special areas (writing center, learning centers, etc.)
    _____ post classroom expectations and consequences posters
    _____ organize filing cabinets

_____ Set up student mailboxes/cubbies

_____ Create Day of the Week folders

_____ Create individual student folders

_____ Set up gradebook

_____ Write welcome postcards to students
    _____ mail postcards/letter

_____ Create a class schedule

_____ Create a substitute folder

_____ Organize a Teacher Binder

_____ Write out lesson plans for first day
    _____ second day?
    _____ third day?

_____ Meet with grade level or academic department

_____ Meet with special education and special areas teachers (as needed)

_____ Meet with mentee (as needed)

Conclusion

There are so many different tasks that must be done before school starts; it can be overwhelming for us. However, these tasks are necessary to ensure that we start the year well-prepared. As we know, the more prepared we are at the beginning of school the more effective we are throughout the year. It is important to keep in mind that the more time you spend in your classroom before school starts, the more you will get done and the better prepared you will be. If you are really interested in revitalizing your classroom, now is the time to brainstorm and make that extra effort.

Questions to Ponder

What is included in your substitute folder? Could you add anything else to make the transition easier on the "guest teacher" and your students when you are absent?

Is the Day of the Week folder a concept you feel you could implement in your classroom? How would you adapt it to fit your needs?

Do you think you have a positive learner centered environment in your classroom? If not, what could you do to create a stimulating learning atmosphere?

Do you feel prepared to start the school year? What do you always feel has been left undone? How could you rearrange your priorities so that those items are completed?

Additional Resources

Wonderful Rooms Where Children Can Bloom
by Jean Feldman

So Much Stuff, So Little Space: Creating and Managing the Learner Centered Classroom
by Susan Nations, Suzi Boyett, Steven Dragon

Begin With the Brain: Orchestrating the Learner-Centered Classroom
by Martha Kaufeldt

Sink Reflections
by Margaret Cilley

The Organizing Sourcebook: Nine Strategies for Simplifying Your Life
by Kathy Waddill

Notes/Reflections on Chapter

Creating a Balanced Classroom Environment

In order to have a roaring fire, you must have just the right elements. If the fireplace is too drafty or you have wet firewood, the fire will never start. It is the same in the classroom. It is vital to build a balanced classroom environment where students can learn. In order to do this you need to nurture certain elements. These elements include our surroundings, our leadership style, our daily procedures, and our relationships with students. Since we've covered the physical aspect of our classroom, we'll take a look at the last three in this chapter.

As teachers, we are much more than just babysitters, managers, and timekeepers. We are also leaders. This role has much more importance than most realize on the overall classroom climate. A leader guides, shapes, teaches, motivates, corrects, directs, and encourages his/her "platoon." In a teacher's case, the proper leadership style is crucial so that chaos doesn't rule.

We also need to make sure that we have routines and procedures in place to begin building healthy habits from the first day. It is important to have those routines clearly defined ourselves in order to communicate them to our students.

Lastly, we need to strive for positive relationships with our students - one that has clear expectations, but is based on mutual respect, communication and kindness. Just because we are in control and expect appropriate behavior does not mean that we need to be cold or distant.

Throughout this chapter you will see that we can create a positive and motivating classroom environment by:

√ Being proactive
√ Being organized
√ Being well-prepared
√ Effectively communicating our desires and expectations
√ Understanding that students cannot read our minds
√ Having a positive and not hurtful sense of humor
√ Having a good rapport with students

Classroom Leadership Styles

The three main leadership styles teachers use in the classroom are:

Teacher as Dictator
Teacher as Free-Spirit
Teachers as Balanced Leader

Teacher as Dictator

The teacher who acts as a dictator is often afraid of losing control, so he/she resorts to maintaining a very distant and stringent relationship with students. This often results in a relationship that is businesslike, firm, and authoritarian.

Characteristics of a Dictator Leadership Style:

- No room for group discussions or banter of any sort

- Routines are strictly adhered to

- Flexibility is not commonplace

"The Dictator Leadership style does not promote a positive classroom climate."

- Tasks are performed in a quiet and efficient manner

- Students are not encouraged to be individuals and active participants in the lesson

- Students are required to conform to the teacher's way of learning

- Creative thinking is not encouraged

- Memorization and "skill and drill" are the main learning styles of this classroom

Although predictability and routine can be a positive classroom feature, this type of leadership is often boring and squelches creativity. It promotes a dull and resentful environment instead of one filled with active learning and excitement.

Rarely does a teacher accomplish a smooth running classroom by resorting to dictatorship. Students are more likely to rebel, complain, and misbehave because they are not intrinsically motivated.

In addition, when student resentment occurs, often times parental concerns arise. *Is the teacher being fair? Is she too demanding? Is my child's dislike of the teacher justified? What will the teacher think of me as a parent?* These concerns can be barriers to a positive parent partnership.

Teacher as Free Spirit

An ingredient in the free-spirit recipe is a teacher who is more than likely unorganized and unprepared which results in a choppy and incomplete presentation. Students are kept waiting while the teacher mentally decides what to do next and looks for materials. Students get confused and distracted easily which results in disruption after disruption. This in turn results in more "breaks" as the teacher must stop to deal with unruly behavior.

Characteristics of a Free Spirit Leadership Style:

- Teacher wants to be a "buddy" with the students rather than an authority figure.

- Students end up making most classroom decisions without guidance.

- Lesson plans are loosely sketched and student digressions dictate the course of the lesson rather than the teaching objective.

- Students are given maximum freedom to work and move about the classroom.

- The teacher gives the students the responsibility to make the decisions by themselves, in other words to "be their own boss."

- When students are not actively engaged in learning, this teacher is often quick to anger because he/she feels they are giving students freedoms which are being abused.

This leadership style would be fabulous in a world where all students had the same set of values—honesty, integrity, responsibility, and determination. We would love for every classroom to be totally student centered, where students were always intrinsically motivated. However, this is unrealistic. It is the nature of most children to push the limits as far as they can. Therefore, this laissez-faire, or lax, style of leadership will most likely be a recipe for disaster and anarchy.

Parents are apprehensive of this "loose" classroom environment and wonder what kind of education their child is getting. Will my child be able to keep up in future years after a year of "fun and games?" What learning objectives are being met? Is this chaos with purpose or simply a lack of preparation on the part of the teacher? This can affect the appearance of the teacher as a professional. These concerns can act as a barrier to a positive relationship with both students and parents.

"The Laissez-Faire Leadership style does not promote a positive classroom climate."

Teacher as Balanced Leader

This leadership style blends both of the other styles to achieve the greatest results. As they say, "Everything in moderation." A teacher using this balanced approach to classroom management will:

- Set limits
- Communicate expectations clearly
- Follow routines and procedures
- Provide students with freedoms and responsibilities
- Offer choice
- Value students
- Invite student involvement on a daily basis

Other Characteristics of a Balanced Leadership Style:

- Is organized in order to maintain a productive classroom.

- Maintains discipline as a key component to this teacher-student relationship.

- Encourages students to be responsible for their own actions and holds them accountable.

- Allows students to be actively involved in the classroom.

- Explains and reinforces clear expectations from the first day of school.

- Consequences are consistent when behavior is inappropriate.

- Students feel valued and motivated.

- Students are given freedoms and choices in order to discuss, move, and work about the classroom freely.

Students tend to be much more cooperative with this classroom environment because they feel respected, appreciated, and valued. This leads to students who are intrinsically motivated! In addition, parents are more apt to discuss concerns with the teacher knowing that action will be taken and they will not be judged for their home situation.

Idea Share:

Discuss the use of choice with parents as a way of motivating and discipling students at home. Choice is a very powerful tool which is not utilized as often as it should. Parents who use this tool at home are teaching children to make positive decisions in their lives and to self-regulate their behavior.

Creating a "Balanced" Classroom Environment

As we just discussed, the balanced leadership style results in a balanced classroom which creates a non-threatening environment where students and teachers feel safe. This comfort allows students to be better learners.

In providing a balanced classroom, teachers need to be prepared to accept additional roles of:

- Mediator
- Tutor
- Leader
- Caregiver
- Listener
- Problem solver
- Disciplinarian

Accepting that you have these roles is the key to having positive student relationships. How does one manage to perform all of those roles as well as the tasks required of us as teachers? The answer is effective time management and organization.

Classrooms are very complex, busy places! During a typical day we are required to perform many tasks:

- Organize learning activities
- Present lessons
- Prepare materials
- Manage student behavior
- Manage classroom equipment
- Handle administrative/housekeeping duties
- Beat the Clock!

All of this must be accomplished while being interrupted for various reasons, such as assemblies, intercom announcements, office assistants, helping a sick student or getting a brand new one!

The challenges we face daily often wear us down over time. The remainder of this chapter is dedicated to providing strategies for recharging your classroom management style so that you can have a balanced and positive classroom environment.

| Quick Tips on Successful Classroom Management |

Below are some quick "refresher" tips and ideas for classroom management. Many of these you are already doing in your classroom. Some ideas may be new to you, and some may be "oldies, but goodies" that need to be unearthed and used again.

√   Read up on Brain-based learning. This research clearly shows how a non-threatening environment increases student learning and leads to open communication between teachers and students. See our discussion in the Teaching Strategies Chapter.

√   Distinguish between "Teacher Time" vs. "Student Time." A productive classroom allows for teachers to instruct without interruptions, and then gives students opportunities for debriefing, disscusing and assimilating the new information.

√   When joking with students, be sure to set a limit and end with a phrase such as, "Well, that was fun, but now it's time for us to get back to work. Everyone needs to focus on chapter…" Remember that all humor should be free of derogatory references and sarcasm.

√   Use eye contact to make sure that everyone has understood the move from "play time" to "work time."

√   You'll find that when your lessons are motivating for students, they beg to stay in the classroom!

√   Post basic classroom procedures so that in the beginning students and parents know what to expect and can become accustomed to your classroom management style.

√   When students are actively participating in classroom activities which are meaningful and motivating, they are too focused to misbehave.

√   Students crave consistency. Your class will run smoothly if students always know what to expect.

√   Consistent behavior builds trust.

√   Trust then builds respect.

√   Frustration builds when students are confused. When frustration builds, behavior breaks down. Don't let this happen to you! Structure your daily routines!

√   Personal choice and group discussions are daily occurrences in a classroom which thrives on student involvement.

Being Prepared Every Day

Students can immediately tell when the teacher is not in control due to lack of planning. When this happens the class quickly becomes rowdy or unmanageable. As we get more and more comfortable with our teaching it also becomes easier to put off preparing for lessons until the last minute. This can cause extra stress and ultimately can result in not being as prepared as we should for each class. Below are some tips/reminders to help us stay on track.

Planning Lessons

√ Stay a little longer after school in order to plan and prepare for the next day. (Use the Day of the Week folders explained in the previous chapter)

√ Before you start an activity, all materials should be organized and ready.

√ Never use class time to prepare for the lesson.

√ Always prepare warm-up assignments and sponge activities ahead. Write them in your lessons and prepare your board ahead!

Plan for Transition Times

Don't just let things happen! Take time in your lesson plans to decide what you expect and give appropriate directions to students. This includes transitions between activities and classes. Otherwise chaos can occur. It is helpful to have these procedures or directions written down in the lesson plans or posted in the room so a substitute will know how your classroom operates.

Between activities/ When students are finished

- Clapping rhythms - (helps to focus students on you)
- Circle time - (have primary students meet in a common area)

- Straighten up
- Logic Puzzles
- Jig-saw puzzle
- Silent reading
- Thinking Games
- Read Aloud

Primary Idea Share:

Tape letters to the floor in your "circle" area and assign each student a specific letter to go to when you meet up again. You could also use colors, numbers, or shapes.

You might even think about putting up a "Finished" Poster that lists what activities are acceptable for students to do if they finish their class work early.

Between classes, lunch, recess, or even activities as a class:

- Quiet game
- Quick questions (for Math, Science, Geography, etc.)
- True or False Facts
- Vocabulary/Spelling Review (one students says one letter as you go down the line)
- Other "sponge" or ice-breaker activities *(See next chapter)*

Create a Calm and Welcoming Climate

Maintain Your Composure

Create a classroom climate that is calm by not overreacting to situations or problems that arise. Stay alert for behavioral problems and initiate strategies to dissolve the problem before it gets worse. Saying hello to each student as you check their calendar or focus assignment gives you a chance to assess potential issues.

Avoid Yelling

When you find yourself losing your temper, turn around and count to ten or take several deep breaths while you close your eyes. This will help you remain calm and focused. Yelling only makes things worse. It upsets students and causes them to lose respect for you. Also, increasing the volume does nothing more than add to an already chaotic situation.

Use Non-Verbal Cues

Use a quiet signal to help students focus on you while you are giving directions. This allows you to use a quiet and deliberate voice. We often have a tendency to want to continue speaking because we are aware that there is limited time for our teaching. However, do not speak until EVERYONE is silent and looking at you. In the long run, this will earn you more teaching time as the year progresses.

Redirect Inapproprate Behavior Immediately

Unnecessary commotion must not rule your classroom. If things get out of control, rely on your non-verbal cues, such as eye contact or a quiet signal, to bring things back to order. Ignoring the situation does not work as effectively as redirection.

Keep Students Actively Engaged in Learning Activites

"Busy hands are happy hands," our grandmothers always say. Challenge students and keep them involved with lessons by planning meaningful activities that have connections to other subject areas and real life.

Give students project type activities where they must create some sort of a product. This can be as simple as a scavenger hunt of important concepts within a chapter, or as complex as a diorama and oral presentation.

We offer specific strategies for this in the latter half of this book! Please read on!

"When Students are interested and engaged, behavior problems are at a minimum and positive student - teacher relationships are at a maximum."

Dealing with your regular classroom duties with efficiency and calmness allows for positive student relationships. Students feel flustered and uneasy when their teacher is in a panicked or unorganized state. Too much unstructured time or too many pauses in instruction result in misbehavior. Also, loss of respect and trust for the teacher can result in additional misconduct. Here are some tips to help you streamline your classroom routines.

Have Specific Procedures Every Day

It is important to have procedures ready for students to follow upon entering the classroom from the very first day. Examples of daily routines which need teacher expectations and procedures:

- What to do before the bell rings
- Checking attendance
- Giving directions
- Collecting classwork and homework
- Distributing materials/ papers
- Bathroom breaks during class
- Transition times between lessons/activities
- Working on projects
- Reading workshop
- Writing workshop
- End of the day

"Having procedures in place saves stress."

Teacher Talk

"My first year of teaching 5th grade I had a horrible feeling at the end of every day! It seemed like chaos as students grabed their backpacks and began shoving everything inside! Some students were asking me questions about homework, while other students were responding to a lesson we had just finished, and most students were excitedly chatting with each other about after school activities. I felt so scattered and disjointed when the bell rang and the students rushed the door. After several weeks of this, I decided to enact an End of the Day Routine that we would follow everyday. If the procedure wasn't followed, then students didn't get to leave my classroom. This included cleaning up the room, copying homework into their daily planner, packing up their backpacks, and then writing quietly in their journal until the bell rang. I gave them topics that provided closure to my lesson or that stimulated interest for the next day. When the bell rang, we all sat in silence until I said "Go!" Then they put their journals away and off they went! I felt so much more collected and relaxed at the end of the day from then on!"

> • Follow your procedures religiously. You may want to post them so that students can see what to do every day.
>
> • Procedure posters will help students and substitutes throughout the year (Susan Kovalik, 1997).
>
> • Sample procedure posters that you may use can be found in the back of this chapter.

An example morning procedure (intermediate grades):

1. Check student mailbox & get out Journal, Math folder, and graded work
2. Get supply box & supplies
3. Sharpen pencil
4. Copy homework in calendar
5. Copy Word of the Day
6. Write in Journal
7. Complete other Morning assignments

An example opening class procedure (Secondary):

1. Check student mailbox, retrieve graded work and class materials
2. Get class or lab supplies, if necessary
3. Sharpen pencil
4. Copy homework in calendar
5. Complete focus assignment

An example morning procedure (primary grades):

1. Put backpack on hook
2. Get folders and book
3. Check "Cubby"
4. Sit at desk
5. Begin D.E.A.R. time

Other Sample Procedures

Writing & Reading Workshop Procedure:

1. Get your writing folder, reading folder, and novel from your mailbox
2. Be ready to take notes
3. When writing, write quietly for the entire 20 minutes.
4. When reading, quietly get your book and reading folder. Find a place to read.
5. When time is up, record your reading in your reading log and answer the reading response on the board
6. Put your materials back into your mailbox.

Beginning of Class Procedures

√ Have the chalkboard, an overhead transparency, or your presentation station made out with important information and morning assignments.

√ Students should enter the classroom, begin copying important announcements, and work on morning assignments.

√ Some possible warm up assignments are daily journal, daily vocabulary words, daily oral language, daily math and daily geography activities.

√ For the middle school teacher, warm ups, or sponge activities should not last longer than 10 minutes.

√ Students should KNOW every day to come in and get busy with their morning work.

Here are a few examples of how you could set up your chalkboard or presentation station before class begins.

ELEMENTARY SCHOOL

Objectives:	Date:
Homework:	Agenda:
Journal:	
Words of the Day:	

Idea Share:

A detailed, well-organized board will keep you and your students on track!

It also prevents those pesky questions of "What are we doing next?"

"Setting up the board for the next day before going home reduces stress in the morning."

You can adapt this board to fit any grade level. Knowing your objectives are equally important in Kindergarten as they are in the upper grades!

Teacher Tip: If you are using a thought-provoking introduction and want students to be guided into discovering the objective rather than being told, leave it off the board until after the activity is finished. Then, review the objective with students and write it on the board.

Secondary Guidelines

√   Type up a sheet with the date, class objectives, class agenda, any project or homework assignments, due dates, and the focus assignment for the day. Be sure you type up one per prep (course taught).

√   Type up this sheet along with your lesson plans so that everything is ready at the same time. Do not wait until the night before to type up your Beginning of Class Information.

√   Get some copier transparencies. You might also try finding transparencies for laser or ink jet printers. Copy these typed sheets onto a transparency.

√   Place each sheet in the Day of the Week folder with the appropriate lesson plans and other materials.

√   This cuts down on having to change board information in between each class period. Simply put the new course transparency on the overhead and you are ready to go.

Administrative Routines

These are our daily routines where we check attendance, check the academic calendar, and complete other "housekeeping" tasks while students are engaged in another learning activity. A good time to take care of these tasks is while students are completing their focus assignment.

Ideas for Checking Attendance

√   One easy way to do this is to use a seating chart, check who is missing and record it.

√   Another method which works well with teachers who group students together would be to call out, "Group 1" and have the students tell you who is missing.

√   One last method is to place student journals or folders out for students to pick up when they enter the room. Folders that are left on the table are absent students.

√   With secondary classes, an easy way to keep track of attendance is to create a manila folder for each period. Staple the attendance sheet to the right hand side and a seating chart to the left hand side. This way you can easily see who is absent and tardy.

Checking Academic Calendars (Daily Planners)

After roll call, you may want to go around the room, while students are still working on their morning/focus activities, to check to see that the homework has been copied down correctly. This gives you an excellent way to say hello to each student personally and check on their well-being. This can be such a positive way to start each class and provides useful information on the emotional state of your students. It also can be used to your benefit during parent conferences, because it shows that you have taken a proactive role in teaching students to be responsible and reminding them on a daily basis. Lastly, you can use the academic calendar to encourage two-way communication with parents.

Class Jobs

Do you use student helpers or student jobs in your classroom? Giving students different jobs in the classroom makes them feel important and gives them a sense of cohesion in your class. It also helps you build relationships with individual students throughout the year. Lastly, assigning jobs to students helps with the work load! Why not let your students help you take care of routine classroom tasks? In our classroom we organized our jobs this way and found it to be a fabulous success!

Host and Hostess
A boy and girl each week serve as Host and Hostess.

➔ Once everyone has had a chance to serve, then you may assign this job as a privilege to responsible students.

Responsibilities:
- Line leaders
- Turn off/on lights
- Close/open doors
- Pass out papers
- Teacher helper and errand runner
- Washing transparencies
- Board eraser
- Other miscellaneous jobs

The following jobs require an application and letter of interest. These jobs are assigned for an entire semester.

Checkers

At the very beginning of class two students get homework papers from bins, check in grade book that it was turned in (pencil only), make out a list of students who did not turn in assignments and give to the teacher.

➔ **Qualifications** - Student must get to class early and finish AM assignments (or warm ups), be responsible, neat, have homework done on time, and upstanding behavior.

Graders

Two students help the teacher grade easier assignments that have a KEY. This can be done when these students finish their class work, or during study period.

➔ **Qualifications** - Graders must be responsible, neat, and have upstanding character and behavior.

Filers

Three students help file graded work in student mailboxes. One student helps teacher file materials in folder, notebooks, and student information files.

➜   **Qualifications** - Students must be responsible, neat, and have upstanding character and behavior.

MORE IDEAS...

There are many jobs that are easier to assign to all ages of children. Take a look at these classroom jobs listed below and think about having your students join the team, and take part in the classroom community.

- Board eraser
- Errand runner
- Handout monitor - passes out papers
- Media person - sets up overhead projector, turns on TV, collects videos, CD's and other computer programs from Librarian

- Pet monitor
- Lights monitor
- Table washer
- Filers
- Teacher helper

- Door monitor
- Transparancy washer
- Trash monitor
- Line leader

> *"Relinquish some of your responsibility and let the students take part in the class community."*

Here are some other methods used by teachers to sort out and assign class jobs:

➜ **Student/Job Wheel**

For this method, mark several clothespins with different classroom jobs. Make a wheel with student's names on it. Clamp the clothespins on different names. You can rotate jobs every week, two weeks, or month.

➜ **Pocket chart**

Get a clear pocket chart (primary grades use these as calendars). Label each pocket with a different job. Mark each student's name on an index card in bold letters. Place a card in each job pocket. You can rotate jobs as needed.

➜ **Alphabetically**

Go down your student list and assign jobs alphabetically.

Student Discipline

As we stated earlier in this chapter, student discipline problems will be at a minimum if you keep your students challenged and busy.

If students are working and having to **think** the entire time they are at school, they will be less likely to misbehave. This does not mean that piling worksheets upon worksheets will keep your students out of trouble. They need meaningful assignments that are motivating as well as challenging.

Activities which are meaningful to students:

- Show connections between content areas
- Require active student participation
- Offer choices for students
- Relate to the real world and real world scenarios
- Require thinking rather than regurgitating information

Many teachers confuse the terms "Classroom Management" and "Classroom Discipline." What do each of these really mean?

Classroom Management - The way you organize and manage your daily classroom events minimizing problems occur. This includes:

- Creating a positive classroom climate
- Implementing classroom procedures
- Organizing both the teacher and the students
- Preparing lessons and activities ahead of time

Classroom Discipline - Behavior modification for students who are not meeting classroom expectations. This can include both rewards and consequences for behavior displayed in the classroom.

Do not confuse "Classroom Discipline" with a "well-disciplined class." When your students know exactly what to do and when to do it, and meet the expectations of the teacher each and every day, you have a "well-disciplined class."

When students misbehave and do not meet classroom expectations, you will need some sort of "Classroom Discipline" plan in place to help those students modify their behavior.

"Without effective classroom management on the part of the teacher, you will NEVER have a well-disciplined class!"

Recipe for a Well-Disciplined Class

√ Teacher who has planned ahead and is well planned

√ Flexibility   √ Confidence

√ Established routines and procedures   √ Positive attitude

√ Consistent follow-through

√ Brain-based classroom
   - non-threatening environment
   - offers guided choice
   - teacher as a learning facilitator
   - relates to real world
   - motivating
   - discovery learning
   - students actively engaged

Establishing Expectations and Consequences

Teacher expectations do not end with classroom rules.

Oftentimes we get so caught up in the rules that we forget about our other expectations. This can cause us to feel so much more disorganized on a daily basis. Instead, it is important to think about what you expect from your students at ALL times. Don't assume students will know how, when and where you want homework to be turned in if you don't tell them specifically. If you expect for homework to be put in the tray on your desk - explain this to the students. If you don't, then you have students trying to hand you their homework throughout the day, often while you are in the middle of something else!

Also, don't forget about the life-skills you expect from your students each day. Do you expect honesty, integrity, cooperation, dedication, perseverance, and personal best from your students? Make those expectations clear. Explain to your students exactly what it means to be dedicated or to have perseverance. What does this look like or sound like? Some of the most common lifeskills taught in classrooms include:

honesty	integrity	cooperation	teamwork	friendship	dedication
effort	caring	perseverance	initiative	patience	common sense
curiosity	courage	responsibility	flexibility	organization	problem solving

These lifeskills, when integrated into our lives, help us all to have a successful happy life. Some of these lifeskills reflect morals and values while others reflect work habits or attitudes towards others. On the following page are a few ways in which you might communicate the importance of these skills to your students.

Lifeskills which reflect Morals and Values

Without strong morals and values such as honesty and integrity, we can often fall into the trap of harming ourselves and others emotionally, mentally, and physically with our lies and deceptions. Even little white lies can turn around and hurt us later in life. Lack of honesty and integrity can hurt relationships of all kinds including family, friends, and business associates. When a person is not honest and lacks integrity (doing what is right), others begin to lose respect for that person. Once respect and trust are lost, they are extremely difficult to gain back again.

Lifeskills which reflect Work Habits

Many of the lifeskills reflect work habits such as effort, perseverance, organization, responsibility, problem solving, and cooperation. These are work habits which will lead a person to success in whatever job they choose. These skills also provide a person with the ability to become anything he/she wants to be. Without these work habits, a person is more likely to stay unskilled or mediocre in their job and in life. This can affect us in terms of job choice, salary, and upward mobility. A lack of these skills will also affect our ability to get into college or a vocational school.

Lifeskills which reflect Attitudes

Our attitude affects our relationships with other people. The attitude lifeskills include friendship, courage, caring, patience, sense of humor, and common sense. The more of these skills we exhibit, the more likely we are to have long-lasting relationships with other people. Our attitude is generally more positive and a positive attitude goes a long way towards success in life. When we think positively, positive things begin to happen to us on a daily basis.

The more we talk about lifeskills in terms of students' lives and their future, the better they will begin to understand why these skills are necessary. It is our job to encourage and foster these skills within the clasroom so they become a habit.

Next, what kinds of work behaviors and attitudes do you expect from your students? While this is somewhat related to the lifeskills we explained earlier, it is very important that you explain exactly what you want to see and hear from your students each and every day. Show your students a sample of "neat" and "sloppy" work so that they have a visual image of what you expect.

It is also important to understand that students cannot read our minds. Take some time to brainstorm your pet peeves. What behaviors really annoy you? Often our students may hit upon one of our pet peeves and never even know it. These behaviors grate on our nerves and affect our attitude which is not fair to our students. They cannot be expected to read our mind. Be sure to communicate clearly what is and is not tolerable in your classroom.

Analogy

Let's put into perspective this idea of explaining our classroom expectations to students. Imagine that you are visiting a foreign country where you have never been before. When you arrive, a list of cultural guidelines and laws are given to you to help you know what is and is not acceptable. You read over these, and feeling confident that you are aware of everything you need to know, you venture out for dinner. Upon arriving at a restaurant, you enter and wait to be seated. The hostess comes and beckons for you to follow her. You calmly follow her to your table. Suddenly she turns around, looks down at your feet and begins to yell at you. You are startled and don't really understand the problem. The hostess is now quickly ushering you out of the restaurant. As you are being pulled back towards the exit, you realize that everyone else is wearing closed toed shoes and you are wearing sandals. It is an unwritten rule, or expectation, that everyone wear socks and shoes inside buildings in this country. Unfortunately, this was not in the list of guidelines, and no one ever told you about this "unwritten rule." Now you are flustered, you feel stupid, and feelings of anger and resentment begin to build because you are being punished for not knowing the expectation.

Think about these questions:

- How do you expect for papers to be turned in?
- What are your rules regarding neatness?
- Can the students write in print vs. cursive?
- What type of paper do you want students to use?
- Can they use colored ink pens?
- What are your expectations for bathroom breaks?
- How will students get supplies during class or sharpen pencils?
- What do you expect students to do when they are finished with their work early?
- What are your expectations for students in learning centers, the reading corner, or lab stations?

When going over expectations at the beginning of the year, you want to be sure to:

√ Maintain eye contact with each student. This type of body language helps keep students focused on you.

√ Speak slowly and pause after each sentence to emphasize the importance of what you are saying.

√ Practice procedures over and over until they are habits!

√ Have discussions with students to explain why these expectations are important to you.

√ Maybe demonstrate some examples of why it would drive you crazy if students...

Idea Share

Have a student stand at the front of the classroom and read a paragraph. Then as the student is reading, you walk around the room talking with other students, sharpening your pencil, doing jumping jacks, and acting the way you wouldn't want your students to act while you are presenting a lesson.

Then, have the student explain how difficult it was for her to continue reading with all of the distractions.

Teaching Polite Behaviors

Many of our students have not been taught at home how to respond to a greeting such as "good morning." They also have not been taught how to respond respectfully to adults and to each other. These are polite behaviors that you might need to teach to your students as a whole class. Simply telling them that you expect everyone to respect adults and each other will not cut it. Most of your students will nod their heads as though they agree without ever really understanding what you mean.

It is important to take some time to think about what you expect from your students in regards to this issue. Below are a few tips that might help you when broaching the topic of manners expected in the classroom.

Address the class as a whole on both of those subjects.

Word it so that the students understand you are not requesting that they be polite, but that it is an expectation you have for them.

For example

> *"It has come to my attention that we are not showing respect to each other in the classroom the way that I expect to see every day. When I address you with a question or a request, I expect you to reply with, "yes, m'am" (if that is your expectation). Anytime any adult in the classroom or school asks a question or request, not just me, I expect you to reply with, "yes, M'am or yes, Sir." When you reply this way it shows respect for others and shows that you have good manners. Does everyone understand? (the response is the practice for "yes, m'am") If they don't respond, remind them what you just said and you might have to practice a couple of times. ("Let's try that again.")*

Once you've addressed the class, then definitely keep reminding them on a one-on-one basis. Also, you might think about making a poster that shows this expectation. It would prove a nice reminder and you could simply point to it and say, "how are we supposed to repond?" The more they all are required to do this day after day, the more it will become ingrained behavior.

In our house, if my son says, "yeah," I stop immediately and give him "the look." Sometimes I might say, "Excuse me?" or "What do I want to hear?" or "Is that the correct response?" with my firm teacher voice, and he'll say, "yes, m'am." Once you've told the class what you expect of them in terms of responding to you, anytime a student says, "yeah," stop, look directly at them, raise your eyebrow, and wait. This will help remind them without having to go through a three-minute spiel every time.

Additionally, I always respond to yes/no questions from my students with "yes, m'am" or "yes, sir." I respond to my administrator and my colleagues this way as well. As I model this polite behavior, it affects the behavior of those I interact with and those around me. The most powerful message about how you expect students to behave towards you and others is how you behave towards them and others in the school.

Address the greeting at the door with the class

I would have a volunteer student come up and help you show what you want to happen. Model it for the students. Then, take some time to have the students practice it with each other. Walk around and correct students as they need it. When *they've all mastered this skill, let them know that you expect that same kind of response every time they are greeted by someone else.*

Greeting:

When someone greets you with their hand held out:
Grip the other person's hand firmly but not squeezing
Look them in the eyes
Respond clearly with "Good Morning" or "Good Afternoon" or "Good Evening"

OR

When someone greets you, Stop.
Look them in the eyes
Respond clearly with "Good Morning", etc.

At my son's school, the director loves to say good bye to the children. When they leave he will say, "Goodbye _(student)__, I hope you have a wonderful afternoon."

He then teaches them to respond with, "Thank you. You too. I will see you tomorrow." With the younger students this is also an excellent way to practice their days of the week. They might say, "I will see you on Monday." or "I will see you tomorrow which is Tuesday."

This is a ritual that teaches students a polite way to leave the school. It might be something that you could incorporate as part of your end of the day or end of class ritual when students are dismissed.

Train your students on how to accept "No" for an answer

When you get "No" as an answer from an adult:

Look the person in the eye respectfuly (model what this looks like)
Reply "Yes, M'am" or "Yes, Sir"
Walk away calmly

When you get "No" as an answer from another student:

Look the person in the eye respectfully
Reply with "Okay"
Walk away calmly

Train students that if they are angry about this type of answer that they can do one of the following:

1.   Write their feelings out completely in a correspondence journal to the teacher. Place the journal gently on the teacher's desk or hand it to the teacher at an appropriate time. This correspondence journal could have a specific spot in the classroom where students know to find it. Label it clearly. Have students write their feelings as a letter to you and signed with their name. This practices letter writing skills, offers students a chance to vent their frustrations, and lets you know how the student is feeling. Another option is to allow them time to write in their own personal journal.

2.   Ask for an honorable appeal. After responding properly to the "No" answer, students could address the person respectfully and ask for an appeal.

For example

> *"Mrs. McDonald? May I offer an honoring appeal?" or "May I appeal your decision?"*
> *(in a calm and respectful tone of voice -- You definitely want to model what this would and would not sound like)*

The honoring appeal is outlined in the book, *Say Goodbye to Whining, Complaining, and Bad Attitudes in You and Your Kids* by Scott Turansky and Joanne Miller, and goes something like this:

> "I understand that you do not want me to... (or that you want me to...) because....
> However, I (give reason for request and state feelings supporting request).
> Could I (rephrase request)?"

Example

> *"Mrs. McDonald, I understand that you do not want me to leave the class because we are working on an assignment. However, I really have to take this book back to the library before I am fined a late charge. I know that I will not be able to go any other time during the day, and I am afraid that I will forget if I don't take care of it right now. Could I please go quickly to the library? I will return in five minutes."*
> OR
> *"Mrs. McDonald, I understand that you want me to put down my pencil so that I can listen to your directions. May I copy this last part of our homework first? I am almost finished."*

If you say yes to their appeal, hold them accountable to their promise. If they say they will be back in five minutes and return in ten or fifteen minutes, let the student know that they may not appeal again for a certain period of time because they did not stick to their word (promise).

Also, just because a student uses the honoring appeal does not mean that we automatically have to say "Yes" to their request. Be sure you let them know that. If we still say, "No" to their appeal, the student needs to respond politely as we outlined above. However, the honoring appeal is a way for students to voice their own opinion, feelings, and needs in a polite manner rather than, "Awww", huffing, rolling eyes, or storming off.

Remember, to be most effective, you need to address the students in your own personality, but with a firm voice that lets them know you are very serious about these expectations. I personally have used each and every one of these expectations with the students in my classes. They all work as long as you explain, model, practice, and are consistent with expecting this kind of behavior each and every day.

Other Management Issues

Students Leaving the Classroom

Students leaving the classroom to go to the bathroom and for other reasons is a huge issue for intermediate and secondary teachers. Why is this? It is neither right nor fair that we subject our students to the embarrassment of requesting permission to answer nature's call. As adults, we would never stand for that kind of treatment. As long as you discuss your expectations at the beginning of the year, bathroom breaks should not be such an issue.

Example Expectations:

- Students may leave to use the restroom only during "Your" time which is when they are working on assignments. No signing out while the teacher is giving directions or teaching a lesson.

- Students must fill out the sign-out sheet completely and fill in the "time returned" slot when they return. Be sure to take the clipboard to the teacher before leaving the classroom. Only one student may leave at a time for a particular destination.

- Students are held responsible for in-class assignments to be completed.

Idea Share

Create a sign-out sheet that includes: date, time left, time returned, destination, and reason. Use Excel or another spreadsheet program to help you make this easily.

Explain your bathroom policy on the first day of school.

Student Talking in Class

One of the biggest complaints from teachers is the issue of student talking. "They just won't be quiet!" "I constantly have to ask them to be quiet." "They don't listen to my lesson."

Appropriate Talking Times

The first thing you need to ask yourself is *when are they talking?* Are they talking during your instruction, or when you are giving directions? Or, are they talking during a project or work time? There is nothing wrong in allowing students to talk while they are working. Although they may not always be talking about the subject matter, they will stay on task, especially if you are walking around monitoring. Additionally, the more motivating the assignment, the more students will actually be talking about their work.

Human beings are social creatures by nature, and we tend to do a better job when we talk to others. Talking helps us express our thoughts, ideas, and feelings. Students get ideas from one another, judge how well they are doing, and help each other do a good job on their work. Sometimes they are just chatting, but even this helps build a strong community in the classroom.

Talking aloud often allows us to work through a problem, formulate strategies, and organize thoughts. Research done with small children shows that youngsters who are constantly talking are also constantly thinking. Because younger children cannot control their thought and speech patterns, the two are very closely connected. Therefore, a chatty class of primary students should be welcomed as a sign that everyone is using their brains!

Introduce the concept of "My Time" and "Your time."

Students need to know that there will be opportunities for them to talk and move around. In order to help them understand when it is and is not appropriate, introduce this concept. "My time" is teacher time. This is anytime you are teaching a lesson, giving directions, addressing the class as a whole group, or directly working with a small group. "Your time" is student time. This is anytime students are working independently or in groups (excluding testing situations) on classroom activities. Explain to your class that you know they can be quiet and focused during "My time" because after a few minutes, generally five to fifteen, it will be "Your time" and students can take care of their needs.

Introduce this concept at the beginning of the year:

"Whenever I am giving a lesson, directions, am speaking to the class, or am standing in front of the class as a whole, that is MY TIME. During "My Time", I expect for students to be silent, looking at me, and listening. You may be taking notes, but you are expected to pay attention to what I am saying. If you are talking to a neighbor, are you paying attention to me? (No) If you are rummaging around in your backpack, are you paying attention to me? (No) Exactly. Now, let's practice what paying attention looks like."

After practicing a few times on what paying attention looks like, next you might say:

"Now, if I have given you a class or group assignment and have given you time in class to work, that is YOUR TIME. You may get supplies, sharpen your pencil, go to the restroom..."
(These are examples, you DO want to be specific in telling them exactly what they are allowed to do. I let mine get a drink of water or use the restroom if they really need to, because thirsty kids and kids who need to go to the bathroom are kids who won't be thinking about their work - the only things they are thinking about are their bodily needs.)

"When I put up the quiet signal (my hand in the air), or ring the bell (a small dinner bell that I keep in my pocket or on my desk), that is the signal that it is MY TIME again, and I want full attention on me!"

Next, you need to practice this with them several times.

Tell the kids to talk and chatter, sing songs, etc.. Then, time them to see how quickly they can come back to order after you signal them. Practicing this is fun for the students, but also allows them to internalize your expectations.

Teacher Talk

"In my classroom, I schedule talking pauses after new or important concepts are introduced. This allows my students to discuss their thoughts on the topic with a neighbor. I don't just stop teaching, but instead say something such as, "Now I'd like you to turn to a neighbor and discuss what I just presented to you. Write down any new thoughts and ideas you generate so that you won't forget them. Be prepared to share some of your ideas with the whole class."

Then I give everyone several minutes to talk while I walk around listening and engaging in some of the individual discussions.

I got this idea when I went to a district training for in-service presenters, but now I find that is works beautifully with my 6th graders as well!"

Monitoring and Redirect

When you do allow your students to talk during their work time, be sure you are walking around monitoring their conversations. Although it is okay to get off the assigned topic for a minute or two, too much off task talking is not appropriate. While you monitor, you are in more of a position to redirect student talking quietly, rather than yelling out, "Quiet Down Now!" which is completely ineffective. Instead, walk up behind the student who is taking and say (just to them) something like, "So, tell me what you have done so far? I am taking progress checks." That student is immediately back on task and you haven't singled him/her out in front of the class, or yelled at the class as a whole. Standing behind a group of students for several minutes while they are working is also very effective for redirecting off task behavior.

Idea Share

Keep a clipboard with you as you walk around. On the clipboard, have either index cards or a spreadsheet of student names, so that you can take notes on what is happening: who is on task, who is not, problems, etc...

Clipboard Monitoring

1. Using a spreadsheet program such as Excel, Lotus, or ClarisWorks, create a spreadsheet. Down the side, allow for student names. Across the top put one rule or work habit in each box. Leave a couple of boxes blank so you can write in the concept or skill for the day that you want to observe.

Example:

Student Name	1. Stay in Seat	2. On Task During Group work	3. Cooperating wih others	4.
JOHN	1 2 3 4 5	1 2 3 4 5	1 2 3 4 5	1 2 3 4 5
ASHLEY	1 2 3 4 5	1 2 3 4 5	1 2 3 4 5	1 2 3 4 5

2. Use a system of numbers to help you keep track of infractions. Make sure there is enough space for comments as well if necessary.
   With rules, each number represents the number of infractions
   With concepts/skills, you write the skills in the blank columns and underneath, each number represents the level of mastery.
   5 = Excellent, 4 = Good, 3=Fair, 2=Poor, 1=No Mastery

3. Place a week's worth of spreadsheet forms on the clipboard so that you won't have to remember each morning to put a new sheet up.

4. Make enough copies for several weeks. There should be one spreadsheet per day. Label the date at the top of the spreadsheet before using it so that you'll know which day it refers to.

5. Be sure to use the clipboard to record good behavior and to make comments about students who go above and beyond what is expected of them. This will help you when it is time to write progress reports or report card comments. It will also help you if you ever have to recommend a student for an honors position or award.

6. File these sheets in a three-ring binder in chronological order. Use tabbed dividers to separate each six weeks or grading period. Why a binder? Well, a binder keeps all of the papers together in one place with no fear of losing them. Also, it is easier to flip through pages in a binder than it is in a manila folder.

7. Be sure to document behavior disruptions, etc...in the student's folder at the end of the week so that you won't have to bring a ton of extra papers to a parent conference. If you are in a huge hurry, you might just make a copy of the form to put in the students folder. Just be sure to blank out other student names before putting it in a particular students folder.

DATE:_____   CLASS:_____

STUDENT NAMES	1.	2.	3.	4.	5.

Idea Share for Recording Student Discipline

Clipboard

Some teachers use a clipboard. Attached to the clipboard is a spreadsheet like the one illustrated below. Each time a student does not meet an expectation, a mark is given next to their name under the appropriate day of the week. Consequences are met for marks given that day. Each day starts over. This is an excellent way to hold students accountable while out of your classroom as the clipboard follows the class throughout the school.

Student	Monday	Tuesday	Wednesday	Thursday	Friday
Julie	1 2 3 4 5	1 2 3 4 5	1 2 3 4 5	1 2 3 4 5	1 2 3 4 5
Mark	1 2 3 4 5	1 2 3 4 5	1 2 3 4 5	1 2 3 4 5	1 2 3 4 5
Sandy	1 2 3 4 5	1 2 3 4 5	1 2 3 4 5	1 2 3 4 5	1 2 3 4 5

Index Cards

You can mark down the date and the number of the rule not followed on an index card. It is easier and less time consuming to simply write the number of the rule rather than taking the time to make written comments on the card. When you fill the index card, staple another to it. This is helpful when you are contacting parents and want to access a record of student behavior easily.

How are these different?

> **Important Teacher Tip:**
> Writing student names on the chalkboard and placing checks next to the names for misbehavior is not an appropriate way to record behavior problems. Instead, it only serves to embarrass the student. If it doesn't humiliate the child, it could have the opposite affect, and the student enjoys the negative attention. Either way, this will generally result in additional rebellious behavior.

Pocket Chart

Place a clear pocket chart on the wall. Each student should have their own pocket. Next to this chart, place your poster of rules. Attach pockets next to each rule. Place different colored strips next to each rule. (ex: Rule #1 has purple strips)

Each time a student does not follow a rule, have them pull a colored rule strip and place it in their pocket on the chart. Remember to clearly tell the student which expectation they have not followed. This is excellent for primary grades because it is so visual. At the end of the day, you should record each child's infractions in your grade book, on an index card, or on a reward chart. Each day should start over fresh.

Using Rewards

We all know that discipline programs based completely on consequences or punishments are not effective in modifying student behavior. However, there is currently a debate about reward based programs as well. Some researchers contend that rewards can be equally as harmful.

Our belief is that rewards can be used as a motivational tool to help students begin to modify their behavior. As students begin to meet your expectations on a consistent basis, you should rely less and less on rewards as a tool. Remember that students who are actively engaged in their learning do not need outside stimuli such as rewards for motivation. They are motivated by the desire to learn.

For example, in the movie *Dangerous Minds*, Michelle Pfieffer's character walked into an extremely hostile and volatile classroom situation. She wanted to use positive measures to change student attitudes, and began a reward system for classroom participation. As her students began participating more in class and were more engaged, she slowly reduced the number of rewards passed out until finally students were participating because they were truly interested and were intrinsically motivated to learn.

The same should apply to you. If you find yourself in a rough classroom situation where drastic measures are needed, yet you want to foster a positive environment rather than a negative one, a reward based program is the perfect place to begin. As your students' behavior begins to change, you want to wean them off of the rewards until they are participating and behaving because THEY want to, not because you are paying them.

Tips:

√ Use sporadically throughout the day, week, month, year

√ Don't rely on rewards in place of good classroom management

√ Work your way towards students who are intrinsically motivated through engaging teaching strategies

√ Be fair in giving out rewards - each student should have an equal chance

"An effective teacher seeks to modify student behavior by focusing on positives rather than negatives."

Management Program Ideas

Self Manager Program

One discipline program that has been used in Richardson, Texas is the Self Manager Program. This program utilizes the clipboard idea for recording student behavior. Students must go 10 days without a mark of any kind. When they reach 10 days, they are given an application that each teacher must sign. The application is turned in and the student is given a button with their name and picture on it. This "Self-Manger Badge" gives the student extra privileges. The school and each teacher decides on various rewards to happen weekly, monthly, or each six weeks. If a student receives three marks in a one week period, they lose their badge. However, they can earn it back after 10 days with no marks.

VIP Program

Students in Middle School who make the A Honor Roll, or who make all A's in conduct for every class are given VIP badges. These badges give students extra privileges. They may use their badge as a hall pass, may go to the library or computer lab during lunch, and have other rewards given out by individual teachers.

Top Ten

Create a chart for each grading period with student names written down the side and dates written across the top. Each day, record either the number of the rule(s) broken, or place a star or smiley face next to every student's name. When a student acquires ten stars or smiley faces on the chart, the teacher provides a reward. The stars do not have to be 10 in a row, just 10 total. Once a student has received their reward, the process begins again. A fun way to publicly honor students receiving their Top Ten reward is to have a ceremony every Friday for those who earned their Top Ten that week.

Primary Idea:

Tape library pockets on each student's desk. Give each student a popsicle stick. Write the student name on the back of the stick. Everytime a student gets a sticker, they put it on their stick. When they receive 10, students can "shop" in the treasure chest (a chest of dollar toys, small craft projects, pencils, stickers, etc.). To keep track of behavior, paint a yardstick in three sections - green, yellow, and red. Mark the consequences (warning, time-out, etc.) When students misbehave, they move the clothespin with their name on it to the next level. If students redeem their behavior throughout the day, the clothespin can be moved back to green. Students who are still on green receive a sticker for that day.

Thank you to Erica Kruckenberg, First Grade teacher, Prosper ISD for sharing this idea with us!

Tokens of Appreciation

➜ **Weekly Top Ten**

Every Friday before lunch announce students who earned their ten stars/stickers during that week. Students are given a reward during that time.

➜ **Bonus Points**

Use the bonus point coupons in the back of this chapter and add them onto homework/project or test grades. Use coupons in denominations of 1's and 5's.

➜ **Red Tickets**

Buy a roll of red, green, or other brightly colored tickets from a teacher or office supply store. Hand these out for participation, etc. Students write their names on the back and put them into a canister for a weekly drawing.

➜ **Mascot Coupons**

Use school "mascot" coupons, or create your own to give to students for the following: 1st done with morning assignment/sponge activities, parent signatures on binders, life skills shown in class, or best organized binder.

➜ **Class Leader**

Give this award to the student who has shown the most improvement during the week.

➜ **Explorer of the Month**

Award this to the student who has shown the most effort. Invite the student(s) to eat a special lunch with you. Also, take their picture and post it on a special poster on the bulletin board.

> *"You will be surprised at how well your students respond to even the smallest reward for a job well done."*

Example Tokens of Appreciation:

- Special pencils
- Special lunch with the teacher
- Homework passes
- Special helper
- Coke
- Treasure chest with goodies
- Stickers
- Bookmarks

- Children's Books
- Free computer time
- Button or badge
- Small prizes from the dollar store
- Ice cream bar
- Free library time
- Food coupons

BEHAVIOR MODIFICATION PLAN

EXPECTATIONS	MONDAY	TUESDAY	WEDNESDAY	THURSDAY	FRIDAY
1.					
2.					
3.					
4.					
5.					

Cut along the line.

Instructions: Work with the student and/or parent to determine five behaviors you expect the student to perform. Some examples include: stay in seat, use a respectful tone of voice, keep hands to self, take turns when speaking, etc. Then, each day a student exhibits one of these behaviors, place a sticker or initial the box for that day. Reward the student on a weekly basis.

For example:

     5 stickers = a special job to do (erase board, line leader, run an errand, etc.)
     10 stickers = a homework pass
     15 stickers = special lunch with the teacher
     20 stickers = computer time/ library time

NOTICE OF CONCERN

Date_____   Student's Name_____

Student's ID Number_____   Grade_____

Subject_____ Teacher_____

Counselor_____

To Parent/ Guardian

_____   This notice is sent to advise you that your child is having academic difficulties.

_____   This Notice is sent to advise you that your child is at risk for failure.

_____   This Notice is sent to advise you that your child's behavioral conduct may result in disciplinary actions.

_____   Student cannot participate in extracurricular activities due to failure.

Tutorial help: **M   T   W   Th   F   S**   Time:_____

Academic Difficulties

Failure to complete assignments	Failure to make up work/ tests	Excessive absences
Failure to bring materials to class	Poor quality of work	Excessive tardies
Poor test(s) results	Failure to follow directions	Lack of effort

Other_____

Behavioral Misconduct

Talks excessively	Ignores correction	Disruptive
Distracts other students	Displays negative attitude	Displays disrespect

Other_____

Parent/Guardian is requested to have a conference with the teacher at one of the conference periods indicated below:

CONFERENCE TIME: 1st Choice _____   2nd Choice _____

Please Sign and Return

Parent/Guardian Signature _____   Date _____

We Missed You!

Name _____

Date of Absence _____

You missed these cool activities in class today!	Important Assignments
You missed the following Quiz/Test on:	Journal topic/Warm up assignment Other

Conclusion

If we desire a well-disciplined class which is learner centered, it is vital to train our students in our expectations and procedures. Proactive, not reactive, strategies are required to maintain a classroom where students know what is expected of them at all times. Remember, children need boundaries and structure in order to feel safe in their environment. Although they will test and strain these boundaries, children ultimately want to know that they cannot be broken.

When there is consistency in the classroom, trust is built between all members. Where there is trust, respect follows. If we want our students to respect us, then we must respect them as well. This includes setting expectations and being consistent in our requirements. When everything changes from day to day, students never know what to expect and as a result become excitable, unruly, and sometimes angry.

Good classroom management takes time and effort. It is not easy being consistent and it is not easy always enforcing the expectations set. However, without consistency behavior breaks down and learning does not occur. Thus, effective learning on the part of the student is the result of dedication, preparation, and planning on the part of the teacher.

Questions to Ponder

How would you describe yourself as a leader? Does your style of leadership invoke positive or negative reactions from students? How does this translate to your relationship with your colleagues and with parents?

Why is it so important to create a positive climate within the classroom? What are some ways you already work to build this type of climate in your classroom? What are some other strategies you might implement to help foster a positive climate?

What is the difference in your mind between well-disciplined and needing discipline? Which would you categorize your students as being? Why? How can you help your students become well-disciplined if they are not already?

Additional Resources

Choice Theory in the Classroom
by William Glasser, M.D.

Discipline without Stress, Punishments, or Rewards
by Dr. Marvin Marshall

Say Goodbye to Whining, Complaining, and Bad Attitudes in you and your kids
by Scott Turansky and Joanne Miller

Discipline with Love and Logic
by Jim Fay and Dave Funk

The Bully Free Classroom: Over 100 Tips and Strategies for Teachers K-8
by Allan Beane

Revisiting Lesson Plans

When building a fire you need to know whether you plan to have a small campfire or a large bonfire. Prior planning is a must to keep from burning down forests or not getting warm enough on a cold night! The same is true for lesson planning. Without prior planning, our lessons will smoke and fizzle instead of sparking into a flame. But what kind of planning do we need to do to be effective?

Dr. Madeline Hunter, in her research, discovered that effective teachers, no matter what grade level, subject area, teaching style, or background of students, all used a similar method of teaching. From these discoveries, she suggested several elements to be considered when planning lessons. These elements include objectives, standards, anticipatory set, teaching (input, modeling, check for understanding), guided practice, closure, and independent practice. In our teaching courses, this was shown to us as the 7 step lesson design plan. It looked unweildy and overwhelming. If you were like me, perhaps you thought, "Well, I'll get around to using that later." But then later never came.

Over time, I found myself day after day bored with my students, bored with the topics, and bored with teaching. It seemed like I was doing the same thing day after day, and I probably was! It wasn't until I took a class in Curriculum Development that I revisited the elements outlined by Madeline Hunter. Suddenly I realized that I could make my lessons more engaging for both me and my students. There was a way to keep track of what I had taught and to have a road map for what I planned to teach. However, the model still seemed somewhat unweildy in thinking through and writing down each of those elements every single day. In a determined effort to do better for my students, I began setting aside one day a week for planning.

Each Wednesday afternoon I would set aside an hour or two after school to do lesson planning for the following week. At first it was difficult, and it took quite a bit of effort on my part to stick with this detailed type of planning. However, the more I planned in this manner, the easier I found it the following week. At the end of the year, I found the following to be true when writing detailed lesson plans:

- They serve as a way to keep the teacher focused and on target with objectives/standards.
- Students see the teacher as well-prepared and organized.
- Students and the teacher are excited and engaged in the classroom each day.
- Students are less likely to misbehave and interrupt throughout the class.
- No more writing detailed plans for a substitute because they are already done!
- Principals and other staff members view the teacher as efficient and effective.
- Teacher has a smooth flowing day.

Lesson planning affects behavior, motivation, and learning for both the students and the teacher. As we stated in the previous chapter on classroom management, students can immediately tell when the teacher is not in control due to lack of planning. This often causes behavior in the classroom to break down. It becomes easier to get the teacher off topic and before you know it, the class is in shambles.

Additionally, without effective lesson planning, boredom can set in for everyone. Writing out detailed lesson plans can help us make sure that we are varying our activities, that we are meeting different learner needs, and that we are staying on track. Instead of the daily thirty to forty minute lecture or textbook reading, we can make sure we are using the different elements that keep student interest and promote learning.

Let's take a look at the following elements of a detailed lesson plan. Although these are not specifically "7 steps," they do include Madeline Hunter's basic elements.

Focus Assignment

When students first enter the classroom, they need a focus activity of some sort to help them calm down and get ready to start class. It should be easily viewed on the board, the overhead, or the TV/Computer presentation station, and must be done every single day for every class period (when changing classes) in order to maintain consistency. When used here and there, students never know what to expect. This adversely affects their behavior. The focus assignment is sometimes called a bell-ringer, warm-up, or sponge activity.

Types of focus activities:

Teacher Talk

My students all copy their homework into an academic calendar as soon as they walk into my class. Then, while they are all working on their warm-up activity, I go around and check their calendars. I initial each entry that has been copied down correctly. This gives me a chance to say hello to each student and see how everyone is feeling. I can actually diffuse any problems right from the start of class!

- Write in journals
- Creative writing activity
- Calendar questions
- Sentence corrections
- Simple review activity
- Name the season/day of the week/etc.
- Geography questions
- Name the state, scientist, explorer
- Math problems
- Review questions from previous day's lesson
- Vocabulary
- Pop-quiz
- Bulletin board activities—current events, calendar, vocabulary, authors, birthdays, etc.
- Daily Oral Language/Geography/Math/Science
- Quote of the Day

While students are completing their focus activity quietly at their desks, you can use that time to call roll, visit with individual students, and take care of other housekeeping items.

Some quick sponge activities can also be used for transitions when students are finished early, when preparing for lunch or recess, or the end of class/day.

Objectives/ State Standards

What do you want students to be able to do by the end of the lesson/day? Your objectives should be written in a manner that can be evaluated and should correlate with your State Standards.

For example: *Students will be able to identify the main characters in the story, Charlotte's Webb.*
Students will be able to construct a model of a human cell.

You don't want to write objectives that are hard for you to measure student achievement or knowledge.

For example: *Students will understand main characters.*
Students will learn about cells.

First of all, this objective is not specific enough, and secondly, how will you measure student understanding?

Procedures

What will you do during class time to achieve your objectives? This may include direct instruction, modeling, group practice or application, questioning, lab or learning center activities, individual practice, and possibly even assessment. Your procedures should reflect effective teaching practices such as varying learning activities, making connections to the real-world, application of learning, etc. These are very important in developing effective and motivating lessons, and are discussed in the Brain-Based Classroom chapters. ***Make no mistake, if all you do is list your procedures as lecture, textbook reading, and worksheets, you will not see a change in you or your students!***

After writing out your procedures, ask yourself if the activities are:

- Mostly teacher-centered or student-centered
- Varied for different learning styles
- Actively engaging for students
- Helping students meet the objective(s)

Example:

Objective: To be able to identify the three layers of the earth.

Procedures:
1) Student groups cut a wedge shaped slice from the peach on their table.
2) Students make observations about the peach and record on paper as a group.
3) Groups share their observations (should be noting different layers)
4) Lesson - Students take notes about layers of the earth in their notebook.
5) Students draw their own planet earth and identify the different layers
6) Students work in pairs to compare/contrast the earth and the peach in a T-chart or Venn Diagram format. (if time) (extension activity)

Transitions

We often think of transitions only in terms of those blank times between classes or activities. However, it is also important to think about how you transition from one part of your lesson to the next. When planning your lessons, take some time to think about how you will make these kinds of transitions. A good flow to your lessons and activities will help students make better connections in their learning.

How can you accomplish this?

1)   Think through your lesson from start to finish in a logical sequence. Introduce basic concepts first and then build on them throughout the lesson/day.

2)   Does the sequence of the lesson/activity make sense? Does each part follow one another or are they mostly unrelated activities which are just linked together haphazardly?

Below is a sample elementary lesson that may help illustrate this point. Note how each part of the lesson flows into the next. Secondary teachers need to look at the flow rather than the lesson itself. How are you creating this kind of flow between the elements of your lessons? No matter what subject area you teach, these transitions are an important part of an effective lesson.

1)   Blindfold a volunteer student and have him/her try to navigate around the classroom. The rest of the class should be silent.

2)   When finished, ask the student to describe how he/she was able (or not able) to navigate around the classroom. Since sight is not an option, what other senses did he/she use? (Lead discussion to sense of hearing)

3)   What other creatures depend on other senses besides their eyes to help them navigate? (Bats, whales, nocturnal creatures)

4)   I'm going to read a story about one creature who was feeling as out of place as (volunteer student) was earlier.

5)   Read Stellaluna and discuss how she was out of place. What did she discover about herself throughout the course of the story?

6)   Stellaluna learned that she was a bat, not a bird. Let's write down some facts we already know about bats. (K-W-L -- Write on butcher paper or overhead - Older students write on their own paper and then share) What are some questions we have about bats?

7)   Before we can really begin to understand bats, like Stellaluna, we need to know some important vocabulary words. List, copy & discuss vocabulary words.

8)   Which of these words would have helped (volunteer student) if she had this ability? (Sonar) Boats use sonar to test the depths of the ocean. Fishermen use sonar to help them find fish. Why do you think sonar is one of our vocabulary words for this unit? Think back to Stellaluna. At one point the picture shows her with eyes that look like flashlights. Did she really have flashlights for eyes? What do you think this picture is trying to tell us? (Lead students through discussion to the concept that when bats use sonar to navigate in the dark, it is like having a flashlight to help them "see" where they are going.)

9)   Did the birds have sonar to help them see at night? (No) Why not? Why does Stellaluna have sonar? (Bats are awake at night) - What vocabulary word is this? (Nocturnal) Are there other differences between Stellaluna and the bird family? (Yes)

10)   Let's use a Venn Diagram to help us see the differences and similarities between Stellaluna and the birds. (Can be done on chart paper, on an overhead, or by students in pairs/individually.) Think back to the story (This is a great opportunity to cite the source of information/page numbers where the differences are shown in the pictures or in the story - supporting details. It is never too early to begin introducing students to the concept of supporting their information/opinions from the source.).

11)   Review the differences and similarities shown in the chart. If you could be either, would you be a bat or a bird? Draw a picture of the animal you'd choose and explain why this is your choice.

12)   Students share their pictures and reasons.

13)   On a post-it note, students write two (or more) interesting facts about bats they learned in the lesson (closure).

This is just an introductory lesson that is used as part of a unit learning about bats and other nocturnal animals. What we want you to notice is how the teacher continues to refer back to the intial activity and the read-aloud story. Each part of the lesson connects to the next part. There is a flow from one idea to the next. This flow should continue each day building on what was learned previously and introducing/expanding upon further information until the completion of the unit.

Do your lessons have a logical flow from one part to the next? Is this something that you think about when planning your lessons? Reflecting on how we plan our lessons is an important part of being an effective teacher.

"An effective teacher varies learning activities and plans for transitions to help students meet specific learning objectives."

Closure

Closure to a lesson is one of those elements that is so important and yet so misunderstood. In our lives we often talk about needing some closure before moving onto something new. It is the same with lessons. If a teacher spends time and effort teaching a topic, and then immediately switches to a new topic or dismisses students without any kind of a closure, there is a sense of being left in the lurch. We all need a conclusion or summary of some sort before moving on. Here are some tips for providing closure:

- Students should be actively involved.
- Question students about the lesson/ what they learned.
- Students reflect in their journal about the lesson and share.
- Ask students how this lesson/topic relates to the real world or to them personally.
- Use a visual object and/or catch-phrase to sum up the lesson.

Bored with asking the students day after day to review what they learned in class? Take a look at our Motivating Students chapter to get some ideas on ways you can spice up your closure. Try this:

> Have students write one thing they learned on:
> - colored post-it notes or index cards (share aloud)
> - a chart pad or overhead transparency
> - sentence strip (stand in front and share)

Materials

It is equally important to plan for all of the materials you will need for the lesson and activities. Be very specific and include the textbook, student notebooks, etc.. This will help you know to remind students to bring a particular item that they may not use every single day. Planning out materials also helps you stay organized in gathering what you need before you teach a particular lesson.

Assessment

When you plan, you need to know how you will assess student mastery of the objective(s). In order for an assessment to be valid, it must test what the students have learned. Before you plan a lesson, think about how you plan to assess the objective. Will you use a paper/pencil test? Will you use a class activity? Will you use a project or group assignment? Will you require students to recite information or apply it?

Once you've decided how you plan to assess students, then you can check your lesson and activities to be sure that they appropriately prepare students for the assessment. For example, when looking at the sample objective and lesson on the previous page, you might decide that an appropriate assessment would be for students to label the layers of the earth on a diagram. This type of assessment would be valid since students learned and applied the information in a similar manner.

Timesaving Tips

Type out your lesson plans on regular paper

Let's face it, that lesson planning book given out by the school simply does not have enough room to adequately plan. The most you can fit into those squares is a brief outline of your plans. While this seems easy enough, it will cause you more grief later on.

Organize your plans on disk.

If you are using a computer, organize your plans into folders for each six weeks or units. Then, further organize each six weeks into folders for each week. This way you can place typed handouts, tests, newsletters, etc. into the folder with your plans.

> *Example:*
>
> **Disk:** McDonald 5th Grade
>
> **1st Six Weeks** (Folder)
>   **August 6-10** (Folder)
>   *lesson plans* (file)
>   *spelling test* (file)
>   *reading assignment* (file)
>   *science animal matching* (file)
>   *parent newsletter* (file)
>   *field trip form* (file)

Have a chosen planning day.

Choose one day out of the week to write your plans. I like Wednesday because there is plenty of time to gather materials for the next week. Also, many principals request copies of lesson plans on Fridays. If something unexpected happens on Wednesday, then you still have one day to get them finished. Be consistent with this schedule and plan your time accordingly.

"Time taken today will save time tomorrow."

Use a template when planning.

Using a template will help you work out your lesson plans with ease. If you save one week's plans on a disk, you can simply copy them onto a new file and change as necessary. This really saves time since you won't have to change every single item. Also, it takes much less time to highlight and change information on a template than to write it over and over for each day's lesson. *See sample templates in the next several pages.*

Steps of Lesson Planning

These are the steps we go through when developing our curriculum for the year. We want to be sure we are covering our state standards through our objectives and that our students will be prepared for any state assessment to be taken that year. At the same time we want to be sure we are planning motivating lessons that are engaging for both the student and ourselves.

1.   What are you required to teach? Look at a scope and sequence or overview of state required essential elements for your subject and/or grade level. *(Use State Department of Education Webpages)*

2.   How can you organize that material into units? Try to make these units meaningful to students. For example, a unit on Nouns is not going to motivate any of your students, but a Mystery unit might. Later in the book we discuss ideas for Language Arts, Math, and Integrated units that might be helpful to you.

3.   Write an overview for your first six weeks on a calendar. This does not need to be detailed, but should give you an overall picture of what you will cover during that grading period. If you teach several subjects, make a calendar for each subject area. This will be extremely helpful to refer to when you sit down to write daily lesson plans.

4.   Write lesson plans for the first week. In the beginning you may want to go one day at a time unless your principal requires you to turn in your weekly plans. Use the following format:

   • **Date**
   • **Objectives/ State Standards**
     (what do you want the students to be able to do?)
   • **Materials**
     (what do you need to accomplish this?)
   • **Procedures**
     (what are you going to do to accomplish your objectives?)
   • **Assessment**
     (how will you know you met your objectives?)

> *"It is hard work to make lessons meaningful to students, but in the end it is worth it!"*

The following three pages show examples and templates for planning. A sample calendar and daily lesson plan is included for elementary and secondary to show this process in action.

Here is a sample Elementary calendar with a six weeks overview. A sample lesson plan is provided for the day shaded below. A blank template is in the back of this chapter. Secondary teachers can do each prep on one calendar or one calendar per course taught.

Monday	Tuesday	Wednesday	Thursday	Friday	
Get to know/ Team Building/ Organization	Get to know/ Team Building/ Organization	G.T.K./ T.B./ Org. Writing Steps Graphing	Design Team Prewriting Graphing	Design Team Life Map Graphing	(Integrated Science/Social Studies Lessons) (Language Arts Lessons) (Math Lessons)
Universe Magazine Story Place Value	Galaxies Mystery/Horror Thousands	Stars Sci Fi/ Fantasy Millions	Constellations & Myths Advent/ Hist. Fiction Decimals	Constellations & Myths Rough Draft of Story Math Test	(Integrated Science/Social Studies Lessons) (Language Arts Lessons) (Math Lessons)
Gravity Drafting Rdg. Wkshp. Symbols	Tour the Solar System Drafting Rdg. Wkshp. Area & Dimension	Figure Distances Drafting Rdg. Wkshp. Multiplication Quiz	Elliptic Orbit Drafting Rdg. Wkshp. Multiply by 1 Digit	Solar System Fast Facts Drafting Rdg. Wkshp. Multiply by 1 Digit	(Integrated Science/Social Studies Lessons) (Language Arts Lessons) (Math Lessons)
No School	No School	Timeline/ Apollo 13 Global Response Repeated Addition	"The Planets" w/ Patrick Stewart Global Response Addition Practice	Field Trip to Planetarium Revising No math due to trip	(Integrated Science/Social Studies Lessons) (Language Arts Lessons) (Math Lessons)
Intro. Space Project - choose topic Revising Mutiplication - 2 digits	Teach Note Taking/ writing paragraphs 2nd Draft 2 digit practice - Relay Games	Write Paragraphs 2nd Draft Subtraction (take away vs. difference)	Pop-up book Visual Proofread Subtraction with Base 10	Oral Presentations Final Copy Visual Word Problems	(Integrated Science/Social Studies Lessons) (Language Arts Lessons) (Math Lessons)
Space Exploration - Memorial to Space Shuttle Crew Final Copy Due Book Study Long Division Notes & Practice	Moon - One Giant Leap, Music, etc. Book Study (Writing & Reading Time) Long Division Word Problems	Lost on the Moon activity Book Study (Writing & Reading Time) 6 weeks Math Test (No Long Division)	Colonization simulation Book Study (Writing & Reading Time) Long Division - 2 digits into 2/3 digits	Space Test Final Copy Due Share Stories written Share Book Studies Long Division Word Problems	(Integrated Science/Social Studies Lessons) (Language Arts Lessons) (Math Lessons)

Sample Elementary Lesson Plan

Objectives: To be able to demonstrate the Millions Block
                   To be able to identify characteristics of a Science Fiction or Fantasy story
                   To be able to compare/contrast different types of Stars

Materials: Math book, Science Fiction and Fantasy notes on transparency, white paper,
                  Kids Discover Magazine, Mobius handout, Venn Diagram handout

Homework: Math - Math in Space, p. 34-36 (Mobius Loop & experiments)
                 Rdg. - Read for 20 minutes and list the main events from the chapter/section you
                        read

Journal: If I could capture a star, I'd...

Words of the Day: cluster - a group of similar things gathered closely together
                         universe - all the matter and space that exists

Daily Oral Language: Read the following sentence and circle the proper nouns. What is the
                            rule for proper nouns?
                            The Sun is a star in the Milky Way Galaxy.

Daily Geography: a) Name the ocean closest to the Arctic Circle.
                        b) Which one is farthest from the Arctic Circle?

Daily Math: Write the following numbers in expanded form:

                   a) 758 b) ten thousand five hundred nine c) 2,707

Procedures:

8:00-8:30	Announcements, Homework calendar, Word of the Day, Journal
8:30-9:00	Daily Oral Language, Geography & Math
9:00-9:45	- Review homework from last night over Thousands place & expanded form - Give notes from page 18 in Math book- into math notebook - Practice Millions place & assign homework
9:45-9:50	Bathroom Break/ Go to Specials
9:50-10:45	Specials/ Planning period
10:50-11:20	- Reading Workshop - set up folder with paper in middle for responses & choose novel to read - Silent reading
11:20-12:00	- Give notes on Science FictionGenre and pre-write a story in this genre - Give notes on Fantasy Genre and pre-write a fantasy story
12:00-12:50	Lunch/ Recess
12:50 - 2:30	- Read to students about stars from the Kids Discover Magazine & discuss -Student pairs use Venn Diagram to compare/contrast different types of stars - Students create their own Mobius Loop and conduct experiments (See copied directions)

Sample Elementary Lesson Plan in Actual Format (2 pages)

Objectives: To be able to understand Place Value using Base 10
To be able to transfer numbers from standard to numerical form
To be able to write a story as a team
To be able to discuss man's place within the galaxy
To be able to use a timeline to record historical facts

Materials: Base 10 pieces (yellow), long white paper, Timeline copies, Universe video, black construction paper, small white paper

Homework: Math - Place Value
Rdg. - Read for 20 minutes
L.A. - Write one sentence for each word using it correctly

Journal: If you had x-ray vision, what would you use it for?

Word of the Day: galaxy - a large group of stars, planets, gas and dust
Light-year - the distance that light travels in one year - about six trillion miles
Space - the expanse in which the solar system, stars, and galaxies exist, another world

Daily Oral Language: Read the following sentence and identify the helping verb. Is this the only helping verb that can be used for this sentence? Why or why not?

All the stars in the sky are part of the Milky Way Galaxy.

(Answer) *The word "are" is the helping verb. It is the only possible choice because the noun is plural.*

Daily Geography: A) Which ocean is the largest in the world?

B) Which Hemisphere is south of where you live?

(Answer) *a) Pacific*   *b) Southern and Western*

Daily Math: Write the following numbers in numerical form:

A) three thousand four hundred twenty nine
B) nine hundred forty
C) ten thousand seven

Sample Lesson Plan, continued

Procedures:

8:00-8:30	Announcements, Homework Calendar, Word of the Day, Journal
8:30-8:45	Daily Oral Language
8:45-9:00	Daily Geography
9:00-9:45	Daily Math

Introduce/Review basic place value using Base 10 Blocks:

    a) Create a place value chart - divide long white paper into thirds and make
        a Ones column, Tens column, and Hundreds column

    b) Students take out Base 10 pieces - discuss pieces

    c) Give random numbers to students and have students
        place pieces in the correct column (assessment activity)

    d) Continue to practice with students - have students come
        up with their own numbers (extension activity)

    e) Then write out numbers in standard form to get ready
        for homework

    f) Closure - students write in math journal what they learned today

9:45-9:55	Bathroom Break/ Go to Specials
10:50-11:20	Reading Workshop - Students read for 20 minutes. They may sit anywhere in the room - No Talking! Teacher either reads with students on an individual basis, or monitors students reading. After the 20 minute buzzer rings, students return to seats to write response in log.

Reading Response: Where will the main character be 20 years from now?

11:25-12:00 Round Robin Writing - Give each table a different topic

    -A day at the Beach   -I think my mom is an alien
    -Summer Picnic   -A crazy soccer game
    -The day the sky turned black   -the hungry spider

each table gets one topic (on index cards to be drawn), each child has notebook
paper, each person starts their own story, say go, wait three minutes and
stop, pass the paper to right, read the story and continue it. Do this until
you get your story back (approx. 3 or 4 times).

12:00-12:50	Lunch/ Recess
12:50-2:30	Set up Mission Log - White folder - title it Student Log

Middle section -Cover page - (Mission Log, name, teacher & grade), Timeline
pages, Blank paper

    • Students write in the dates on their timeline
    • Students write in the first timeline event and discuss it
    • Watch Galaxy film to introduce Galaxy unit
    • Students make model of galaxy by punching holes in black paper and back
       it with white paper (use pencil to punch holes)

Assessment will be finished timeline at end of unit

2:30-2:50   Read Aloud or Journal and Clean up Room

Blank Template

Date:

Objectives: To be able to
To be able to
To be able to

Materials:

Homework: Reading. -
Lang. Arts -
Math-
Science -
Social Studies-

Journal:

Words of the Day:

Daily Oral Language:

Daily Geography:

Daily Math:

Procedures: (note: these times are in half hour blocks, but you may need to
individualize your schedule – See the sample lesson plans for examples)

8:00-8:30
8:30-9:00
9:00-9:30
9:30-10:00
10:00-10:30
10:30-11:00
11:00-11:30
11:30-12:00
12:00-12:30
12:30-1:00
1:00-1:30
1:30-2:00
2:00-2:30
2:30-3:00

Closure Activity:

Assessment:

Sample Lesson Plan - 9th Grade Creative Writing

Objectives: To be able to compose a narrative using real life experiences
                   To be able to design a life-map of important events

Materials: Real Life story (from my life), object to go with the story, large white paper, markers, crayons, color pencils, large sheets of paper for each student

Homework: Write a draft of a story based on real life experiences

Focus Activity: Read the news article about the ozone layer on the overhead (or the handout) and relate the events in that story to your life. How is this affecting your life, or how might it affect your life in the future?

Procedures:

9:00-9:05   Student enter and work on focus assignment. Teacher checks attendance and
(1:20-1:25)   visits with each student around the room, checking homework calendars

9:05-9:10   Share a few journal entries as a class
(1:25-1:30)

9:10-9:25   Lesson - Real Life Writing
(1:30-1:45)

                  a) read own real life story to the students, "My Golden Puppy"

                  b) discuss - what made this story enjoyable? Did you think it was good? Why or why not? What about it was fun or interesting? Move into class discussion about how real life experiences can make a better story because we are able to add more details. We are writing about what we know.

                  c) show students the object related to the story and explain that the story was based on a real life experience

9:25-9:45   a) Pass out large sheets of paper
(1:45-2:05)

                  b) Explain to students that we will be writing and illustrating a life map which will help us remember important events in our lives

                  c) Students create their own life-map

9:45-9:50   Closure - Students write on index cards -- why should we use experiences &
(2:05-2:10)   knowledge from our own lives in our writing? Pass in cards/Clean up to leave

Blank Template (Secondary)

Date:

Objectives: To be able to
To be able to

Materials:

Homework:

Journal:

Word of the Day:

Daily Sponge Activity:

Procedures:

1.)

2.)

3.)

4.)

5.)

6.)

7.)

Assessment/ Evaluation:

Homework

Homework for tonight is...Groan, whine, whimper! These are often the responses from our class as we dole out their duties for the evening. Why do we put ourselves through the aggravation of assigning homework only to hear loud protests? Often we only receive a half-hearted effort, if it gets completed at all. Is homework really necessary?

Over the past century our society has gone from the belief that homework is essentially bad to the belief that homework is good and back again. In their book, *Who's Teaching Your Children?*, Vivian Troen and Katherine Boles trace this transition from the 1900's to recent times. It seems we have come full circle.

Although ten years ago the consensus was that homework was good, Troen & Boles point out that "parental backlash against the ever-growing burden of homework is clearly spreading nationwide." Additionally, current research shows that while homework given in sixth grade and increased through high school is beneficial, it is a complete waste of time for students in Kindergarten through 5th grade. (p. 125-126)

From our experiences in the classroom, we have seen that homework in the elementary grades is not necessary to enhance student learning. During this crucial learning period it is vital to give students time to complete their work in class rather than at home. Why?

- Teacher can supervise student work

- Students get immediate feedback on their efforts

- Teacher can correct misunderstandings and incorrect answers immediately

- Students do not repeat wrong information over and over which must then be unlearned during class

- Teacher can assess student learning/acquisition of skills while monitoring students

Student practice of skills/knowledge during class time is a much more effective measure of assessment and/or extension of learning than sending it home where it may or may not be completed by the student.

> *"What is the goal of your homework assignments?"*

Assigning homework in moderation can be useful to instill values of self-discipline and responsibility in older students. Homework is effective in helping to build a work ethic in our students. However, it must be done in moderation!

Teachers should remember that when homework is assigned, one student could easily spend hours on the same assignment that takes another student just 15 minutes to complete. Why do we need to assign 25 two-digit multiplication problems when 5 will show us whether or not students can apply the concept?

Keep in mind the following factors which influence a child's ability to complete homework:

- A chaotic home environment with many children - the student may have adult responsibilities within the home

- Students who are without parental supervision for most of the time after school hours

- Students living in poverty who may not have a place to complete homework nor the supplies needed

- Older students who might work after school

- Busy family and extra-curricular lives including sports, church, clubs, community service activities, and family events

Must Teach Organization Skills

If you must assign homework due to parental and/or school demands, it is vital that you teach students how to keep themselves organized. It is difficult to keep up with homework assignments for several classes along with the materials needed to complete those assignments.

- Keep an "Unfinished" folder or "Homework" pocket-folder where students can place work to be done on one side and work completed on the other side. Label each side clearly.

- Train students to keep materials, handouts, and work completed in a specific section of their 3-ring binder for each subject area.

- Train students to use an academic calendar to copy down homework for each class. Check that this information has been copied down correctly and initial it each day.

"It is vital to teach students organization skills which will help them in the future."

Write out Homework Procedures

Procedures are important to help students and parents know what you expect in regards to homework assignments. Type out your homework procedures and expectations to give to students and parents. One copy should go in the student's binder and the other should be posted on the refrigerator at home. *(An example can be found in the next chapter.)*

• What homework stays the same each night or each week?

• Do you expect parents to sign the academic calendar once a week?

• When and where do you expect assignments to be turned in?

• What is your policy for absences and late-work? How long do students have to turn in the assignment? How will their grade be affected?

Tips

• Offer positive feedback for students who turn in their work on time.

• Allow students two days for every one day absent to make up their work. Remember, they are now having to complete double the assignments, so cut them a little slack.

• Take off points each day an assignment is late. I usually take off 5 points for each day. Be sure to clearly explain your policy for latework.

• Remind students of missing assignments each day. Many will forget that they owe you the work.

• Provide before or after-school time to make up missing work or to complete homework with you available for supervision and help.

• Set aside one place in the classroom where assignments are turned in to be graded. Keep this the same all year to cut down on confusion.

• Have parents sign the Homework Procedures/ Policy form to be placed in the students' binders.

• Do not take away recess as punishment for no homework. This is counter-productive and will cause further stress in the classroom.

> Idea Share:
>
> If you must assign nightly homework, make it something the students and parents can do together.
>
> Family reading time where parents or older siblings read to younger children for 20 minutes or longer is a meaningful activity on many levels.
>
> Older students can keep a reading log for accountability.

Grading Homework

Remember that homework should only be used to instill the values of self-discipline and responsibility within our students. As we discussed earlier, it is not a valid assessment tool for student learning since there are so many unknown variables which can influence completion of the assignment. That being the case, homework assignments can be graded with a system of checks for the level of completion. This holds students accountable for the work, but no more.

> **Example:**
> (√)   (homework completed)
> (√–)   (homework partially completed)

These types of grades might count towards a participation grade, but individually should not account for much of the student's overall average. In-class assignments and assessments should make up the majority of the student's grade in order to accurately reflect learning.

Defense of No Homework

If you feel that you will have a difficult time defending the decision to not assign homework, whether to your administrator, district administrators, or parents, we suggest that you read the book, The End of Homework: How Homework Disrupts Families, Overburdens Children, and Limits Learning by E. Kralovec and J. Buell for supporting research. Additionally, there are several articles available on the internet which point out the deficiencies in assigning homework which may help you defend this position.

OVERVIEW

When thinking about homework, keep the following in mind:

- Do more work during class time.

- Do not assign homework to younger students.

- When assigning homework to older students, lighten the load.

- If homework is necessary, make the assignments meaningful.

- Do not use homework to assess student learning.

Conclusion

Detailed lesson planning is one of the major keys to a successful classroom. Without it teachers are unprepared and unorganized which causes students to be unruly and disruptive. Rather than broad topics in a small box, lesson planning encompasses so much more. It involves thinking through objectives carefully, developing engaging activities to motivate students and enhance the lesson, and creating meaningful assessments of knowlege learned. To use an analogy, lesson planning is the jar that contains our methods for teaching students. When used properly, everything flows out smoothly into each container. Without it, our ideas and strategies have no guidance and spill hapazardly around the room.

Questions to Ponder

Why do you think it is important to write out detailed lesson plans for each day instead of simply writing "fractions" in the planning book?

Do you feel it is important to have a focus assignment for every single class? Why or Why Not?

What is your opinion of giving students time in class to do assignments rather than as homework?

How can you prepare yourself and your class for a formal teacher observation?

Additional Resources

Daily Planning for Today's Classroom: A Guide to Writing Lesson and Activity Plans
by Kay Price and Karna Nelson

The End of Homework: How Homework Disrupts Families, Overburdens Children, and Limits Learning
by E. Kralovec and J. Buell

Rethinking Assessment

Part of planning is knowing how you will evaluate the results of your efforts. In laying the foundation for a fire, you know that you will see and feel the results of you work. You'll be able to see whether the fire is large enough, whether it provides enough light, and whether it generates enough heat for your purposes. The purpose of the fire is determined during the planning stage. Having the ultimate purpose clear in mind, you are better able to evaluate the results. In turn, the results of your evaluation may cause further action on your part or not.

It is the same with learning. Assessment must be considered in the planning, implementation, and evaluation stages in order for it to be effective. We need to know what we will evaluate (our objectives). Then we need to conduct ongoing evaluation to determine necessary changes. Lastly, we need to evaluate the final results.

Often we skip the first two parts of assessment and focus solely on the third, the final evaluation. This may come in the form of an end of the chapter or end of the unit test. It may be multiple choice, essay, fill-in-the-blank, or something in between. But what about those informal assessments that help us to determine whether students are on track? What about the prior planning for assessment within our lesson plans?

Also, if we do decide to pull in assessment in the planning and implementation stages, how will we accomplish it? What strategies will we use? How effective will they be in evaluating student knowledge and/or progress?

When thinking about Assessment, let's remember that...

- It is important to continually check our assessment philosophy and techniques. By doing this, we make sure that our assessment presents a true picture of student achievement.

- Proper assessment can be a challenge.

- It is important to vary and adapt assessment tools to fit different learning styles an instructional needs.

"Effective teachers continually re-evaluate their assessment techniques."

Philosophy of Assessment

Here are some thoughts to help you reflect on your philosophy of student assessment:

Assessment is so much more than just assigning a letter grade. It should provide teachers with detailed information to share with parents.

- Proper assessment throughout the school year will:
  - Measure the progress a student has made
  - Show students' strengths and weaknesses
  - Allow a teacher to check for understanding

By varying the ways we measure student achievement, we can tap into different kinds of learners and accurately represent student progress and achievement.

> *For example:*
>
> If a student has difficulty with writing and every single method of assessment in a Social Studies class is an essay test, what kind of grades do you think this student will get in Social Studies? If, however, you vary your assessment tools and give an oral interview or observe the student discussing concepts with other peers, then that student has a chance to really show you what has been learned! This student may be able to tell you the entire history of the Civil War if you asked him, but when he has to write it down, he fails and receives a poor history grade. Is that a fair assessment of his historical knowledge? This is an important issue for teachers!

Your lesson should reflect the type of assessment tool you use.

- Are you going to have students create a timeline of important dates during the American Revolution? Then you need to teach your lesson or give students notes in a timeline format.

- Essay questions require a classroom discussion where students can express their thoughts and opinions.

If a student does not understand what the teacher's expectations are, it will be difficult to get a true picture of what that student has really learned.

- Do you expect your students to be able to compare and contrast fractions with decimals? Make sure that students know this. Students cannot meet your expectations if you do not tell them what they are.

Directions for any evaluation should be clear and precise. When students are confused, they cannot show their knowledge of the skill or concept being assessed.

- Use simple language and sentences. Too many compound or complex sentences will cause your students to bog themselves down in your instructions.

- Follow your own directions exactly as you have written them to double check the clarity.

Alternative Assessment Tools

There are a variety of ways to assess student work and learning. A common dilemma among teachers is how to find different ways to assess students other than paper and pencil examinations. Here we have provided for you different ways you can evaluate your students' learning. You might not use every method, and you may vary your assessment tools with each class and/or each student. Whatever methods of appraisal you choose, just be sure to use a diversity.

Observations

Teachers can observe students in various situations and can keep records for grading purposes.

- **Walk around the room**
  If you walk around the room, you can more accurately observe students without them necessarily knowing that you are grading them. Students often freely share their knowledge when they are not intimidated by the pressure of getting graded!

- **Observe students in cooperative group discussions**
  Are they participating? Are they showing knowledge of a concept or comprehension of a reading passage by the comments they make in a discussion? Are the students correctly using a skill that was taught?

Clipboard Cruising is one way of keeping records on observations of each student. Have one clipboard for every subject (Math, Language Arts, Social Studies…)

Make up a large index card for each student, and tape the top of the cards vertically along a clipboard in alphabetical order, so that you can easily flip through them. For each observation, date the entry and make a short, but detailed statement of what you observed. You do not have to make a record of each student every time! Just record noticeable observations on that day. You'll want to replace the index cards each grading period, and put the old card in the student files.

We have another example of clipboard monitoring in the Classroom Environment chapter with a spreadsheet that is also effective in the classroom.

Example:

Suzy Smarts – Social Studies	
9/20/98	Great discussion and reasoning of why the Southern Confederacy was fighting to preserve their way of life. Logical thinking and specific examples used!
10/05/98	Provided few specifics – conference with Suzy about reading requirements.
10/15/98	Excellent work on timeline project, showing knowledge and comprehension of material – good improvement!

Student Reflection

When students are asked to reflect on their own growth and knowledge of a concept or theme, it forces them to take reponsibility for their own learning. Students create their own meaning instead of memorizing and regurgitating information, which provides the teacher with a clear picture of what the student actually learned and internalized. You might use this assessement tool after students read a book or passage, after students have studied a unit, or with student projects.

Clear and Unclear Windows

This is another variation of student reflection. In this format, students fold their paper into two or more sections. They label half of the paper as clear windows, and the other half as unclear windows. In the clear window boxes, the students write what they have learned and understand about a topic, reading, or concept. In the unclear window boxes the students write about the concepts that they do not understand or where they need clarification. This is a great resource for teachers as they can shape future lessons to accommodate for unclear windows.

Semantic Web or Mind Map

This is a fabulous method of assessment as well as a great way to teach students how to organize information. Students need to learn how to make connections and find relationships among varying facts and concepts. The students place a main topic in the middle of the paper, and then branch off with related details. Each branch then might have another branch off of it and/or connecting that fact or statement with another detail. This can be written or drawn. Using this as an assessment really shows the teacher how a student's knowledge is organized in their brain, or if they don't understand a concept at all.

"A Mind Map is an excellent assessment tool for students who like to draw."

As with all of these different types of assessment, it is important that you model for students what you expect to see when they turn in their work. Model how they would create a mind-map around a specific concept or skill.

"I learned..." Statement

This assessment can be used after a short activity, such as a lesson or film, in order to measure whether or not the teacher's objectives were met. It could also be used as a culmination to a large thematic unit in place of the dreaded unit test! In the "I learned..." statement, the students simply express what they have learned either orally or by writing the sentences. It is best to narrow this assignment to five or less statements so students are forced to prioritize the information instead of throwing out trivial little facts. This is another assessment where Bloom's Keywords can come in handy.

Summary Statement

This is longer and takes more depth than the "I learned" statements. The students are asked to summarize what they have learned in a coherent paragraph. This may also be an oral or written assignment. A summary should require the students to make connections among the various facts they learned instead of simply stating isolated data. This type of activity requires higher-level thinking skills on the part of students.

Interviews

Oral interviews can be held with individual students on any topic to see how much a student learned, or to check for understanding. The interview should be short and last no longer than five minutes. The questions should include a range of lower level to higher level thinking. The lower level questions will provide opportunities for success and build student self-esteem. The higher level questions will allow you to assess student reasoning ability. Teachers should take notes during the interviews for grading and record-keeping purposes.

> **Teacher Talk**
>
> *"My second year of teaching I had one student in particular who was a concern. It seemed that he could not pass any test that I gave him. However, I knew that he understood the content because of discussions we'd had in class. After a while, I gave him some oral examinations to see how well he would do. He passed every time. This student had a hard time getting the information from his head onto paper. Had I not ever thought of varying my assessment for him, he would not have passed my class."*

Visual/Pictoral Assignments

Visual learners can often express their knowledge beautifully through many different types of artistic and creative assignments. Here are some great examples of visual assessment tools: Illustrations to go with writing and to show comprehension of material, pictures with captions, cartoon drawings, murals, mobiles, dioramas (shoe box scenes), students creating their own maps, charts, graphs, posters, travel brochures, and mind maps. There are several different activities of this nature in the Motivating Students chapter which can be used to assess student learning.

K-W-L Chart

Prior to a lesson or unit have the students create their own KWL chart. Students fold their paper into three sections. Label each section K, W, or L. The students complete the K section (what they already know about the topic), and the W section (what they want to know about the topic) prior to the lesson or unit. At the end for an assessment, the students finish the L section (what they learned about the topic). In primary classes, this chart can be done on large butcher paper as a class. Then you can use individual interviews to determine each student's answer for the L section. After the interviews, put student answers on the chart and discuss them as closure to the unit.

Checklist of Objectives

When students have a lengthy assignment, a helpful tool for teachers to evaluate student progress is to have the students fill out a checklist. When students are given time to work on the project in class and you don't want to grade in depth until the final project, you can ask to see the student's checklist along with corresponding work. That way a brief glance shows you whether or not a student is on track. An easy grade can be given at this point for effort and progress, or completeness of that particular section. Earlier we discussed how Bloom's keywords can be used to create a checklist so students are required to use all levels of thinking.

See our example below:

Native American Project

_____ 1. Identify, locate, and illustrate on a map the area(s) where your tribe lived. (Knowledge)

_____ 2. Explain the culture and daily life of your tribe. (Comprehension)

_____ 3. Construct a visual teaching tool to demonstrate the lifestyle of your tribe. (ex: diarama, model, poster, video)   (Application)

_____ 4. Compare and Contrast your tribe with another tribe when looking at food, dwellings, religious ceremonies, and geographic location. This will require you to communicate with one other group. (Analysis)

_____5. Organize a presentation that incorporates all of the information you have gathered about your tribe in order to teach others. (Synthesis)

_____ 6. Determine how well your tribe would be able to survive in America's modern environment. (Evaluation)

Student Evaluations:

Evaluate your group on the following:

___ Cooperation within the team
___ Individual participation
___ Information gathered
     ___ amount   ___ correctness
     ___ elaboration

___ Visual teaching aid
     ___ creativity   ___ best quality
     ___ accurate   ___ use in presentation

___ Presentation
     ___ individual participation
     ___ clearly spoken
     ___ loud voices
     ___ creativity

Portfolio Assessment

Many teachers do not rely on portfolios when assessing students because they are confused about what a portfolio is and what it should be used for. Do we only use the best student pieces or do we put both "good" and "bad" work in to show improvement? Also, how do we grade the portfolio? If the work is already graded, do we grade it again? The following is a brief "How To" on portfolios.

Goals

- Decide what your goal is. What is the purpose of the portfolio? What is unique about you and your students? Your goal should reflect your classroom and your students. Some possible goals might include the following:

  - Student Improvement
  - Mastery of Certain Skills
  - Amount of learning occurred
  - Collection of student work

*Remember that your goal should reflect you, your classroom and your students.

Assessment

- Before using portfolios, you need to decide how you will grade them. Once again, what is the pupose of this portfolio? Assessment of the portfolio is closely tied to your goal.

  - Quality of work in the portfolio
  - Amount of work in the portfolio
  - Improvement
  - Knowledge of skills

The easiest way to assess a portfolio is on a rating scale. The rating scale must also reflect your goal. You must decide for yourself what you are looking for in each portfolio entry, or in the portfolio as a whole, and then create a rating scale to reflect that. For example, let's say your goal is to show the amount and quality of learning that has occurred over the semester. You might evaluate each entry as Correct (mechanics), Complete (information), and Comprehensive (thought provoking) with the student receiving a score of 1-4 in each area:

    1 = not at all   2 = somewhat   3 = mostly   4 = entirely

The scores then would be added up to give a grade for the entire portfolio.

Ask another teacher to help you assess the portfolios in order for them to be a reliable form of evaluation. Why? Well, we often grade according to the student. If the work in the portfolio is absolutely terrible and not up to standards, but we know that this is the best the student can do, then we might be more lenient on our rating scale than another teacher who doesn't know the student. Thus, the impartial evaluator helps to make the portfolio a much more reliable and accurate form of assessment. The two grades can be averaged and used as the grade for the portfolio.

Student Involvement

Student involvement is a very important part of the portfolio process. After all, it is the students we are evaluating. There are three main components to student involvement.

- **Understanding** -

It is very important that students understand what the portfolio is, your goals, your rating scale, the pieces you want included, and how it will be used. This needs to be explained at the beginning of the year. If you wait until the end of the semester, your students will not be as involved with the portfolio and you will not get a true reflection of their thoughts and feelings about their work. If your students understand what is required of them, they will be much more likely to create what you want in a portfolio.

- **Choice -**

Choice is an extremely important aspect of the portfolio. There are some pieces that you will want them to include so that you can accomplish your goal, but there should be some entries that express and reflect the student's personality and preferences. You may be able to give students some choice even in the work you require, but it is absolutely vital that your students be allowed to choose work that is a reflection of them or their progress whether it is bad or good.

- **Reflection -**

Students should write a reflection of their thoughts and ideas about each portfolio entry. You may want to ask students to write why they chose to include certain pieces, or how they felt about an assignment. These reflections will give you an even clearer picture of the student's work, learning, and progress throughout the year.

Another important aspect to reflection is a discussion between teacher and student of each piece and reflection in the portfolio. Some sort of dialogue needs to occur between student and teacher so that a clear understanding of the portfolio occurs. The student and the teacher should be able to explain each entry.

> **Teacher Tip**
>
> Student reflection on portfolio entries is an important part of the process. However, it is important to remember that student reflections must be done in a timely manner. If you wait until the end of the year to do reflections, most students won't remember what the assignment was for in the first place.

Sample Portfolio Outline

An outline of details regarding how you plan to use the portfolio will make things much easier for you in the long run. It will also help you to remember what you decided at the beginning of the year. Below is a sample portfolio outline for a Language Arts class. It is not absolutely necessary that you produce an outline with the same detail, but it does help.

PORTFOLIO ASSESSMENT

GOAL:	To show the amount of learning that has occurred over the semester.

FOCUS:	The focus will be on the reflection statements for each entry since most of the work has already been graded.

ITEMS TO BE EVALUATED:	Students must include one narrative, two expository (how to; compare/contrast, etc.), journal entries, and three poetry pieces. In addition, students must choose 5 other assignments from class to put in the portfolio.

STUDENT INVOLVEMENT:	Student choice of 5 assignments should show what they have learned over the semester. These entries can be both good and poor work samples. Students must write a reflection over each entry. The reflection should express the purpose of the entry in the portfolio, the skill(s) it shows accomplished (or working on), any thoughts or feelings about the entry and why they put it in the portfolio. Before the portfolio is evaluated, the student and teacher will have a conference to discuss the entries included and the portfolio as a whole.

CRITERION:	Each reflection/entry will be evaluated as being Correct (mechanics), Complete (information), and Comprehensive (thought provoking) with the student receiving a score of 1-4 in each area where 1 = not at all; 2 = somewhat; 3 = mostly; and 4 = entirely.

RELIABILITY:	Two teachers will score the portfolio. One teacher will be myself, the main instructor, and the other teacher will be one who is not as familiar with the students. These two scores will be averaged and used as a final grade for the semester.

VALIDITY:	This portfolio will have content validity because it measures the student's awareness of what was taught in class. Students reflect on what they learned through each experience or project done in class.

Portfolio Conference Sheet

Student Name _____   Date_____

Teacher Name _____

Directions: Make comments about the discussion under each entry of the portfolio.

Title of Entry

1. _____

2. _____

3. _____

4. _____

5. _____

6. _____

Name _____   Grade _____

Class _____   Teacher _____

Description of Entry	Complete (1-4)	Correct (1-4)	Comprehensive (1-4)
1.			
2.			
3.			
4.			
5.			
6.			
7.			
8.			
9.			

The grade is marked in the smaller box with comments in the larger box.
Each student should have a reflection of about 5 to 10 sentences for each entry (upper elementary).

© 2005 McDonald and Hershman

Grading with Rubrics

Subjective grading is one of the hardest parts of evaluating students. How do we judge their work? Is there a specific criteria we use? Do we compare different student results? It is important to grade writing, projects, and other types of subjective assignments in a fair manner.

The rubric is one way that you can evaluate student performance in a manner that is equitable and judges students on his or her own merits. It also provides an overall picture of the assignment and a set criteria to use when grading. Below are a few strategies for using a rubric when grading.

- Decide what skill(s)/objective(s) you want the student to show

- Write these down in a checklist format

- Grade each skill/objective on a scale of 1 to 4 where

    1 = poor, 2 = fair, 3= good, and 4 = excellent

- Average the numbers to get a total score for the assignment

- Final scores might look like this:

1- = 60	1 = 65	1+ / 2- = 70	2 = 75	2+ / 3- = 80
3 = 85	3+ / 4- = 90		4 = 95	4+ = 100

Diorama of American Revolution

Score	Criteria	1	2	3	4
3	Scene from American Revolution	1	2	3	4
3	Correct Information	1	2	3	4
4	Complete sentences used on index card	1	2	3	4
3	Colorful	1	2	3	4
2	Creative	1	2	3	4
3	Neat	1	2	3	4

18   Total Points =   18/ 6 = 3   = Grade   85

Comments:

Grading Writing Assignments

Technically writing assignments are subjective, and it is one of the hardest areas of grading. Here are a few strategies to help you with this challenge:

- Use a rubric like the one on the previous page. Grade only the skills you have already covered in class.

- Use an overall rubric. With this students will receive one grade for their entire paper. A sample overall rubric is provided in the back of this chapter. Also, your district, school, or perhaps the state, may have developed a writing rubric that they expect you to use. Ask other teachers or the Language Arts department chair for this information.

- Give students two separate grades for their paper. One for content and one for mechanics.

When giving two separate grades on writing assignments –

The content grade can be a 1-4 on the ideas expressed and how well they followed the writing mode. The mechanics grade can be on a scale of 1-100 with one point or 1/2 point taken for each grammar error in the paper. You can then average the two grades, OR keep them separate for your grade book. Be sure you are grading grammar learned previously. Correct the mistakes, but do not count off for rules not yet taught or learned in a previous grade. How do you know? Check with the students' teachers from the year before.

Teacher Talk

"It really concerned me as I was grading student work that they were receiving a grade which reflected their effort as well as the grammar skills demonstrated. During my student teaching, my cooperating teacher told me to grade one and then judge the others according to that first paper. They would be either better or worse. In my mind that is not acceptable. It does not take into account the individual differences of my students. In the end I decided to give students two grades, one for grammar and one for content. This way they are able to see some success and get the constructive feedback they need to improve. With an overall grade, students do not receive the specific feedback in either grammar or content to become better writers."

A Sample Writing Rubric

Score	Characteristics	Score	Characteristics
4	Correct purpose, mode, and audience Elaboration for each point and in each paragraph Consistent organization Clear sense of order/completeness Smooth flow - almost no grammatical errors	2	Correct purpose, mode, and audience A little elaboration (one point/paragraph) A few specific details Lists items rather than describing them Gaps in organization A lot of grammar and spelling errors
3	Correct purpose, mode, and audience Moderately well elaborated (a few points/paragraphs) Somewhat organized Clear language - few grammatical errors	1	Attempts to address the audience Brief/ vague/ No elaboration at all Off topic/ thoughts wander/ No organization Wrong purpose/mode Major grammatical errors

Testing and Test Anxiety

Whether or not you agree with standardized tests as a valid assessment tool for student performance, they are here and it doesn't look like they will be going anywhere for a while. In fact, it seems that the public is leaning more towards these types of tests than they ever have before. What does this mean for us and our students? Well, basically it means more stress.

We are stressed out because, for many of us, our jobs are directly affected by how well our students perform on these tests. Some of us feel the need to "teach to the test" while others take a "back to the basics" approach with students.

One factor that is not often discussed, though, is student test anxiety. I believe that low student scores are often a result of fear and frustration rather than lack of knowledge. This is especially true of our border-line students, or the students who are on the verge of a passing score.

Just imagine yourself in their place. *You know how to work multiplication word problems. You've done it a hundred times in class and most of the time you pass with an average grade. Then a test is placed in front of you. You are told that this is a very important test, and that how well you score will determine what you have and have not learned. You might even be told that this will effect whether or not you go up to the next grade level. Now you are getting nervous and your palms are sweating. You have butterflies in your stomach. You think that you can do this, but you aren't quite sure. The more you think about it, the more nervous you get. Suddenly all you can think about is how nervous and/or scared you are. The teacher announces that it is time to open the test booklet. You see the first question and your mind goes blank.*

Have you ever experienced that same sensation? I know I have, both as a student and as an adult. This is test anxiety. It is a fear that, as we mentioned in the previous chapter, causes your brain to downshift to a lower "gear." When going through test anxiety, it is virtually impossible to concentrate on working through individual test questions.

Understanding How the Brain Works

It doesn't take long to teach your students how their brain works. No matter how old or young, your students should be able to understand the basics. On pages 143 and 144 we discuss the theory of the Triune Brain. Here is just another way you can use this research to help your students.

- Explain the basic theory to your class. Be sure to put it into terms they can understand.

- Discuss/brainstorm different events that can cause them to shift from their "thinking" brain to one of the smaller sections of their brain. These might include being hungry, having to use the bathroom, fighting with someone, being angry, being frustrated, being tired, being afraid, etc.

- Work out with students ways to overcome these stumbling blocks during a test. Prepare, with your students, a classroom environment that will help them stay in "thinking" mode throughout the test.

Create Favorable Testing Conditions

*   Have healthy easy snacks, high in carbohydrates if possible, available for students in the classroom. Always approach this as both a necessity and a privilege for students. Be sure that you explain your expectations regarding food in the classroom in detail. When students understand why food is available and your expectations, they will be less likely to take advantage of the situation. Goldfish crackers, triskets, apple slices, trail-mix, and popcorn are good snacks for testing days. Be sure that you have disposable bowls and napkins as well.

*   If you teach younger students, or have a morning testing class, provide a small breakfast. You might offer muffins and juice or a ready-to-eat fruit.

*   Be sure the lighting in your classroom is adequate. If not, bring a few lamps from home to add more soft light. Also, check the temperature of the room. If the conditions are too cold or hot, students will be more concerned about the temperature than the test. Lastly, are students moderately comfortable? You don't want things too cozy, but if a large student is crammed into a small desk, his/her brain will not be on the test.

*   Explain restroom procedures to students. Make sure they understand that they are not required to "hold it," but that they need to give you a signal. Some teachers like to give each student a small piece of colored construction paper folded in half. The student places this card on their desk to signal the teacher when they are in need of assistance, a snack, or a restroom break. You might want to laminate these cards and use them all year long.

*   Encourage students to eat a good meal and get at least eight hours of sleep the night before a big test. This will help students arrive to school rested. Also, you want to encourage students to arrive a little bit early so that they do not feel rushed before taking the test.

Teach Students Calming Exercises

What do you do with a student who has severe test anxiety or who clams up suddenly during a test? Here are the steps you can teach your students when they are feeling nervous or tired during a test.

1. Close your test booklet and place your answer sheet in the middle of the booklet (or turn the test over).

2. Close your eyes.

3. Imagine yourself in your favorite place - somewhere quiet where you feel calm and relaxed.

4. Slowly count to ten or take several slow deep breaths.

5. Don't think about the test, but try to keep your mind empty/calm (in other words, don't start thinking about what you are going to do later in the day).

6. When you feel ready, open your test booklet and begin again.

Teacher _____

Modified Grading System Grading Scales

	50%-75%		55%-75%		60%-75%		65%-75%		70%-75%
A	75 = 100	A	80 = 100	A	85 = 100	A	90 = 100	A	95 = 100
	74 = 99		79 = 99		84 = 99		89 = 99		94 = 99
	73 = 98		78 = 98		83 = 98		88 = 98		93 = 98
	72 = 97		77 = 97		82 = 97		87 = 97		92 = 97
	71 = 96		76 = 96		81 = 96		86 = 96		91 = 96
	70 = 95		75 = 95		80 = 95		85 = 95		90 = 95
	69 = 94		74 = 94		79 = 94		84 = 94		89 = 94
	68 = 93		73 = 93		78 = 93		83 = 93		88 = 93
	67 = 92		72 = 92		77 = 92		82 = 92		87 = 92
	66 = 91		71 = 91		76 = 91		81 = 91		86 = 91
	65 = 90		70 = 90		75 = 90		80 = 90		85 = 90
B	64 = 89	B	69 = 89	B	74 = 89	B	79 = 89	B	84 = 89
	63 = 88		68 = 88		73 = 88		78 = 88		83 = 88
	62 = 87		67 = 87		72 = 87		77 = 87		82 = 87
	61 = 86		66 = 86		71 = 86		76 = 86		81 = 86
	60 = 85		65 = 85		70 = 85		75 = 85		80 = 85
	59 = 84		64 = 84		69 = 84		74 = 84		79 = 84
	58 = 83		63 = 83		68 = 83		73 = 83		78 = 83
	57 = 82		62 = 82		67 = 82		72 = 82		77 = 82
	56 = 81		61 = 81		66 = 81		71 = 81		76 = 81
	55 = 80		60 = 80		65 = 80		70 = 80		75 = 80
C	54 = 79	C	59 = 79	C	64 = 79	C	69 = 79	C	74 = 79
	53 = 78		58 = 78		63 = 78		68 = 78		73 = 78
	52 = 77		57 = 77		62 = 77		67 = 77		72 = 77
	51 = 76		56 = 76		61 = 76		66 = 76		71 = 76
	50 = 75		55 = 75		60 = 75		65 = 75		70 = 75
D	49 = 74	D	54 = 74	D	59 = 74	D	64 = 74	D	69 = 74
	48 = 73		53 = 73		58 = 73		63 = 73		68 = 73
	47 = 72		52 = 72		57 = 72		62 = 72		67 = 72
	46 = 71		51 = 71		56 = 71		61 = 71		66 = 71
	45 = 70		50 = 70		55 = 70		60 = 70		65 = 70
F	44 = 69	F	49 = 69	F	54 = 69	F	59 = 69	F	64 = 69

Source Unknown

Mid-Term Progress Report

The grades below reflect your child's grade mid-way through the current grading period.

Student's Name _____

Reading _____   **Language Arts** _____   **Art** _____

Math _____   **Science** _____   **P.E.** _____

Social Studies _____   **Foreign Language** _____   **Behavior** _____

══ CONCERNS ══

_____ **Low grades on homework**

_____ **Does not complete assigned work**

_____ **Poor homework/study habits**

_____ **Does not pay attention in class**

_____ **Does not make up missed work**

══ COMMENTS: ══

- -

I have seen my child's mid-term grades.

Student _____

Parent _____

© 2005 McDonald and Hershman

Weekly Progress Report

Student Name _____   Date _____

WORK HABITS	E.E.	M.E.	N.I.	COMMENTS
Completes assignments on time				
Follows directions readily				
Uses time wisely				
Contributes to activities/ discussion				
Works neatly and carefully				
Works Independently				
BEHAVIOR				
Follows school/class rules				
Respects authority				
Considerate of peers				
Cares for school property				
Is self-disciplined				
ACADEMICS				
Reading				
Writing				
Social Studies				
Math				
Science				
Extra-curricular				

EE = Exceeds Expectations   ME = Meets Expectations   NI = Needs Improvement   *(Developed by Spring Branch ISD Summer Program)*

MISSING ASSIGNMENTS:

Parent Signature _____   Date _____

If you have any questions, feel free to call me at _____ .

Missing Assignments

Name: _____

Assignments:

_____

_____

_____

_____

_____

_____

_____

_____

_____

_____

_____

_____

_____

_____

_____

_____

_____

Parent Signature: _____

Conclusion

In order to be effective, we must think about how we will assess students in the early stages of lesson planning. The fact that many of our classroom activities can be used as a way to assess student learning is a time saver. However, if we do not take this into consideration, we could find ourselves trying to evaluate students in a manner that is neither valid nor reliable. Always be sure that your assessment matches what you have taught and that it addresses different learner needs. This can be done by varying the type of activities you use. Also, take into account your special needs students, and determine ahead of time how you plan to modify assessments so they are valid. In short, student assessment should not be an after-thought to lessons, but rather a pre-planned effort in order to effectively evaluate learning.

Questions to Ponder

What is your philosophy of assessment?

Are your assessment techniques accurately representing student achievement and progress? Why or why not? What could you do differently?

In what ways can a portfolio be used in the classroom? How might you implement a student portfolio as an assessment?

Are you concerned with the issue of test anxiety? Is this something that you have faced yourself? What issues do you think affect your students' ability to take a test? What can you do to help them?

Additional Resources

Classroom Assessment: What Teachers Need to Know
by W. James Popham

Rubrics for Elementary Assessment: Classroom Ready Blackline Masters for K-6
by Nancy Osborne

Great Performances: Creating Classroom Based Assessment Tasks
by Larry Lewin and Betty Jean Shoemaker

Classroom Assessment for Students with Special Needs in Inclusive Settings
by Cathleen Spinelli

Lighting
the Fire

" When you appeal to the highest level of thinking, you get the highest level of performance."

--- Jack Stack

"The mediocre teacher tells. The good teacher explains. The superior teacher demonstrates. The great teacher inspires."

--- William Arthur Ward

Great Beginnings

It's summer and I'm sleeping. The house is quiet and all is peaceful. The phone rings. I stretch and lazily reach over for the phone. "Where are you? Your classroom is empty and school starts in ten minutes." I hear the principal say calmly into the phone. I jump out of bed and start stressing. I'm not even ready, I think to myself. I don't have plans for the first day. I haven't set up my classroom. My heart beats rapidly and I can feel myself starting to sweat.

Suddenly I sit up in bed. It is still summer and school doesn't start for another three weeks. I breathe a huge sigh of relief and start to calm down.

Why do we have these kinds of dreams? Probably because we all realize that the first day of school is the most important of the entire year. You make or break your classroom environment on this day. The first day and first week is your best chance to build a classroom climate of mutual respect and understanding. You want the students to go home with a feeling that the year will be fun as well as challenging, but also have a clear sense of your expectations.

This is just like lighting the fire. You need a good spark from the match to get the fire going. If you have a dud match, you'll never get it lit! What we do on the first day and during the first week of school is the match for our fire. If we want that fire of learning to become a blaze, we must have a great beginning! This chapter contains ideas and strategies to help that spark along. While most will be a "refresher", perhaps a new idea or two will help light the fire in your classroom.

Prepare seating assignments and/or have grouping arrangements ready.

Being prepared with a way to seat students as they arrive shows planning and organization on your part. It sends a positive message to both parents and students that you know what you are doing and that you have certain expectations from the start.

Have you slacked off on this first day strategy? Chaos in the first ten minutes of the school year is not going to help you light that fire of respect and learning in the classroom. Maybe it's time to start using this oldie but goodie again! If you are still on target with this strategy, the next page offers a few ways you might seat students as they enter the classroom.

Random Seating

Using random seating will give you a good idea of who should and should not be sitting next to each other as you develop your class seating chart. Additionally, it is easier to have a general note of welcome ready at each spot which will be appropriate for all circumstances. Some strategies are listed below.

- Cut up and laminate several different colored squares. Each color should represent either a table or a row of desks. Have enough of each color squares for the seats at that table, or in that row. Tape one colored square to each table or on the first seat of each row. When students enter the classroom, greet them and have them pull a square from a bag or basket. They then locate a seat for that color. This is an organized way of seating students, yet it is random and does allow for some choice. It is also less time consuming as students enter the room.

- If you are working with tables or groups of four, another fun way to seat students randomly is to use the four suites of playing cards, or numbers. This works the same as the colored squares.

- Label each row with a team name. Have laminated cards with the team name ready to pass out to students. You could also use subject area vocabulary, names of famous people, or objects that relate to your subject area.

Primary Idea

Use the same idea as above, but cut out shapes for each table or use the die-cut machine to punch out animals, stars, etc.. Laminate the shapes/ die cuts so that they can be used all year long.

Welcome Note/Nametags

- Have a welcome packet ready on each student's desk. This packet could include a desk nametag, a note from you, a peppermint or pencil, and any other information you want students to have from you.

> *"Welcome students to your class with a note at each seat along with a peppermint or pencil."*

Secondary Idea

Type up your general welcome note and copy it on brightly colored paper. It makes for a nice way to say hello and welcome to students entering your classroom. You might even think about having a student information sheet copied on bright yellow paper for students to start filling out as soon as they sit down.

Here are some short, fun, and easy assignments for students to complete as soon as they walk in the classroom:

- **Name plates** - Give students short pieces of white paper and instruct them to create a name plate. It must be colorful, creative, and fill the entire page. The students may use a theme such as favorite things or family. Have the instructions written on the board or overhead. (Have crayons & paper ready on the table/ desk.) This is a great, colorful way of decorating the classroom. Hang them up as students finish or laminate them to hang up the next day.

- **Journal topic** - Write a fun and interesting journal topic on the board or overhead and have students write and illustrate.

- **Student fun facts sheet**

- **Crossword or Word search puzzle** about you and the school

- **A welcome packet** which could include a student information sheet, a puzzle, a fun story to read, and a page to color

- **Coloring pages** work well for younger students as do wooden puzzles and books. Primary teachers may want to have several activities ready to be used on each table.

- **Brain Teaser or Challenge** is a fun way to start of every class, not just the first day. It is fun to do, yet it also stimulates the brain into thinking mode.

- **A Quick Quiz** to assess what students already know. This activity can be used to help you assess student prior knowledge.

Know where you want students to put their supplies.

- Do you want each item stacked separately?

- Do you want certain items and have the kids keep others?

- You can also ask students to hold on to their supplies until later in the day/class. Just make sure to decide this in advance so that you are consistent.

- You should have received a supply list for your grade/ team before school started. If you don't have one, go ask for it before the first day.

> **Idea Share**
>
> You want to have students busy and engaged while you chat with parents and take care of housekeeping duties. Otherwise you will get off to a bad start.

Planning Ideas for the First Day

√ Alternate your class time between formal procedures, expectations, and fun team building or ice breaker type of activities.

√ Take some time to discuss your personal standards. "I believe in doing your personal best." "Character counts!" "Honesty and integrity are traits that I value highly."

~ You may also have students write down the character traits that are important to them. Older students may even write a personal statement of their values. This could be a personal vision statement and could be used to help you better understand each of your students.

√ **Have a poster or overhead that lists the daily schedule and explain it.**

Students like to know what to expect in the flow of the day. This will deter them from asking you the whole morning long, "When is lunch?" or "What's next?" Additionally, if you get questions such as these, it takes less class time to say, "Look at the schedule."

Secondary teachers can help prevent this question by writing the class agenda on the board for students to follow.

> **Idea Share:**
>
> I like to use the poem, Pretty Good, by Charles Osgood, to introduce the concept of personal best. We take some time to discuss the poem and to discuss how it relates to each of us in the classroom, myself included. It usually stirs up a great discussion and I get across my point of how important it is for each student to do their own personal best.

√ **When presenting rules and consequences speak clearly and firmly.**

- Your tone of voice and attitude are crucial at this point.

- Pause after every expectation/rule, and look each student directly in the eye. Do not go on to the next expectation until you have looked at each and every student. This sends the message that these expecations are not to be taken lightly.

- You need to set distinct expectations and leave no questions about discipline unanswered.

> **Idea Share:**
>
> Pausing after an important statement sends a powerful message to students that they had better pay attention to what you are saying. Direct eye contact completes that feeling of seriousness. You'll find that if you pause long enough, everyone will lift his or her head to look at you. In a world where we are bombarded by noise, silence gathers attention.

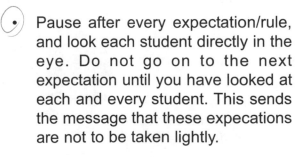

- Make sure your rules and consequences posters are displayed where all students can see them. Also, make sure the writing is large enough to read from anywhere in the classroom. Most districts have a media center where you can take your typed up rules and consequences to be enlarged to poster size and laminated.

- It is important to have the students complete an activity where they will demonstrate knowledge and understanding of each rule and consequence

Example Activities:

- Visual Presentation - Students work in groups to create a visual poster or a skit showing a specific rule and/or consequence and present this to the class. All groups should present!

- Is/Is Not - Students tell and/or show what each expectation Is and Is Not.

- Looks like, Sounds like, Feels like -Students tell and/or show what each expectation would look like, sound like, and feel like if properly followed.

- Have students brainstorm and chart behaviors falling under each rule/ expectation.

Remember: Copying the rules does not help students internalize the information!

BRIEF OVERVIEW:

- Take time to train students in expectations and procedures.
- Expectations are not just class rules, but also life-skills to be exhibited in the classroom
- Demonstrate the "why" behind different expectations for visual learners
- Introduce the concept of "My time" vs. "Your time"

> We discussed setting expectations for students in detail within the Student Discipline section of the Classroom Management chapter. Take some time to review that information in order to apply those strategies on the first day.

Teacher Talk

"I never realized how much my tone of voice influenced the way students responded to me. Although I had gone over the class rules with them several times throughout the year and trained them in my procedures, I was still having trouble with certain students ignoring my directions or acting familiar with me. Then I heard myself on a recording, and realized that when I speak I have a very soft and timid sounding voice. No wonder they weren't taking me seriously. That summer I practiced using a more forceful voice. I used the tape recorder to help me analyze my voice, and could really tell a difference by the end of the summer. The next year I felt that my students showed me more respect because my tone of voice demanded it."

Checklist for the First Day

Use this checklist to make sure you are ready to start your first day!

_____ **I know how I am going to seat my students when they first walk in the door.**

_____ **I know how I am going to greet students and parents when they arrive to the classroom.**

_____ **I have a short note welcoming my students along with a pencil, peppermint, or other small token on each desk. (Remember, you don't have to write names on these notes)**

_____ **My board is set up with the date, my name, an agenda for the class/ day, and opening assignment instructions.**

_____ **My lesson plans are written out in detail and are where I can get to them easily.**

_____ **My class list(s) are with my lesson plans.**

_____ **My attendance sheet(s) are with my lesson plans.**

_____ **I know what students are going to do with their supplies when they bring them to me.**

_____ **I need the following materials for today:**

_____ **The materials are out and ready for students to use.**

Sample Lesson Plan for the First Day

Intermediate Elementary

Objectives: To become familiar with rules, schedule, and procedures
To be able to work with others in a team situation

Materials: cut white paper, crayons, student information sheets, schedule, class procedures, rules, Themes and units, regular sized white paper & construction paper, progress report, welcome letter, "If You Were" handout

Procedures:

8:00-9:35   Students come in and work on nameplates – create a nameplate on a small piece of white paper. Be creative using crayons and lots of colors. You can use a theme such as favorite things to decorate it, or just make it colorful. Make sure that your first name is very clear – no white spaces. Name should be large.
While students are doing activity you need to:
roll call, take up supplies & check off on student list

- Teacher introductions
- Introduce and practice the quiet signal
- Name game – students get in a circle. 1st person says name, 2nd repeats name & says own name. Go around the circle. Teacher should be last and should say everyone's name.

9:35-9:45   Quickly go over line/ hallway rules with students
Bathroom Break/ Go to Specials

9:45-10:30   Specials – Art, Music, PE rotation

10:35-10:50   Simon Says – after playing, discuss objectives of the game – listening skills and following directions

10:50-12:00   Review school rules, discipline policy, reward system, and consequences
Student groups create a written and oral presentation of one assigned rule telling what it looks like, sounds like, and feels like. Presentation can be a simple discussion or a skit.

12:00-1:05   Bathroom Break/ Lunch/ Recess

1:05-2:30   Student presentation of rules
- Introduce the year-long theme and six weeks units/ Lifeskills
- Object activity – write down the first object that comes to your mind when you think of yourself – draw that object. What does it reveal about you?

2:30-2:55   Clean up
End of the day journal – First day jitters/ Go home

Sample Lesson Plan (One 50 minute Prep/Course)

Objectives: To be able to know everybody's name
To be able to understand the classroom policies and procedures
To be able to share orally

Homework: Create a mind-map or web of the expectations discussed in class. Be prepared to share.

Materials: white paper, index cards, classroom policies and procedures

Procedures:

5 min.	Housekeeping - Students complete information cards - include name, address, phone number, parent's names & phone numbers (if different), birth date, class schedule **While students are working you should – call roll, and do other opening day procedures**
5 min.	Teacher introductions
10 min.	Name game – students get in a circle. 1st person says name, 2nd repeats name & says own name. Go around the circle. Teacher should be last and should say everyone's name.
20 min.	Classroom expectations and procedures
10 min.	Closure - Emphasize importance of working together to learn. I am your guide. What you put into your learning/this class is what you will get out of it. Etc. Journal -- What are your goals for this course? What expectations do you have from me as the instructor?

The first few days should be spent getting to know students and training in classroom procedures/expectations.

If you have Blocked scheduling and have 90 minutes with each class, you will want to alternate between going over classroom procedures/expectations and fun activities.

For example, you might add the following before the closure:

15 min.	Student pairs develop a mind-map of the expectations discussed.
10 min.	Student pairs group together and share mind-maps. How are they similar? How are they different? Can you see the thought patterns of other students? What does this tell us about working together in groups as opposed to working individually?
10 min.	Share results as a class. Why is it important to know expectations up front?

More First Day Strategies/Ideas

- Throughout the day you want to have several fun team building and ice-breaker activities. These should be structured and organized activities, not a free for all. Make sure to have clear instructions for each activity.

- Prior to the students leaving your classroom for any reason, you need to explain hallway rules and procedures.

- Prior to lunch and/ or recess, be sure to go over any cafeteria and playground rules. This will save you if a student misbehaves on the first day. You can tell your principal that you already explained the rules!

 • Students feel appreciative when you display their work. Have them do activities on the first day that you can hang up in the classroom or hallway right away. This is a great way to show the students that you value them and their work.

- Have the students fill out a student information sheet with all necessary information. A sample is included in the back of this chapter.

- Go over your procedures and expectations with the students. It is helpful to provide them with a copy to take home! This will include homework expectations, daily assignments, quizzes and testing information.

> *Teacher Tip:*
>
> Displaying student work on the very first day really goes a long way to showing students that they are valued. While this may not seem like much to you, our students want to know that we value the work they do in the classroom. Younger students especially like to see their work posted on the walls for everyone to see.

On the following page is an example of a list of procedures for an intermediate classroom. Notice how EVERYTHING is listed so that students and parents know exactly what is expected each day. Parents can put a copy on the refrigerator.

Primary teachers may want to use a calendar format rather than listing out procedures and regular assignments. A list can be overwhelming and shouldn't be used with younger students.

For secondary teachers, the syllabus should outline as many assignments and projects ahead of time with due dates. This will help prepare students for the eventuality of college and/or vocational school.

> *"Take some time to think about everything you require from your students. Now include that on your procedure page to send home with students."*

PROCEDURES & HOMEWORK

MONDAY

Homework: Read for 20 minutes and write a response in log
Vocabulary sentences – Due Thursday
Other homework written in calendar

TUESDAY

Tuesday envelopes go home with information from the school and grade level. Look for parent newsletter from grade level each week and progress report every three weeks.

Homework: Testing skills practice
Read for 20 minutes and write a response in log
Vocabulary sentences
Other homework written in calendar

WEDNESDAY

Tuesday envelopes returned with parent signature
Testing skills practice due from previous week

Homework: Read for 20 minutes and write a response in log
Vocabulary sentences
Other homework written in calendar

THURSDAY

Vocabulary homework due

Homework: Read for 20 minutes and write a response in log
Study for vocabulary test
Other homework written in calendar
Parents check over and sign student binder

FRIDAY

Spelling and vocabulary test
Teacher checks binder – parent signature and reading
response log

*This is for a 5th/6th grade class. Modify as needed. Younger students may not have homework as part of these procedures, older students may have more.

All About _____

My Favorites

Sport: _____

Kind of Book: _____

T.V. show: _____

Color: _____

Movie: _____

My Interests

Hobbies: _____

Places I've traveled: _____

_____

Future occupation: _____

My Wishes

Where I'd like to travel: _____

_____

My one wish for me: _____

_____

My one wish for the world: _____

_____

Welcome!

Dear Parents:

Hello! I am very excited to have your child in my class this year! I feel confident that we will have a terrific year full of learning and fun! I look forward to talking with you throughout this year.

Communication is very important to me, so please feel free to ask any questions and express any concerns or ideas you may have. Your child's education and well being is my #1 priority this year. I want to work together with parents and students to make this year a success for all of us!

Sincerely,

— —

Name of child _____

Name of parent/ parents _____

Daytime phone _____

Evening phone _____

Explain any special interests, sports activities, and hobbies your child has:

List any allergies your child has toward foods, or other products:

List any medications your child is currently taking:

Are there any special notes or comments you would like to make?

Student Information Sheet

Name _____

Address _____   Phone_____

_____

Mother's Name: _____   Work phone_____

Father's Name: _____   Work phone_____

Guardian's Name: _____   Work phone_____

Brothers or Sisters:_____   Age _____
_____   Age_____
_____   Age _____

Your Birthdate: _____

Age, as of today:_____

What is your favorite...

Sport:_____   Food: _____

Book: _____   Movie:_____

T.V. show:_____   Subject:_____

In my spare time I like to: _____

_____

I collect: _____

I enjoy playing: _____

I like to read: _____

Do you have any special talents and interests? If so, what are they?

_____

_____

_____

Get-to-Know Activities

Here are some activities you can do during the first few days/ weeks of school:

Name Game

Students get in a circle. 1st person says name, 2nd repeats name & says own name. Go around the circle. Teacher should be last and should say everyone's name.

Scavenger Hunt for Signatures

Students use the sheet found in the back of this chapter and walk around the room trying to find other students to fit each description. When they have found someone, they need to get that person's signature in the box.

> **Idea Share**
>
> One way we show students that we value them is by remembering their name. The Name Game is an excellent way to help you remember student names from the first day of school. As the students go around repeating the names, you do the same. Silently mouth along with each student during their turn. As you silently say each name, look clearly at the student for name/face recognition. By the time it is your turn, you will have said everyone's name several times in your head and should have no difficulty in remembering on the following day. This method has actually been published in *Reader's Digest* as a way to help people better remember names.

Picnic Basket

Tell students that you are going on a picnic. Say your name aloud and one or two items that you are taking with you on the picnic.

For example, "My name is Julie Rogers and I am taking Jam."
Then ask students, "Who wants to go on the picnic with me?"
Students raise their hands and tell their name along with an item.

The item MUST start with the same letter as their name, but do not tell your students this. They should discover it for themselves. Tell them they cannot go on the picnic if they bring the "wrong" item, but they can try again.

Back to School Bingo

Similar to Scavenger Hunt. See the sheet in the back of this chapter.

M & M Game

Pass around a large jar/ can filled with M&M's. Instruct students to take some as it comes around. Then, after everyone has taken some M&M's, they must tell one fact about themselves for each M&M they have BEFORE they eat any!

People Scavenger Hunt

Find someone in the classroom for each phrase below and have them sign on the line. You may use each person's name only twice.

New to this school this year _____

Has on something red _____

Has an older brother _____

Has a younger sister _____

Was born in September _____

Read a book this summer _____

Has a dog for a pet _____

Went swimming this summer _____

Has blue eyes _____

Can play a musical instrument _____

Walks to school _____

Went on a vacation trip this summer _____

Has visited a foreign country _____

Has visited at least five different states _____

Has exactly seventeen letters in entire name _____

Is the youngest in their family _____

Knows how many centimeters are in a meter _____

Has brown hair _____

Is an only child _____

Back to School BINGO

Try to find classmates to initial each square. Try to get five in a row (across, down, or diagonal). If you want a REAL CHALLENGE, try filling the whole box!

Read more than five books this summer. _____	Moved into a new house this summer. _____	Flew on an airplane this summer. _____	Has traveled to a foreign country. _____	Has visited five or more states. _____
Likes to play soccer. _____	Has a younger sister. _____	Has visited Washington, D.C. _____	Has a dog as a pet. _____	Plays more than one sport. _____
Is wearing a watch. _____	Has exactly 15 letters in their full name. _____	FREE _____	Has a four digit house number. _____	Has blue eyes. _____
Has a bike. _____	Earned perfect attendance last year. _____	Will celebrate their birthday this month. _____	Has relatives in other states. _____	Can play a musical instrument. _____
All of their grandparents are still alive. _____	Has relatives in other countries. _____	Has an unusual pet. _____	Made Honor Roll last year. _____	Was born in June. _____

Back to School BINGO

Try to find classmates to initial each square. Try to get five in a row (across, down, or diagonal). If you want a REAL CHALLENGE, try filling the whole box!

___	___	___	___	___
___	___	___	___	___
___	___	___	___	___
___	___	___	___	___
___	___	___	___	___

© 2005 McDonald and Hershman

Star Activity

Students use the star on the opposite page and fill in each point with their own answer. Then, they walk around the room to find another student with the same answers. If they find someone, that person needs to sign the back of that particular point.

Partner Interviews

Introduce other students

Students pair up, or are paired up with someone they do not know. With the class as a whole, brainstorm five or six questions to ask. Students then interview each other using index cards. When everyone is finished, each person must stand up and introduce their partner to the rest of the class and share the interesting new facts they learned about their partner. This activity is one used often in a middle school setting.

Groups Activity

Have each student brainstorm for 2 to 3 minutes and list the different groups they belong to. These groups include any and every way that students could categorize themselves. For example, they might be:

-daughters   -African American   -Texan
-sons   -student   -football player
-pianist   -babysitter   -shopper
-Christian   -sister   -friend

Be sure you give examples of the groups you belong to in order to help students begin their brainstorming.

Once everyone has their list, go around the room and allow each person to introduce him or herself and share the groups they belong to. Ask students to listen for commonalities in the lists.

This is an excellent activity to jumpstart a discussion about tolerance of others, accepting differences, and focusing on our similarities as ties to friendship. It is also a great way to help us identify different strengths and talents among our students.

Setting Goals

Setting goals is another important activity that can and should be done during the first week of school. Have students think for a few minutes and jot down their goal for the class or for themselves for the year. This would also work well with the personal vision statement we mentioned earlier in this chapter.

Go around the room and have each person share their goal(s) with the rest of the class. Compile these into a list of Learning Goals for that class.

Use the goals set by students to help you get to know them better as well as to set goals for your teaching throughout the semester and/or year. Post these goals immediately, or at the very least type them up so that each student can have their own copy.

Star Activity

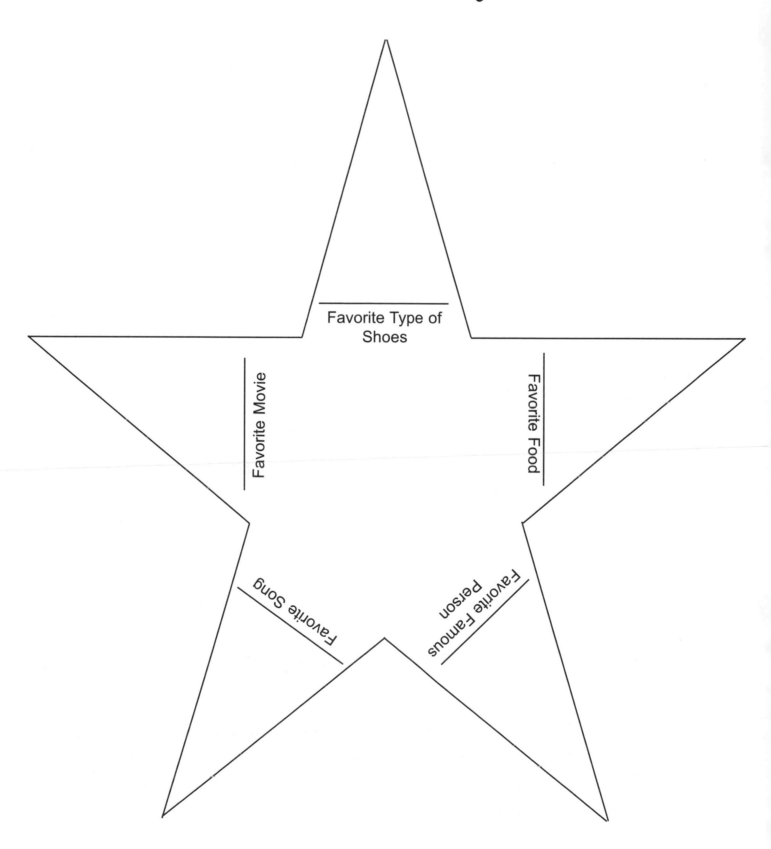

Favorite Type of Shoes

Favorite Movie

Favorite Food

Favorite Song

Favorite Famous Person

Team Building Activities

If You Were …
In this activity the students all answer the questions and then share them with the class. This is a great way to get to know each students' personality!

Sample questions:
→   If you were a car, what kind of car would you be?
→   What kind of animal are you like when you are angry?
→   If you were a bug, what kind of bug would you be?
→   Name something that always makes you smile.
→   If you could be like any other person, who would it be?

Assumption Game

Students work together as a class to try to figure out "what happened" or "why" by asking yes or no questions.

For example,
"A man on his way home saw the masked man coming towards him so he turned and ran. Why?"

Students might ask, "Was the first man scared of the other man?" You have to answer yes or no. "No" answers are just as helpful as "Yes" answers. For example, if the answer is, "No, the man is NOT scared" then students do not need to ask if he is a burglar, etc. There is no limit to questions unless you want to set one.

(The answer to the example is that it is a baseball game. The man is running to home plate and the catcher is coming towards him with the ball.)
You can make them up yourself, or have students create them and share.

** This is a great activity to develop critical thinking skills. You can get these kinds of scenarios in books with logic games.

Cooperative Learning Games

There are many books available with cooperative learning activities to help students learn how to work as a group. One example is the book, Cooperative Group Problem Solving: Adventures in Applied Creativity by Douglass Campbell. We have an adapted version of a commonly used team-building activity, the Desert Survival game, in this chapter. These types of activities are fun to do at the beginning of the school year and help students see the importance of working together as a team.

Desert Survival

You are on a small airplane that is forced down in the Sahara Desert in North Africa. The plane is off course. It was traveling at 200 miles per hour and lost radio contact 5 hours ago. All passengers are okay. There is no guarantee of a rescue, nor of continued survival. It is a 3 day journey north, to a city.

As a group, you must choose the items to take with you. Only 7 of the 20 items can be chosen to help your group survive the desert trek.

Your group must be ready to tell why the seven items were chosen.

Desert Survival Box

a hand mirror	a long sleeve jacket
a parachute	an umbrella
a pencil	a safety pin
1 book of matches	T.V. guide
2 cans of coke	nail clippers
scissors	a compass
an electric fan	a portable radio
1 tube of toothpaste	1 case of water bottles
a 10 dollar bill	a hunting bow and 1 arrow
1 school math book	1 box of saltine crackers

Chicken Hawk Game (from ROPES)

1. One person is the chicken hawk. Everyone else is a chicken.
2. The chicken hawk tries to tag chickens. Everyone must stay in the boundaries.
3. When a chicken is tagged, he/ she must stand on one leg and flap wings and say, "Help me! Help me!"
4. A chicken may be untagged when two or more chickens hold hands in a circle around him/her and sing "Happy Birthday"
5. The chicken hawk may NOT tag any chickens who are in a circle, holding hands singing "Happy Birthday"
6. If all the chickens are tagged, the chicken hawk wins.
7. If the chicken hawk CAN'T tag ANY chickens, the chickens win.

IT IS POSSIBLE FOR THE CHICKENS TO WIN!!!

Answer: If all the chickens get in a huge circle holding hands and sing "Happy Birthday" It is important that the kids work together to try to solve this together. Do Not give them the answer, but let them figure it out on their own. It will take a while before they get it and you may have to stop the game periodically to repeat the instructions. If it goes on too long, you may want to start giving hints. This game has instructional value because the kids learn that they have to listen to each other and work together to solve the problem.

Paper Plate Game (From ROPES)

1. Place the nine paper plates in a row

2. Each team of four students stands on the four plates located at each end of the line. One empty plate should be in-between the two teams.

3. One team is from Jupiter and the other is from Mars (or you could make it two cities, two cultures, or two indian tribes). Tell the teams that there is a bridge between the two planets and they have to cross the bridge to get to the other side. If they fall off the bridge, then they are sucked into the voidless vacuum of space.

4. The goal of each team is to change places with the other team. They may NOT step off the plates.

RULES

Stay on the plate. If your foot touches the floor, everyone starts over.

You may jump around one person at a time. You may only jump around people on the other team (NOT YOUR OWN TEAM)

You must go from your space to an empty plate. You may step forward onto an empty plate.

When your team gets stuck (no one can move), you have to start over.

First team to finish wins and must show the other groups.

Answer to Paper Plate Game
READ THIS CAREFULLY AND WORK IT OUT ON PAPER PRIOR TO THE GAME.

- → Label each team A1-4 and B1-4.
- → A1 steps forward
- → B1 jumps A1
- → B2 steps forward
- → A1 jumps B2
- → A2 jumps B1
- → A3 steps forward
- → B1 jumps A3
- → B2 jumps A2

- → B3 jumps A1
- → B4 steps forward
- → A1 jumps B4
- → A2 jumps B3
- → A3 jumps B2
- → A4 jumps B1
- → B1 steps forward
- → B2,3, and 4 all jump one space
- → A1,2,3 & 4 move into final place

Draw an Alien Activity

- Break students into groups of four.
- Have each student select a different colored marker or overhead pen.
- Give each team one transparency or large sheet of white paper.
- Students are to draw a team alien without talking.
- Each student must use only the marker they have chosen and may not switch colors. Set a time limit for this activity. Two to five minutes is a good limit. Directions for students are in the back of this chapter.

This activity is designed to show students the importance of EVERYONE working together and communicating with each other. You will notice that some colors are used more than others. Lead students to the idea of team roles. There are leaders and followers in every team. Who are your leaders? Which colors were not used at all or were used very little? These are students who need to be encouraged by the group to participate.

Design Team Activity

Break students into groups of four. Choose what you want students to design according to your unit or theme. Our theme was space, so we had students design their ideal spaceship or space station. It is nice to offer students a choice of two or three designs. Another idea might be to design the perfect classroom, cafeteria, gym or playground. Students need to work together as a team on this project. Make sure you give them lots of time to brainstorm, sketch and do a final copy.

Instructions for Team Draw Activity

In your teams, have each person select a marker. Using only your own color and with no oral communication, create a team picture on your blank paper.

Once your illustration is complete, discuss your handiwork and name your creation.

Conclusion

Remember that the first day and week of school is like a match that lights a fire. Although the first day is often hectic, it is vital that you strike it just right. If students see you flustered and unorganized, they will store that picture of you in their heads for the rest of the year. Following expectations and staying organized will not be a priority to your students because of it. However, if students see before them an organized teacher who is prepared, cares enough to learn about each student, and sets clear expectations, they will be more likely to develop into a class that loves to learn.

Remember that your tone of voice and posture also affect how students view you as a teacher. Be firm when going over expectations, but also let students see your unique personality. Take the time to get to know your students and to train them in what you expect to happen within the classroom. In essence, the first day is a time for you to "strike the match" and light that fire of learning!

Questions to Ponder

Why is the first day of school so important?

How do you think having a poster clearly visible with the daily schedule listed will help you? Why should you go over this schedule at the start of class?

Why do you think it is important to alternate between giving information about class rules and procedures, and fun get-to-know or team building activities?

Additional Resources

Cooperative Group Problem Solving: Adventures in Applied Creativity
by Douglass Campbell

Team Building Activities for Every Group
by Alanna Jones

Notes/Reflections on Chapter

Learning-Centered Classrooms

Don't let the spark of a great beginning go to waste. Some fires have a great start, but then fizzle and die because necessary elements, such as oxygen, are missing. We want to build a roaring fire of learning in our classroom that will last all year long. How can we do this? One way is by developing a student-centered classroom. We need a place where students feel comfortable to take risks and know that they are safe from emotional, mental, or physical hurt. We need a place where the students and teacher collaborate throughout the learning process. We need a place where relationships are built and develop into mutual trust and respect. However, this special environment takes thought, preparation, and work on our part to be successful. In this chapter we will discuss the three elements we feel are essential in creating a learning-centered classroom. They are:

- An understanding of the content
- An understanding of human nature
- An understanding of how the brain learns best

Knowing Our Content

Why? Well, the more knowledge we have about a particular event, concept, or skill, the better we are able to teach it. The wealth of information stored away in our brains through study and experiences makes it possible for us to expand upon the basic information presented to students in textbooks.

Could we teach a subject straight from the textbook and cover the required objectives? Probably. Would it be considered effective teaching that will follow the students throughout their lives? No way. Knowing your subject material brings with it the confidence that you know what you're talking about. You'll be able to share stories and fun facts that add depth to student learning. And, you'll be better prepared to help students apply this learning to their lives and the world around them.

Example: A class is reading a chapter in Social Studies about the early United States government and the first president.

Teacher A:	Teacher B:
After students read the chapter, the teacher discusses the information from the text and assigns a worksheet with various questions to assess comprehension of material read.	While students read the chapter, the teacher stops at various points to check for understanding. When students read about the first president, the teacher pulls out two white squares the size of teeth and passes them around the class. When students ask about the squares, she tells them, "How do you think George Washington may have used these?" Students brainstorm and they discuss the possible uses. The teacher then goes on to tell them that George Washington actually used false teeth. Students are then encouraged to look on the internet for other interesting facts about the U.S. founding fathers or early presidents.

Which lesson do you think students will remember and retain?

Look at the example for Teacher A. Did this person discuss the history of U.S. government? Yes. Did they cover a required objective? Yes. Will the students remember this information? Most likely not.

Look at the example for Teacher B. Do you think that using the fun fact and concrete object of "false teeth" grabbed student attention? Definitely! Additionally, the extension activity is motivating for students and encourages further thinking on their part. This type of lesson is likely to be remembered by students for years to come.

Taking information about a famous person and relating it to students' lives helps make that person real to them. Getting students actively engaged in a discussion about the pros and cons of false teeth will stick in their mind and will stay with them longer than a two sentence or two paragraph statement about George Washington from the textbook.

Staying Knowledgable

How can I be sure that I am able to extend and enrich student knowledge on topics/concepts that I don't know much about or understand?

1) Read and Keep Reading

-biographies
-science journals such as Discover
-historical events
-non-fiction books

Non-fiction books and magazines can be very interesting and sometimes fun to read. Remember, the more you read, the more you know!

Idea Share

Kids Discover Magazine is an amazing source of interesting information, fun facts, and great photos on a variety of topics including Science concepts, Famous People, Historical Events, Current Events, and World Cultures. Check the school library to see if they subscribe to this magazine.

2) Research

√ As you do your lesson planning, write down key words from the textbook and/or other resources from which you plan to teach

√ Use those keywords to do an internet search for information
Type in "fun facts" along with the keyword(s) to see what comes up in your search.

√ How is this skill/concept applied in the real world?

> *"Other types of professionals must stay well-informed of content for their field as well as current practices, and so must we!"*

Example of real-world application:

Last year my husband and I were remodeling our bathroom when he found that he needed to enclose a vent at an angle. Neither of us knew how to figure out the measurements to cut the 4 X 4 board. So, I turned to the internet, went to Ask Jeeves (http://www.askjeeves.com) and typed in "How do I figure the measurements to cut an angle?" and "construction." The information was right there. Needless to say, we found that we needed the Pythagorean theorem. This is a real world application of geometric skills. You could also type in "real-world geometry" (or any other skill) and get plenty of information to help you when planning lessons.

Idea Share

When do you have time to read all of this? Try one or more of the following:

-in the bathroom

-while taking a bath

-while walking on a treadmill

3) Do the following before planning lessons.

√ Practice the math skill to be taught

√ Read the chapter or selection you plan to use in class

√ Practice the experiment

By doing these things BEFORE you plan out your lesson, you'll find that this helps you prepare for potential questions, glitches in procedures, problems, and misunderstandings that might occur during the lesson. It will also help you know what to expect when you actually present the lesson with students.

Understanding People

Why do teachers need to know about human psychology? Well, the more you know about human behavior, the more you will be able to motivate students to want to behave and learn in your class. Take some time to review the concepts you learned in your psychology course and brainstorm ways you can adapt your own behavior to create positive relationships with your students.

Each student in your class is a unique individual who has specific needs. It is easy to forget that fact when dealing with a classroom full of faces. We can get caught up in curriculum, deadlines, grades, accountability, and forget that we hold in our hands the fragile psyches of children who often need more than just good grades to help them bloom into successful adults.

Know your Students

1) Get to know your students as individuals.

> *"It is so important to take the time to get to know students as individuals."*

2) Be flexible and know that you can't react exactly the same to every situation and every student.

3) Be understanding.
   Look further into what may be causing the problem rather than immediately assuming the child is a troublemaker or is "out to get you."

4) Take the time to talk with students.
   Don't make assumptions, but rather talk out the problem, assist with mediation between students, or just take time to talk with the student about life in general.

Boys in today's classrooms

In talking about human psychology and meeting individual needs, I want to bring up a topic that may cause some controversy - Boys. Most classroom teachers, being female, do not understand boys and how they operate. They find themselves at a loss in trying to help these boys find a place within the classroom.

For the longest time girls have been a major focus in teacher training because they were often being left out of class discussions. The goal was to help our girls become more assertive in the classroom and receive the attention they deserve. This has been an issue of concern in the past and is currently being addressed. The following information is not in any way intended to propose that we stop encouraging our girls to be successful in the classroom, only that we need to understand our boys so that they can also see success.

Psychologists and social scientists are warning our society that we are in the middle of a major crisis among boys. We can see this ourselves when we look at the number of boys commiting horrifying types of violence in our schools. So why are we addressing this issue here? We feel that the more you know about the types of behavior you are likely to see from boys, the better prepared you will be and the more effective you will be as a teacher.

> **Teacher Talk**
>
> *"One of the boys in my room was very active and had difficulties with prior teachers in the school. He was brilliant, but often caused disruptions because of his need for movement. I moved his desk to a place where he would not distract others, and let him stand or wiggle while working. This gave him the outlet he needed.*
>
> *The year before he had been in and out of the Principal's office all year long. The year I had him, he went to the Principal's office maybe two times all year. His parents were pleased with the progress and he was able to be a positive member of my class."*

Dr. James Dobson, in his book *Bringing Up Boys*, states that understanding how boys are "hard-wired" is the first step. Let's take a look at the information he provides.

1) **Higher levels of Testosterone** (T) in boys cause traits of high risk including physical, criminal and personal risks. The more (T) in a person, the more risky behavior is exhibited.

2) **Boys have lower levels of Serotonin**, the hormone which calms the emotions. This hormone also facilitates good judgment.

3) **Boys have a large amygdala** which is the fight/flight part of our brain. It does not think or reason, but puts out a chemical that causes a "knee-jerk" reaction which can lead to violence in some instances.

Taking away recess from boys will only increase your frustration level.

All of these elements are the backbone for why boys generally engage in risky behaviors including acting out in class, wrestling with other boys, and a seeming lack of common sense.

Does this mean that your boys are a hopeless case? Absolutely not! What it does mean is that we must understand the need of most boys to be physically active. We also need to have an understanding behind the cause of often irrational reactions by boys to events and people in the school. For example, boys are much quicker to "shut down" when in a controversial situation with a teacher.

What can I do?

1)   We strongly recommend that you read *Bringing Up Boys* by Dr. James Dobson, *The Wonder of Boys* by Dr. Michael Gurian, or *Raising Cain* co-authored by Dr. Michael Thompson. All are excellent books on understanding and helping boys.

2)   Keep in mind the strategies for knowing your students that we discussed earlier in this chapter.

3)   Provide opportunities for your active boys to move around or wiggle. You would want to seat them in the back of the room where they cannot distract others. **ex:** *let them stand, wiggle a leg, bounce up and down, use squeezy balls while working, etc.*

4)   Provide a place where students can calm down until they are ready to join the class. I used my reading corner as "Australia" for them to get away.

Difficult Students in today's classrooms

There are different reasons for angry or difficult students.
- picked on by other students
- assumes he/she will always get in trouble (from past experiences with teachers)
- issues at home
- feels no one likes/appreciates them
- feels the need to "prove" they are tough
- feels stupid
- doesn't trust the teacher because of past experiences

Steps to Determining Root of Problem

1.) Identify the specific behaviors exhibited by the student.

2.) Is this happening in just your class or in other classes as well?

3.) Is this behavior recent (past few days or months) or has it been going on for several years?

If behavior has changed recently:
        -you've seen a change in behavior/attitude
        -student was not behaving this way last year

Then ask:
Has something happened recently to the student either at school or home?
        -bullied   -family issues   -changes in family life
        -a recent move   -a friend moved   -death in family

These types of events can affect a student's attitude and behavior resulting in a shut-down in the classroom.

© 2005 McDonald and Hershman

4.) Once you've identified the cause of the change in behavior, work towards a solution

√ Offer a place for students to go to calm down. They may rejoin the class when they are ready.

√ Talk one-on-one with the student to determine the cause of the anger or problem. Talking out issues is oftentimes enough to help the student build a sense of trust in you.

√ Allow students to talk to the counselor.

> *"Sometimes all it takes is a kind word or "I believe in you" to turn an angry or difficult student around."*

If the student's behavior is long-term, begin to work with parents and the counselor to resolve the problem.

• Be flexible rather than overly rigid.

• Offer a place for the student to calm down every time he/she is angry or frustrated and allow them to rejoin the class when they feel ready.

• Encourage positives shown by the student.

• Utilize leadership qualities within the student and use in a constructive way to help you. *"I could really use your help as a leader in my classroom."*

• Talk with the student instead of making assumptions.

• Slow down and take your time when working with the student. This shows you care.

The more time spent=building trust=building respect

• Many angry/difficult kids are ignored, yelled at, and/or demeaned at home. They need something better from you if you want their cooperation.

• Implement a non-threatening environment in your classroom.

Teacher Talk

"One year I had a 5th grade student who was the angriest child I had ever seen. He was in complete shut-down. The merest hint of another kid touching him would result in a total melt-down. I looked in his Cumulative folder and saw that he had been a problem since the first grade. He was in Special Education, but for Speech reasons only. However, he kept telling me, "I can't do that. I'm stupid." After talking to the mom, who threw up her arms in exasperation, I decided that extra care was needed with this one. Whenever I saw him get angry, I would let him go to the quiet corner to calm down. When possible, I would go and talk with him about whatever had happened. After a while he began going to the corner less and less. One day, I saw him doing some of the more complicated math problems with ease. I said to him, "Boy, you sure are smart. Look at what you can do!" He simply beamed. I told him this over and over. By the Winter Holidays it was like I had a totally different child in my class. You know the best part? Last year he graduated in the top ten of his high school class. I was so proud of him!"

Understanding How the Brain Learns

Studies done by researchers show us that there are certain elements which increase students' chance of learning. We're going to use a very simplified explanation and application to the classroom, but in order to fully understand how the brain learns best, we strongly suggest that you read authors including Eric Jensen, Howard Gardner, Leslie Hart, and Susan Kovalik. We have listed several different books in the back of this chapter as additional resources for your review.

The first element of a brain-based classroom is a non-threatening environment. What is a non-threatening environment and why is it so important that our classrooms be this way? An environment is non-threatening when students feel comfortable sharing their thoughts, ideas, and dreams with the teacher and also with other students. We want to strive to have an atmosphere in the classroom where no one is judged by anyone else. Every idea is welcomed, no one is ridiculed, no one is fearful of overly harsh punishments, and no one is put down. Our classroom should be a place where students can make mistakes and still be cherished.

As teachers we can create a non-threatening environment by:

- Insisting upon positive life skills.
     kindness, cooperation, team-work, flexibility, friendship, integrity, honesty, dedication, loyalty, etc.

- Character education is an additional way to create a positive classroom climate.

- Do not stand for bullying, teasing, gossiping, and other negative behaviors in your classroom.

- Implement your consequences and defend those students being hurt by others. Show that you will not tolerate it.

Of course, all of this is well and good, but if you do not practice what you preach, you will never have a non-threatening classroom environment.

Why is this so important? Remember that amygdala we mentioned earlier in the chapter? When our classrooms are full of negativity and hurtful behaviors from either the teacher or students, the amygdala kicks in and student learning shuts down. Let's take a look now at how the brain operates.

The Triune Brain

Current research on the brain continues to change and/or improve our understanding, but it is also very complex. Here we are merely trying to give an overview for teachers to get the basics.

Simply put, the brain is made of three parts. This is called the "Triune Brain." There are technical terms for each part, but I use more simplified terms to explain this concept to my students.

1. The "Thinking" Brain
    This is where we learn, store, and retrieve knowledge. Our memories are housed here as well as our creativity.

2. The "Regulating" Brain
    This part of our brain is much smaller and somewhat below the thinking area. This part of our brain takes care of all our bodily needs such as eye blinking, swallowing, digesting, heart beating, eating, etc.

3. The "Reflex" Brain
    This is the smallest part of our brain (the amygdala) which resides just below the regulating brain and just above our spinal cord. This is the control of our emotions, as we discussed earlier. The "fight vs. flight" reflex is exhibited through this part of our brain.

I like to explain this concept to my students so that they will better understand how they learn and why sometimes it seems so hard for them to learn.

There are several things that can keep us from using our "Thinking" brain. For example, if we are starving because we haven't eaten anything all morning, our brain downshifts into the "Regulating" part and all we can think about is our hunger. No learning can take place because every thought we have revolves around food.

Another strong example is anger. If someone makes us angry, our brain downshifts to the "Reflex" part, and all we are able to do is be angry. All of our thoughts revolve around our anger. No learning can take place while we are still emotional. This goes for all emotions including joy and fear.

Take a moment to think about a time someone made you really angry. Were you able to think straight? Often this is how people describe a haze of anger. How can our students learn if their thoughts are consumed by hunger, bodily needs, anger, or other emotions? Also, how can we teach well if we are consumed by those same things?

Anger inhibits learning

Let's apply this theory to the classroom. What would happen if our students walked into a classroom where they were constantly picked on by other students, ridiculed or belittled by the teacher, and punished for every little mistake they might make. Can learning occur in this classroom? Definitely not! Students will enter the room and immediately downshift to their "Reflex" brain so that they are better able to protect themselves from possible harm, be it physical, emotional, or mental.

Now, what about a classroom where chaos rules? Before long, the teacher is the one who becomes fearful. The entire class is spent with the teacher operating in survival mode. No quality teaching can take place when the teacher is spending every minute using his/her "Reflex" brain.

Teach Students about the Triune Brain

At the beginning of the year, explain to your students the concept of the Triune Brain. Give specific examples from your own life of when you have "downshifted".

> **Example:**
> "When I was taking the GRE exam, I arrived very early and brought a book to read while I waited. Although the test had not yet been passed out, a test-monitor came by my seat, snatched the book out of my hands and threw it on the floor near the opposite wall. "No outside materials aloud," she harshly told me. Well, let me tell you, I was so angry that I couldn't think of anything else except for that woman for a full fifteen minutes or more into the test. I couldn't concentrate on the test until I had calmed myself down."

This is a perfect time to explain to students the implementation of the other ideas presented in this section. I discuss at length my expectations for student use of these privileges and freedoms along with the consequences if they are abused.

Keep Healthy Snacks Available.

To help students stay in their "Thinking" brain, I keep a huge jar of pretzels, goldfish crackers, or some other healthy type of snack available for everyone. If a student comes to me and is hungry for whatever reason, I let them grab a handful of crackers to help ease that hunger.

"What kind of classroom environment do you promote? How does it affect student learning? These are important questions to consider."

Allow Students some Freedoms

When students need to use the restroom, I allow them. All they have to do is let me know they are going (not during my instruction of course) and sign out. When they return, they sign themselves back in. This allows me to keep track of where and when everyone has gone. I feel that this shows students more respect than demanding that they ask permission to leave when "nature calls." However, if students abuse this freedom, there are consequences.
(See "My Time vs. Your Time")

Conclusion

A brain-based classroom is one where collaboration between students and teacher occurs on a daily basis. It is a place where everyone feels comfortable working and sharing ideas with one another. Can it really occur in the real world of teaching? You bet! We've been there and have experienced it ourselves. However, it is up to the teacher to create this type of an environment through their knowledge and actions. By being life-long learners ourselves, we foster a love for learning in our students. How? By reading and researching all we can about the concepts we teach, our students see our own desire to learn more. Additionally, when we take the time to get to know each of our students as individuals, they begin to trust and respect us as their guide. Lastly, when we understand how the brain works, we can better meet student needs. When these needs are met, learning takes place every single day, which, after all, is our ultimate goal.

Questions to Ponder

How has your level of knowledge and experience helped you to make your lessons more interesting for students? How could you improve in the areas that are less familiar to you?

How does knowing about the Triune Brain affect your teaching style and your classroom? What are some strategies you might implement in your classroom?

What are you doing, if anything, to encourage a non-threatening environment in your classroom? What could you do differently to develop this type of classroom environment?

Additional Resources

Multiple Intelligences: Theory into Practice
by Howard Gardner

The Unschooled Mind
by Howard Gardner

Brain Based Learning
by Eric Jensen

Human Brain and Human Learning
by Leslie Hart

Bringing Up Boys
by James Dobson

The Wonder of Boys
by Michael Gurian

Raising Cain: Protecting the Emotional Life of Boys
by Dan Kindlon and Michael Thompson

Notes/Reflections on Chapter

Engaging Students in Learning

Another necessary element to building a roaring fire of learning in our classrooms is actively engaging students. We need students to be active, not passive participants in the learning process.

Take a look at this learning pyramid to see the average retention rate for different styles of teaching. Which of these encourage passive learning through listening or watching and which encourage active learning through doing?

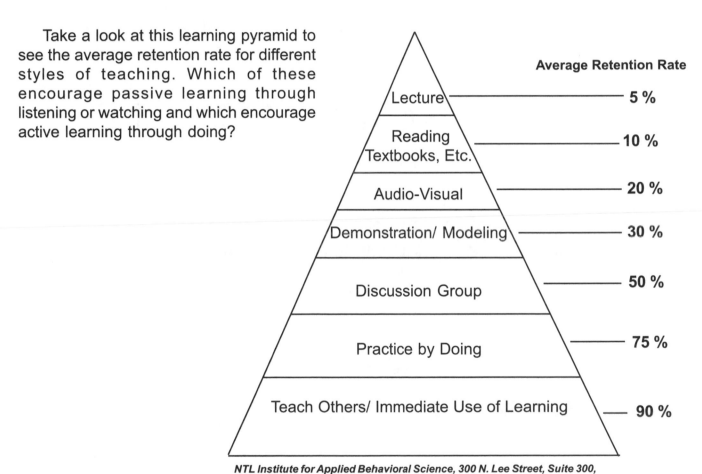

Average Retention Rate

Lecture	5 %
Reading Textbooks, Etc.	10 %
Audio-Visual	20 %
Demonstration/ Modeling	30 %
Discussion Group	50 %
Practice by Doing	75 %
Teach Others/ Immediate Use of Learning	90 %

NTL Institute for Applied Behavioral Science, 300 N. Lee Street, Suite 300, Alexandria, VA 22314. 1-800-777-5227.

Students need to be actively manipulating information through a variety of activities in a learning-centered classroom. Being actively involved is motivating and you'll find that students won't want to leave your class because they are having so much "fun." Can you imagine a classroom where students are being challenged to think at higher levels, create products that demonstrate and apply their learning, and teach others what they have learned? This is what a learning-centered classroom looks like. Let's start by taking a look at higher level thinking skills.

Bloom's Taxonomy

Bloom's taxonomy of cognitive skills includes:

KNOWLEDGE

COMPREHENSION

APPLICATION

ANALYSIS

SYNTHESIS

EVALUATION

Knowledge is the lowest and most basic skill while evaluation is the highest cognitive skill. Our students should be assessed using each of these cognitive levels. This helps our students to stretch and challenge their critical thinking skills rather than always testing basic facts.

Below are some terms you can use to help you create different types of activities:

KNOWLEDGE	COMPREHENSION	APPLICATION
define	explain	demonstrate
list	summarize	show
identify	interpret	operate
describe	rewrite	construct
match	convert	apply
locate	give example	
ANALYSIS	**SYNTHESIS**	**EVALUATION**
compare	create	judge
contrast	suppose	appraise
distinguish	design	debate
deduct	compose	criticize
infer	combine	support
categorize	rearrange	

Here are some sample activities for each level in Bloom's:

KNOWLEDGE

- Define the following vocabulary
- Identify the main characters
- List the properties of a gas
- Locate England on the atlas
- Describe the scientific method

> *"Use Bloom's taxonomy to help you assess different levels of student learning."*

COMPREHENSION

- Retell the story in your own words
- Give an example of how the main character is a hero
- Explain how a gas is different from a solid
- Explain how an island is born

APPLICATION

- Predict what will happen in the sequel to this book
- Demonstrate how a liquid becomes a solid or gas
- Demonstrate how a volcano can create an island in the ocean
- Show how to cross the street safely

ANALYSIS

- Compare and contrast the hero and villain in this story
- Compare and contrast the desert and savannah climates
- Distinguish between "Pangaea" and today's continents on earth
- According to the theory of Plate Tectonics we just read, infer how a mountain is "built"

SYNTHESIS

- Imagine that the villain and hero are friends. What might happen in the story because of this?
- Suppose we breathed liquid rather than a gas (air), how would our lives be different?
- Design your own island using three different land features
- Design the front page of a newspaper that might have appeared in Great Britain in the year 1100

EVALUATION

- Choose an issue from the story to debate
- Which is better to breathe, solid, liquid or gas? Support your opinion
- Using what you know about landforms and tectonic plates, criticize or support the notion that California will one day "fall into the ocean"

Team/Group Activities

Another aspect of the brain-based classroom is cooperative learning. Working together as a team is an important skill students will need throughout their lives. Also, when students work together as a group they learn from one another.

Although we may not see some of the benefits immediately, our students are learning important social skills. They are also learning different ways to think and respond to situations by observing the others in their group. If handled properly, group activities not only motivate students, but also enhance student learning.

Expectations

Take some time to brainstorm your expectations for collaborative groups in your classroom. What would you like to see when students are working in groups? What behaviors are acceptable and not acceptable? What kinds of outcomes do you expect from group work? Write these expectations down to help better clarify them in your own mind. This will also help you to communicate your expectations clearly to your students. You might even work up a procedures or expectations chart/poster for students to use as a reference while working in groups.

> **For example:** *I expect to see students taking turns to talk in a group. I expect to see each student participating. I expect to see each student doing his/her "job" within the group. I expect to see a completed project/assignment at the end. I expect for students to learn how to work through their differences. I expect for students to learn how to work with students who are not necessarily their buddies. Students talking quietly and working quietly is acceptable. Loud discussion or yelling is not acceptable. Students walking around the classroom with a purpose (i.e. - to get supplies, resources, etc.) is acceptable. Students walking around the classroom to chat with friends is not acceptable.*

Team Roles

It is important to discuss team roles with your students so that they each know what is expected of them. In the beginning you need to model what you expect each "role" to look like and sound like. Just telling students, "Okay, you are the leader," does not teach them how to be a leader. Instead model what the leader of a group might say and do. Even if your students have worked in a group situation before, they still need a "refresher course."

> **Example:** *(leader) "We are supposed to read this chapter and respond using the questions on this sheet. Why don't we break up the chapter and each read a section aloud. Who would like the first two pages? " When getting off task leader might say, "I think maybe we are getting off topic. Who is supposed to read next?"*

Primary Teachers -- Give the students some simple guidelines for each role. You might even "script" out what they should say to help train them in this role. Your goal at this point is to begin training students for each role within the group.

> **Idea Share**
>
> Looking to get students actively engaged in a lesson? Try putting them together in a group to become "experts" of a section in the chapter or to create a product using the skill/concept you just taught.

A good book to read besides Johnsons *Cooperative Learning* is *Learning Thru Discussion* by W. M. Fawcett Hill. It will give you additional ideas on how to model a good team for your students. Additionally, *Choice Theory* by William Glasser also discusses the concept of teaming within the classroom.

We have seen that to get the best results from cooperative learning, it is vital to have students review the roles and rules of working as a team before starting the activity. This should happen each time you use cooperative learning groups. Here are a few roles you might use:

Leader - The person guiding the group. This person begins discussion and leads the team in the activity. They also redirect when the group gets off task.

Cube It → (handwritten)

Recorder - The person who writes down the specifics of the activity, takes notes, etc.

Reporter - The person who presents information to the class.

Materials - The person who gathers necessary materials.

TimeKeeper - The person who watches the clock and makes sure the group meets their deadline.

(These roles are taken from different Learning Group Models)

Strategies for Successful Teaming

- **Provide structure for the activity.** Have a list of questions for reflection/discussion, an envelope of tasks, or a checklist of activities ready to give each group. This helps make sure that students have a clear understanding of what they are to do in the group. It is so much easier for them when they have a specific starting point rather than a vague command of "discuss this."

- **Constantly monitor students.** We use the Clipboard Monitoring method mentioned in the Classroom Management chapter. A simple spreadsheet on a clipboard will help you keep track of student behaviors and academic progress.

- **Using bonding type activities** at the beginning of the year, or anytime you change groups, to help students work better as a team. We have several activities listed in the Great Beginnings chapter that you could use for this purpose. Additionally, you might look up information on ROPES activities which are designed to build trust between groups of people and emphasizes problem solving skills.

Idea Share

Use Bloom's Keywords to help structure group discussions or group activities.

We sometimes use a concept called "Cube It" shared with us at a G/T training.

The idea is to take a box, cover it with colorful paper, and put the keywords for each level on each side of the box.

Give one cube to each group of students and have them create their own questions or activities based on one or more of the keywords listed on each side.

You could tell students to "Cube It" and have them do one question/ activity for each level.

Or, you could assign a level to the student groups depending on what you wanted them to do.

Teaming Strategies Continued...

- **Remember, your students will not do this perfectly the first time.** It will take constant practice before they become adept at working together as a group.

- **Remind students before group activities what your expectations are.** Take some time to model what you want to see and hear, not just one time, but throughout the year.

> *Example: "We had some problems during group work today. Let's remind ourselves of what group work looks like and sounds like."*

Please don't think that you can say to your students, "Okay everybody. Get into groups of four and discuss the implications of war on a new country," and they'll do it. Oh no, not by a long shot. You probably won't even be able to get them to do a simple activity such as illustrating a concept just taught.

You have to show them how to work together, or how to guide and participate in a discussion. It is a lot of work on your part, but you'll find it is so worth the effort in the long run! Just stick with it and keep reminding your students what is expected of them. Before you know it you'll have students actively engaged in their learning rather than bored to tears.

Grouping Strategies and Ideas

Think-Pair-Share
With this strategy, have students take a minute to think about the topic or question you have posed. Then have them share with a partner or neighbor. After a few minutes of sharing, have the pairs choose another pair and share again as a larger group. This activity gives students a chance to think both independently and gain new ideas from others.

Jig-Saw
This strategy calls for small groups of two-four students. Each small group becomes an "expert" either with reading a selection, with research, or with a partiuclar skill or concept. Every group is responsible for a different passage or concept.

The second step is to have one "expert" from each group get together in new larger groups and share their information with each other. This activity helps make an otherwise boring assignment exciting and different. It also allows students to see how others work and it keeps them moving.

Group to Individual
Anytime you are presenting a new skill or concept for students to manipulate, work through an example as a whole class. Next, have students do the activity as a group. Then, have students do a similar activity with the skill in pairs. Lastly, have students show application of the skill/ concept as individuals.

This strategy allows students the opportunity to practice the skill or concept several times and gather input from other students before having to show comprehension and application on their own.

Any Activity to Enhance Learning

Pretty much any activity that engages students actively in their learning can be done as a group. Below are a few ideas to jumpstart your thinking:

"It is a good idea to use a variety of teaming strategies so that group work does not become as dull as lectures."

Games - Playing board and other types of games such as Scatergories, Mastermind, and Monopoly encourage thinking skills and require students to take turns

Scavenger Hunt - Students read through a chapter or part of a chapter and work together to create scavenger hunt questions for the class to answer.

Scripts - Students work together to turn a historical event or a story into a play. Students could work together to explain a concept or skill through a skit or play. I always require a written out script to show the different reading parts.

Problem Solving

Problem solving is an important life skill that we need to make our students aware of! Here are some tips on how you could teach your students about the concept of problem solving.

As we work on a project for another person, for school, for work, or for home, we naturally go through several steps in order to complete our goal. However, most of us are not consciously aware of the mental steps we are using.

Problem solving cannot be memorized from a book and is never done exactly the same as another person. We each have our own unique process of solving problems. Your methods are different from your parents, your students, and your friends.

Theorists have generally defined problem solving through six steps that everyone should use to reach the most efficient results. The following, offered by Hacker and Barden in their book, Living with Technology, is an organized process that people practice in order to conserve time, materials and money when problem solving. The point we need to get across to our students is that if they will use these steps, less time, materials, and money will be wasted.

1. Define the problem clearly
2. Set goals (desired results)
3. Develop alternate solutions
4. Select the best solution
5. Implement the solution
6. Evaluate the actual results and make necessary changes

Thank you to Terri Richards, Plano ISD, for sharing the idea of teaching problem solving with us.

It is important to explain to your students that through experience they will each develop their own technique for problem solving. Eventually they will become aware of the mental steps used when working on a project. When they become aware of this process, they will be able to refine that skill and improve on it in order to be more efficient.

Discovery and Experiential Learning

Another aspect of the brain-based classroom is discovery, or learning through experiences. Students learn best when they experience something and add that experience to their knowledge base, or schema. Science and Social Studies provide excellent opportunities for this type of learning. Instead of telling students about the Civil War, take them to see a reenactment of a battle. If a student asks a question about whales, have them research the answer for themselves and share it with the class.

Allow your students to find and experience the knowledge for themselves. If that seems the easy way out to you, you are wrong! From an outsider's point of view it may seem as though the teacher is doing nothing. However, students need guidance and encouragement to find the right answers. Some students need that extra push to do more than just what is expected of them. Your job, contrary to popular belief, is not always the purveyor of knowledge. It is also to guide your students and teach them how to gain that knowledge for themselves.

> *"Teach your students HOW to learn so that they can become life-long learners."*

Here are some ways of allowing students to discover knowledge for themselves:

Expert Advice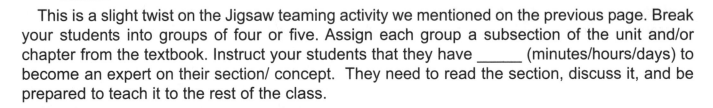

This is a slight twist on the Jigsaw teaming activity we mentioned on the previous page. Break your students into groups of four or five. Assign each group a subsection of the unit and/or chapter from the textbook. Instruct your students that they have _____ (minutes/hours/days) to become an expert on their section/ concept. They need to read the section, discuss it, and be prepared to teach it to the rest of the class.

Encourage them to ask questions of each other and you. Also, their presentation should be creative. Then hold EVERY student accountable for the information presented through a test or other assessment. You will be surprised at how motivated students are to read when THEY are the ones who have to teach everyone else.

Independent Study

Have each student choose one concept/ person/ idea related to your unit to research. Create a checklist for them to follow. Have them write a research paper, create a visual, and present the information to the class. Hold students accountable through an assessment over the information presented.

Discovery   *" I Wonder Questions"*

Pose a question to your class and discuss it. Help them to discover the information through questions and discussion. For example, you might ask your students, "I wonder why George Washington was elected the first president?" Then guide them through a discussion to help them discover the answer. This is a wonderful way to encourage questioning skills that will help in student research.

Use objects to jumpstart "I wonder" questions. Pass around an object and ask, "I wonder what this is used for?" Encourage students to come up with their own "I wonder" questions about the object.

When students ask a question about a particular topic, or ask a "why" question, help them use the internet to discover the answer for themselves. Then they can share their newfound information with the rest of the class.

Take students on an exploration walk. This is a perfect time to ask "I wonder" questions about the world around them. Your "I wonder" questions do not even need to stay within the confines of nature and the environment. Is there construction going on nearby? As you pass by ask, "I wonder why they are ...?" This may spark some interest in students to research further in order to answer your question. With construction questions, students could learn more about math and science in their quest for knowledge.

> **For example:** You might pose a question regarding the use of triangles and other shapes in building bridges and other structures.

Experiments

Don't just discuss a question or concept, experiment. Are you discussing Egypt and the Nile? Try an experiment showing how the Egyptians were able to use the floods to their advantage in farming.

Discussing space exploration? Experiment with balloons to show how a rocket works. Discussing plant life? Have students design and plant their own garden.

AIMS has some wonderful experiments that are easy and can be connected to all subject areas. The Ranger Rick Big Book Series also come with neat ideas for experiments.

> **Idea Share**
>
> The internet is an excellent source to look for experiments you can do with your students. When doing a search be sure to type in "student experiments" and the keywords of your topic.
>
> You might also try Yahooligans when searching.
> www.yahooligans.com

Scholastic and Teacher Created Materials also have some fantastic books available of kitchen table experiments that could be done in any classroom.

Get your students doing, not just reading!

Children's Stories

Have students read a chapter from the textbook and rewrite it as a children's story. It must be from one person's point of view (ex: Caesar's story about the fall of ancient Rome) and should include all of the important information from the chapter. Have students share their stories. You could even have them share their stories with younger grade levels.

Children's stories are also a great way to introduce a unit and make connections between literature and the subject area. Everyone loves to be read to, not matter what age they are. Additionally, our middle school and high school students often enjoy "reliving their past" through fun activities. Though they may seem childish, we can capture student attention and revive our otherwise dull lessons!

Getting ready to learn about the human body? Why not read the book *Dem Bones*? You could incorporate music into the learning. Primary students especially love the combination of stories and songs! Older students could work together to turn the book into a rap rather than trying to sing the actual song.

Getting ready to learn about Onomatopoeia for a poetry unit? Why not read the book, *Mr. Brown Can Moo*? Although a simple Dr. Seuss book, *Mr. Brown Can Moo* is full of onomatopoeias and provides excellent examples. Your students will get a kick out of listening to an old book from their childhood and you've just used something different to introduce what could be a boring lesson.

Getting ready to study point of view? Start out with The True Story of The Three Little Pigs which is told by Mr. Wolf. There are many such stories out there that take well-known fairy tales and folk stories and rewrite them using a different point of view. Students could then take their own favorite fairy tale and rewrite from another character's point of view.

Getting ready to study Egypt? Start out with a fun book entitled, *The Egyptian Princess*. This is a Cinderella type story that is told in Egypt. Have students point out the differences between the familiar story of Cinderella and this book. This discussion could lead into listing different aspects about Egyptian life and culture and jumpstart your unit!

Getting ready to solve word problems? Introduce your unit with the book, Math Curse. The main character spends an entire day encountering different math problems that he must solve. What a fun way to introduce something that can be such a struggle for students!

There are such a plethora of children's books that reach across all subject areas. Not sure what you are looking for? Do a search through Amazon or another online bookstore with the concept as your keyword. With Amazon you can go to the Children's Books section and then browse only in that area. You're sure to find what you need!

Research Projects

In this "information age" research skills are some of the most important and useful tools we can give our students. These skills should be taught and practiced from first grade all the way up through high school. Children are naturally curious about the world around them, and what better way to learn than to discover the answers to questions through research?

"Oh, no," you may say to yourself, "my kids aren't ready for research." Perhaps you are the one who is not ready. For those of us who remember 20 page writing assignments, the word research can have a very negative connotation. However, research can be as simple as looking up the answer to a question.

Here are some tips to help you along:

√   **Start out simple and easy.**

In primary grades, simply have students use books, their parents, other teachers, and the computer to find the answer to a question.

With older students, have them use primary and secondary sources to find the answer to a question relating to your topic of study. Require a paragraph and a creative product such as a pop-up book or diorama.

With secondary students, set a limit of 3 to 5 double spaced typed pages for each paper. Every 9th grader should be able to write a three page paper and every 12th grade should be able to write a five page paper.

Also, be sure to teach note-taking skills before requiring any formal research. The note-taking strategy we have outlined on the following pages is an excellent tool to help keep students from plagarizing when taking notes from other sources.

√   **Take it step by step.**

When you do your first research project, take the students through the process step by step. Model each step for them as a class and then allow students to complete that step for their own project.

One way to help students get comfortable with research projects is to do the first one as a group project, the second one as a partner project, and the last one, or next ones, individually.

√   **Allow student choice.**

Choose a timely and global topic, but then allow your students to choose the specific area within that larger topic. For example, you may choose the topic of animals, and your students each get to choose the animal they want to learn more about.

> **Idea Share**
>
> The library and librarian are excellent resources. Be sure to talk with the librarian before you begin planning a research project for your students. Know what is available and how you can use the library.

√ **Determine ahead of time what you expect.**

What elements do you expect in the project? Do you want a written part, visual, and an oral presentation? Within each of these, what do you expect? Is this to be a group or individual project? Can the written part be creative like a story or skit, or do you expect a formal essay of some sort?

√ **Create a checklist for students to follow.**

Make sure you include every aspect that will be assessed. Include directions for the project at the top of the page. You can make the checklist as specific and detailed as you feel your students need.

I use mine to show students the steps to follow when completing their project as well as tasks and products to be done for each section. Some students need a lot more structure than others. You might even consider including due dates for completion of each section.

√ **Teach students how to write the formal paper, if required.**

When it is time for students to write their essay, it is important to go through the process with them step by step, especially the first couple of times.

> **Example:** *I teach students how to write an introduction in class. Then, that night they are required to write an introduction for their paper. The next day I read and help students revise their introductions. We follow the same process for the body and conclusion of the paper. It really helps students to go through the process one step at a time, especially if this is their first formal paper.*

√ **Monitor students constantly.**

This is not the time to sit behind your desk. Monitoring is not difficult as long as you are prepared. Use the Clipboard Monitoring form found in the Classroom Management chapter to help you keep track of who is on/off task and who is having trouble with the process.

3 research proj. per yr.

In our opinion, students should be required to complete at least three research projects each year. As students get into upper grades, the requirements should become more stringent. This will better prepare them for college and vocational school where research is a common learning tool.

> *"No matter what time of year, projects are a great tool to use in the classroom.*
>
> *Students are excited to learn and enjoy the collaboration."*

Teaching Note-Taking Skills

   In order to be successful at research projects, our students need to be taught how to take notes from a source. Even the youngest can be taught through modeling. Although you may not ask a Kinder or first grade student to copy down notes, modeling the skill during a non-fiction reading begins building a schema for note-taking.

   The more this vital skill is taught in Elementary and Middle school, the better our students will be at note-taking as they progress through each grade and in every subject area.

√   **Introduce with Big Books**

1) Small chunks of information on each page

2) Large print makes it easier for students to see when reading as a class.

3) Variety of topics

> Ranger Rick puts out a series of Big Books that are Science and Social Studies related. These are very informative, can be easily used to connect to the current topic being taught, and have fantastic pictures.

> **Primary teachers** can Model note-taking skills for the whole class on an overhead transparency or a large sheet of butcher paper.
>
> We want to build those dendrites in the brain that are associated with this concept.

√   **Introduce with Non-fiction Books or Magazines**

   Choose a book or article that is easy to read (never use an encyclopedia to start) and either make transparencies or enough copies so that each student can easily read the information.

   Follow the steps below several times with your students as a class, then have them work in small groups, then as pairs, and finally, individually. This process helps give students confidence to take good notes.

√   **Steps**

- Write the title/general topic of the book as your main heading or topic

- Read each page (including the picture captions) carefully.

- Ask students to tell you what that page was mostly about (main idea).

- Write the main idea as your subheading on a transparency or butcher paper.

- Ask students for details from the page that support the main idea.

- Write these as one or two word details under the subheading.

- Make sure you show the student the pictures and discuss the information in each caption. Is it necessary or extraneous?

THE SOLAR SYSTEM

THE SUN
- a medium sized star
- nine planets orbit
  -Mercury, Venus, Earth, Mars, Jupiter, Saturn, Uranus, Neptune, Pluto
- provides light and heat

INNER PLANETS
- Mercury, Venus, Earth, Mars
- Solid
  -mostly rock
- closest to the sun
- short orbits

Have students apply this knowledge of note-taking skills when researching and taking notes from a source, including the internet. Instruct them to take notes exactly as they have practiced in class. When students begin taking notes in this manner, using only one or two keywords for each detail, you'll find that they are not able to plagarize from the source. You may even want to practice taking notes from an encyclopedia or other non-fiction book to help students make the transition from simple paragraphs to more complex source material. Don't forget to have them write down the title of each source at the top of their notes.

Here is a set of instructions you can give to older students to help them during the research/note-taking process.

Instructions for Taking Notes

1. Read each paragraph - does it contain information you need?
    -if yes, go on to #2
    -if no, read the next paragraph

2. What was that paragraph mostly about?
    - Write the main idea on your paper

3. What are the details in this paragraph?
    -Write the supporting details in one or two words as bullets under the main idea
    -Limit 3 words for each bullet

4. Read the next paragraph

**Remember, you do not need to copy EVERYTHING down. Taking notes is the art of pulling out only the information you need.

Making Connections between Subject Areas

Another effective teaching strategy is integrated study. This section will offer some of our thoughts on why you should integrate as well as some suggestions for your classroom. Most of these ideas come from Susan Kovalik's *ITI for the Classroom*. Another excellent resource for integrating is a book entitled *The Way We Were, The Way We Want to Be* by Ann Ross, written for middle school teachers. Both of these are excellent resources to have in your library!

WHY?

With everything we are supposed to teach each day it often seems as though we can never fit it all in. However, by integrating subject matter, concepts, and skills, not only can we cover everything we need to, but we can also help our students make important connections in their learning.

> *"An effective teacher helps students see connections across their learning."*

Integration is the connection of several subjects under a topic or theme of some sort. Brain research shows us that students learn best when ideas are connected across subject areas. As adults, we know that science cannot be separated from math, and that social studies concepts are closely linked to both language and science.

How then can we ask our students to learn in isolated compartments for each subject? In doing so, we push students farther back rather than leading them forward in their studies. One way we can work towards making connections is through thematic units. Susan Kovalik, in her book *ITI for the Classroom*, states that themes should be motivating to students and relate to the real world.

> *"Making connections in learning encourages higher level thinking and is supported by brain-based research."*

Getting Started

1.) Start with a topic of study required for your grade level
   -Science and Social Studies are the easiest to use as a starting place

2.) Brainstorm skills/ objectives usually taught for that topic

3.) Brainstorm connections with other subject areas
   -find the common links in skills/concepts (ie - graphing is a skill used in math, science, and social studies)

Example:

Let's say that you have an upcoming unit on Volcanoes. You would first want to list skills and concepts to be taught for the topic. Next, you would brainstorm Social Studies, Math and Language Arts connections with volcanoes. Some of your ideas might include:

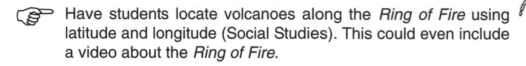

☞ Have students locate volcanoes along the *Ring of Fire* using latitude and longitude (Social Studies). This could even include a video about the *Ring of Fire*.

☞ Students can read about or research famous historical events surrounding volcanoes such as Mount St. Helens or Vesuvius (Language Arts and Social Studies).

☞ A study of landforms could also arise since many mountains began as volcanoes. In addition, students can learn how new islands are created (which goes well with the *Ring of Fire* study). With the study of islands, students can also learn mapping skills. Those skills can be applied by creating their own "island" and using graph paper to create a map of cities, rivers, etc. on this island (Social Studies).

"Can you think of any ways to incorporate art or music into this unit?"

☞ Additionally, there is a very definite sequence to what happens when a volcano erupts and how it creates an island over time. This works well for including the reading concept of sequencing (Reading).

☞ Students can also study the geometry of volcanoes by discussing cones and triangles. Students can also study how seismic instruments work to measure pressure, etc. (Math).

Use a Graphic Organizer when Planning

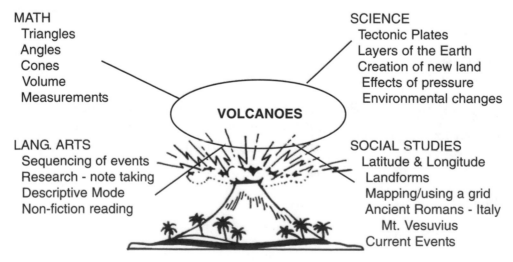

MATH
  Triangles
  Angles
  Cones
  Volume
  Measurements

SCIENCE
  Tectonic Plates
  Layers of the Earth
  Creation of new land
  Effects of pressure
  Environmental changes

VOLCANOES

LANG. ARTS
  Sequencing of events
  Research - note taking
  Descriptive Mode
  Non-fiction reading

SOCIAL STUDIES
  Latitude & Longitude
  Landforms
  Mapping/using a grid
  Ancient Romans - Italy
  Mt. Vesuvius
  Current Events

Start Small

If you jump in with both feet, you will more than likely meet with disppointment. Not only does it take a while to get used to a new idea, but it also takes some time to implement a new type of strategy in the classroom. Just like our students, we all have different ways of learning. Some of us need to go for the gusto, but others need more of a trial period before being ready to undertake a project like this. Integrating takes experience and it takes logical thinking. It works best when you have two or more teachers working together to brainstorm the connections and make them work in a lesson or unit.

For those of you who read the above tips and examples and thought immediately, "That is way too much work for me right now," please understand that you do not need to start out so big. You are probably already integrating without even realizing it. Every time you use a teachable moment to help students reach an understanding, whether it relates to your subject matter or not, you are integrating.

Here are a few ways to start out with small steps:

- When reading a story or novel, incorporate history from the time period used in the setting.

- Provide students with a timeline of interesting events that occurred during the time the author either wrote the novel or during their lifetime. A neat way to do this might be to create a "In the Year Of" poster that shows prices of everyday items, popular music, famous people, etc.

- Point out cities and countries on the map for authors, story settings, famous scientists or mathematicians.

- Point out ways the environment affects a story, historical event, or world culture. This includes landforms, temperature or seasons, climates, and/or animal and insect life.

- Use timelines to show other events happening at the time of a scientific discovery.

- Use research projects in Science and Social Studies to study a topic in further detail.

- When teaching a concept/skill in Math or Science that has a practical application, try to either show or discuss these with students.

Unit used with 5th Grade Students

5th grade Science - Environmental Science - Biomes, Environments, Habitats

5th grade Social Studies - Geography of the United States/ Native Americans

Theme: Trekking Across the United States

Topics of Study: West coast to East coast — tracking the natural movement of early peoples across North America
      Eastern Pacific tribes
        -coastal environment/habitats/weather
      Southwestern tribes
        -desert environment/habitats/weather
      Plains tribes
        -grasslands environment/habitats/weather
      Eastern tribes
        -forested environment/habitats/weather

Skills:
- graphing - Math
- collect current data on precipitation & temperature from each geographical area and graph —Science/Math
- compare/contrast regions — Language Arts (essay)
- discuss effect of environment on Native American culture for each region — Science/ Social Studies
- compare/contrast Native American cultures - S.S./ Lang. Arts
- Native American mythology — compare/contrast stories - Lang. Arts
- environment of each region - Science/ S.S.
- habitats found in each region - Science/ S.S.
- food chain - Science
- energy cycle - Science
- timeline of settlement of early peoples - Social Studies
- research various Native American tribes - Social Studies/ Lang. Arts
- group presentations of research - Social Studies/ Lang. Arts

"An effective teacher keeps a balance between basic skills instruction and integrated thematic units."

Notice that basic Math and Language Arts skills are not included in this integrated unit. We believe that there must be a fine balance between basic skills and integration. We used our daily oral language, daily geography, and daily math to practice these basic skills. We also tied this practice into our integrated lessons. In addition, we added in a "skills" time into our day for math, reading, and writing. An example of an integrated lesson plan can be found on the next couple of pages.

The next two pages contain a sample lesson plan that utilizes integration throughout the day.

Monday, October 21, 20__

Objectives: To be able to average a group of numbers
To be able to create a poetry book using original poems
To be able to complete a book study for a novel
To be able to explain how a habitat, ecosystem, and environment are different and how they are related

Materials: Science book, notes on averaging, large white paper, color pencils

Journal: Imagine that you live in a forest. Describe everything you see: animals, plants, weather.

Homework: Rdg. - Read for 20 min./ Write a response from questions in log
L.A. - Write one sentence for each vocabulary word
Math - Practice averaging/mean

Words of the Day: ecosystem - a community and its nonliving environment

community - all the populations in one ecosystem

population - all the organisms of one species that live in a certain place

Daily Language: Locate the commas used in the following sentences. Explain the two different comma rules used.

Ecosystems can change constantly. They comes in all sizes, and can exist in a puddle, log, ocean, or forest.

(Answer)   Commas are used to separate items in a list. A comma is needed before the "and" in this sentence because it is a compound sentence.

Daily Geography: What sea surrounds Jamaica?

What city is 23 degrees S latitude, 43 degrees W longitude?

(Answer)   a) Caribbean   b) Rio De Janeiro

Daily Math: Estimate the following to the nearest hundreds place:

A) 790 + 3,756 + 2,345   B) 490 + 5,645 + 8,205   C) 608 + 6,457 + 10,790

(Answer)   A) 6,900   B) 14,300   C) 17,900

Procedures:

8:00-9:30   Announcements
Copy homework into calendar, Copy Words of the day
Write in Journal

8:30-8:45   Daily Oral Language - Students complete & go over in class

8:45-9:00   Daily Geography - Students complete & go over in class

9:00-9:45   Daily Math - Students complete & go over in class
- Introduce averaging with word problem —
- Mrs. Hershman went on a shopping spree last week. Monday she spent $20.00, Tuesday she spent $30.00, Wednesday she spend $40.00 and Saturday she spent $50.00. What is the average amount of money she spent last week?
- Give notes in math spiral on average/mean
- Do a few practice problems in the spiral
- Practice with page 95 in Science book — use the diagram of the average number of ants in a particular ecosystem to calculate the total ant population.

9:45-9:50   Bathroom Break/ Go to Specials

9:55-10:45 Specials - Art

10:50-11:20 Reading Workshop - Students complete predictions for main character for Book Study

11:20-12:10 Writing Workshop - Students continue working on poetry book

12:10-1:00 Lunch/ Recess

1:00-2:30   Brainstorm with the students things they might find in a forest environment: pond, fish, bushes, trees, birds, small animals
- Discuss and take notes on ecosystem and difference between habitat, ecosystem, and environment (Use Ecosystem Diversity sheets)
- Students create a visual as a group to show their understanding of the difference between a habitat, ecosystem & environment, AND how these three are related.
- Group presentations

2:30-2:55   Read Aloud - Flight of the Sparrow - poem
- Review Homework
- Clean up

Here are some samples from integrated units that we did for 5th & 6th grade to give you some idea of how to organize your units of study.   The first unit is more detailed to show you how we categorized the concepts taught.

5th Grade
Year-long Theme: Exploring Our World

1st 6 weeks - The Outer Limits -
Topics - Galaxy, Solar System, Moon, Space Exploration

Math
number line
place value
basic operations

Science
galaxies
constellations
solar system
gravity
moon
spacecraft/ exploration
probes

Lang. Arts
news articles
science fiction
narrative (mode)

Social Studies
Timeline
Space Exploration (history of)
Modern American history

Reading
Genres
Attributes of a story - setting, characters, plot
Main Idea

2nd 6 weeks - Our Island Earth -

Topics - formation of earth, volcanoes, islands, rainforests

3rd 6 weeks - A New World -

Topics - Native American tribes, ecosystems

4th 6 weeks - Across the Ocean -

Topics - ocean life, exploration of Americas

5th 6 weeks - Westward Bound

Topics - colonization, growth of America, government, westward expansion

6th 6 weeks - Exploring My Own World

Topics - family, self, 50 states

The following unit was created for a Social Studies/Language Arts class.

6th Grade

Yearlong Theme: On My Own

1st 6 weeks - Knowing Myself

Unit One - This is the Real Me (2 weeks)
- Knowing myself mentally: student information, learning styles inventory
- Knowing myself emotionally: individual values & morals, emotions and the way they affect different people
  - Last Summer with Maizon
- Knowing myself physically: physical appearance, describing people, adjectives, physical skills
  - "Cecilia Dowling"
- Prewriting skills: lifemap, freewriting, looping, brainstorming, mind mapping, jot list, hot topic list
- Reading skills: poetry - "Cecilia Dowing"
  - details - Last Summer with Maizon
- Individual novels
- About the author

Unit Two - My Heritage (2 weeks)
- The Great Ancestor Hunt - Trade Book (Begin reading before unit)
- The World in the Classroom: Map skills, identifying cultures and countries
- Family: family tree, prefixes, suffixes and root words,
  - Child of the Owl
- Traditions: family customs, personal narrative, parts of a book
  - Opera, Karate and Bandits
  - "Fiddler On the Roof"

Unit Three - My Goals (2 weeks)
- Personal: Resolutions, friendly letter, main idea, setting goals
  - Brother to the Wind
- Professional: setting goals, actions have consequences
  - Guest Speaker on Careers

2nd 6 weeks - Finding My Place
> Topics - Continents, map skills, early man, family, communication skills, Early settlements, timelines, ancient civilizations, climates

3rd 6 weeks - Applying Myself
> Topics - Resume, Biographies, charts/graphs, population, government, economics, the "How To" essay, interviewing,

4th 6 weeks - Improving My World
> Topics - Inventions, persuasion, cause & effect, nonfiction, exploration of world, ocean, Renaissance

5th 6 weeks - Dealing With Others
> Topics - Relationships, cultural borrowing, trade routes, economics, conflict/resolution, war, holocaust, governments, advantages/disadvantages, heroes

6th 6 weeks - I'm All On My Own
> Topics - Survival skills, critical thinking skills, freedoms & responsibilities, spread of democracy, world geography, environments

Interdisciplinary Study

Integration is not an impossibility in a departmentalized setting. If you are truly interested in integrating subject matter, there are several ways to go about it.

- You and your team members need to agree that integration is the best thing for your students.
- Share the different skills and topics that will be taught throughout the year.
- Work together to determine a yearlong theme and subsequent six weeks themes.
- Planning together will make integration much easier for everyone.
- Each class will cover a part of the lesson for the day.

For example:
> **If you were doing a mini-unit on volcanoes, each class would build on the others.**

- Science would discuss how volcanoes are formed and would experiment with volcanoes.

- Social Studies might plot various known volcanoes on a map of the world and study latitude and longitude.

- Language Arts might read about some historical volcanic eruptions such as Vesuvius or Mt. St. Helen's and may write a How To essay on making a model volcano.

- The art teacher could be a part of this unit by actually allowing students to make a volcano (or it could be done in another class).

- Lastly, Math might be able to study cones, ratios, percentages, and probability.

Learning Centers

Another way of enhancing your instruction is through learning centers. Upper elementary and middle school teachers often do not utilize the learning center for the following reasons:

- Takes up too much room

- Takes too long to create and organize

- Takes too much effort to monitor

- Takes too long to evaluate students

In our classrooms, we finally found a way to utilize learning centers so that they were not a burden, but instead were a helpful tool.

Enrichment Centers

Students use the enrichment center when they are finished with a class assignment and have nothing else to do. We also used it as a reward. Here is how you set it up:

- Create a "thinking folder" for each student with a manila folder
- Place these folders in an easily accessible place
- Copy logic puzzles, think-a-grams, and other word puzzles, glue them on colorful construction paper and laminate them
- Separate puzzles by type & place them in clearly labeled manila folders
- Write the directions for the center on the manila folder
- Place vis-a-vis pens in a can on a table
- Students choose a puzzle, complete it and write the answer on their own sheet of paper.
- Then they put their paper into their "thinking folder."
- Lastly, have students wipe the original puzzle clean and put it away.

Thinking Folder

A Thinking folder is an easy way to monitor student work from the learning center.

- Students can work these puzzles at their own seat which means that you don't have to have a whole "center area" prepared. All you need is a spot to keep the puzzles.

- Every three weeks check the folders & grade the puzzles.

- Give students extra credit for correct answers and feedback for wrong answers to help them do better the next time.

Rotating Centers

Another fun idea for learning centers is to use rotating centers. Set up each center on a table/ group of desks. Separate students into rotation groups. Each group works on a center, then at a pre-determined time, rotates to a new center. The only problem with this type of rotation is that some students finish more quickly than others and may become behavior problems.

A variation on this type of center is to create a checklist and allow students to work at their own pace. Each student visits each center when he/she needs to. For management purposes, set limits as to how many students can be at each station.

In order for this to work, you must MONITOR, MONITOR, MONITOR! Have your clipboard in hand and be ready to help students, note hardworking students, and mark behavior problems. Have an alternative activity ready for those students not mature enough to handle this type of assignment.

Setup

- Type/ copy directions for each center
- Paste directions on colorful construction paper
- Laminate directions
- Set directions and materials on each table/group of desks
- Pass out checklists to students
- Students record data/answers on their own paper
- Students turn in their checklist, answers & any products they made in a manila folder to be evaluated.
- Evaluate the centers using the checklist. Give each activity a score of 1-4 and then average the scores to determine the overall grade.
  - 1 = 65   2 = 75   3 = 85   4 = 95

(See the Assessment chapter for more information about Rubric scoring)

> *"Planning structure and guidelines helps students get the most out of labs or rotating centers."*

STUDENT CHECKLIST

_____ How Does Salt Water Help Keep Whales Afloat?

_____ How Big Are Whales?

_____ What Keeps Whales Warm?

_____ What Helps Keep Whales Afloat?

The center activities are from the Ranger Rick Big Book, Whales.

Note: **Each of these questions in the student checklist goes with a science experiment to perform to find the answer.**

Field Trips

Field trips are important discovery learning tools. As we all know, they provide hands-on learning for students and serve as a great way to get children to experience the community around them.

Students love field trips! However, without planning and organization, field trips can be a nightmare for teachers. We have discovered, over time, that prior-planning is the key to a positive field trip experience. This does not mean just planning out where, when, and how you're going on the field trip. It also includes providing structure and guidance for both your chaperones and your students.

Although you've probably been on a thousand field trips, we thought we'd just take a little bit of time to refresh our memories of some different strategies for having a successful and effective field trip.

Remember...

- The more chaperones you have, the lower the student to adult ratio. Smaller groups give parents/ volunteers greater control over their charges.

- Whenever you go on an inside field trip, you want lots of structure and control to maintain a quiet and non-disruptive environment.

- Sign up parent volunteers well in advance of your trip.

- Notify other teachers in the school of the dates and times for your field trip.

- Notify the cafeteria if you will be out during lunch time. This helps them better prepare for lunch that day. Also, you may have several students who need a sack lunch from school. A lunch count needs to be done at least 2 weeks before your trip.

- Put in a request for a field trip to your principal as soon as you begin your initial planning.

- Have a clear educational objective for your field trip. Why are you going? If it is just for a free day or to give students a break, the trip probably won't be approved.

- When signing up parent volunteers, write down their names on your calendar so that you can remember to call them with reminders.

Holding Students Accountable for Their Learning...

- Be ready with some sort of a scavenger hunt or focus questions for adult volunteers to use with their groups to help make the most out of this great educational experience.

- Organize and write down your expectations of both students and adult volunteers during the field trip. Give each adult leader a clipboard with the following information attached:

  - Their assigned bus
  - A list of students in their group
  - Teaching tips for the trip

    ⇨ questions volunteers should ask students during the trip
    ⇨ topics that need to be discussed during the visit
    ⇨ special exhibits for students to focus their attention
    ⇨ back up procedures for supervising difficult students

- Visit your destination ahead of time so that you can prepare this information for the field trip.

- Visiting a field trip destination ahead of time does not have to be drudgery. Take a date, a friend, or a member of your grade level and enjoy the outing. Just be sure to take a little notebook and jot down questions/ideas for a field trip activity.

Working with Chaperones...

- Have name tags ready for everyone. This helps the volunteers know the students in their group AND the other adults in the group.

- Thank the volunteers for joining you even BEFORE the field trip begins.

- Ask volunteers to arrive 15 minutes before the departure time to receive instructions.

Organizing...

- Have signs made up for the buses (especially when taking a large group) so that students can easily identify their assigned bus. (Bus #1; place in the front passenger window)

- Get several large plastic tubs on wheels to hold lunches. I like to have one for each group, but some people simply have one for each class.

- If you or the school can't afford to get these types of tubs, gather several large empty boxes to use. They aren't as easy to get from the bus to the eating area, but they do work to keep lunches together.

Idea Share

Give each adult a clipboard with important information for the field trip.

Have each student bring a clipboard or pocket-folder to hold focus questions, scavenger hunt, or some other type of activity.

Field Trip Permission Form

Dear Parents,

    We are taking a field trip to _____. For the students' safety and well-being, it is important for you to know where we will be going and the purpose of this trip. Please note the following important information about our upcoming event.

Place: _____

Date: _____

Time: _____

Purpose: _____

_____

_____

Please fill out and sign the form below. Detach the bottom portion and return it to me in the next couple of days. If you have any questions or concerns, please feel free to contact me at school during my planning period, or leave a message with the school secretary for me to return.

Sincerely,

- -

I,_____ give my permission for_____

to attend the field trip to _____ .

I will _____ send a lunch for _____ purchase a school lunch

My child has the following special needs to take into consideration _____

_____

Parent Signature:_____ Date:_____

Field Trip Instructions

DATE:_____

TIME:_____

PLACE:_____

GROUP:_____ VOLUNTEER NAME:_____

LIST OF STUDENTS	SCHEDULE FOR THE DAY: (including rotation schedule of exhibits if necessary.)
Please be sure to ask your group to think about or discuss the following:	Be sure to visit the following places/ exhibits:

© 2005 McDonald and Hershman

Conclusion

A brain-based classroom is also one in which students are actively engaged in the learning process. Human beings naturally have a sense of curiosity about the unknown. Unfortunately, the isolated nature of traditional lectures and textbook reading has a tendancy to squelch that curiosity. Students become bored and refuse to learn. We hope that this chapter has inspired you instead to use cooperative learning tools such as discovery learning, integrated content, and learning through experiences to foster life-long learning within your students.

Questions to Ponder

Why is it important to keep students actively engaged in the classroom rather than passively listening?

What are some different ways you can keep your students actively engaged?

How might you implement discovery or experiential learning in your classroom?

Why should you consider using research projects throughout the year rather than just once a year?

What is your opinion of integrating subject areas? Is this something you might implement in your classroom? Why or why not?

Additional Resources

Learning Thru Discussion
by W. M. Fawcett Hill

Teaching with the Brain in Mind
by Eric Jensen

Integrated Thematic Instruction
by Susan Kovalik

The Way We Were, The Way We Can Be
by Ann Ross

Synergy
by Karen Olsen

Making Connections:

Reading and Writing Across the Curriculum

When striving to build a fire of learning in the classroom, we cannot forget about the foundational skills of reading and writing. Whether you teach the actual subjects of English and Reading or not, these skills are vital in all aspects of learning and life. Without the ability to read and write, students cannot function effeciently and successfully in the classroom and the world, not to mention on those "oh-so-important" standardized tests.

While most of us will admit to the importance of these skills, there are many teachers who feel that the teaching and practicing of reading and writing is solely the domain of the Language Arts teacher. This is absolutely not true. With the current crisis in student achievement and the recent *Leave No Child Behind Act*, more than ever it is important for every teacher in the school to incorporate reading and writing skills in the classroom and across subject areas.

And yet, none of us has the extra time to add another item to our overloaded curriculum. How can we reconcile this need with the reality we face? Within this chapter we have striven to provide a variety of strategies that will not only help students practice vital reading and writing skills, but will also enhance the teaching of your subject area. The question and challenge we put to you is this:

How can you rekindle your own subject area by integrating important reading and writing strategies into your lessons?

The Classroom Library

Every classroom, no matter what subject area, should have a classroom library with books and other materials to encourage students to read. Below are a few tips on creating and managing a classroom library.

• Choose one corner of your room to be dedicated to reading. It doesn't have to be huge, just a space big enough for two or three kids to sit comfortably. However, if you have a nice big room, make your corner as big as you like!

• Partition it off a little from the rest of the room to make it seem like a special quiet place.

• Books and other types of reading material are an important part of a reading corner and should include non-fiction as well as fiction. Be sure materials is available for a wide variety of reading levels.

What to include?

- How-To books
- Fun Facts books
- Magazines
- Newspapers
- Biographies
- Historical Fiction
- Non-fiction books related to subject
- Student publications
- Poetry books

Idea Share

Magazines, How-To books, and other non-fiction books provide great sources of information for in-class research.

There are several wonderful books put out by Scholastic and other educational publishers on Science, Social Studies, and other subject area topics. Check out Scholastic's webpage: http://click.scholastic.com/teacherstore/ or Amazon.com: http://www.amazon.com to browse for good non-fiction books to include in your reading area.

Educational Magazines:

Kids Discover
Discover
Ranger Rick
Scholastic DynaMath
Scholastic Math
Chem Matters
Current Science
Science Weekly
3-2-1 Contact
Smithsonian Magaznie
World Kid
TIME For Kids
Midlink Magazine
Sports Illustrated for Kids

A reading area can be a place for students to sit quietly and read, a place for research, or a quiet area to be used by students needing to take a break and get calm. Design your area so that it can meet one or all of these purposes throughout the school year.

Make the corner seem inviting to students:

- Add pillows and a beanbag
- Add chairs or even a small couch (if your room is big enough for that)
- Add small lamps or floor lamps. This will give your students the impression of a cozy reading place. Not everyone has room for these nice extras, but if you do - go for it!
- Put down carpet squares if your room isn't carpeted.

Make the corner conducive to research:

- Add a long skinny table
- Add several trays or containers to hold supplies
- Include paper, pencils & pens, highlighters, and post-it notes

Teacher Talk

"As a middle school teacher teaching LA/Social Studies classes, I really wanted to set my reading corner apart from the rest of the room. I decided to pull in a comfy rocking chair, some bean bags, colorful carpet squares, big pillows, and a floor lamp. There was no window near my corner, so I created a window out of butcher paper and "hung" curtains to make it seem homey. I also stuck a big palm tree way in the back of the corner. All of my kids enjoyed that corner and I often used it for more than just reading."

Getting the Materials

Here are some tips for getting materials at low or no cost:

Gathering Books

√   **Hold a book drive**
- Make it a contest between either your students or your classes.

- Send home a letter to the parents explaining what you are doing and why you are doing it.

- Ask for both fiction and non-fiction reading material.

- When students bring in their books, have them write "Donated By:" and their name on the front cover.

- Another option is to create book plates using large labels on the computer. You can print these with the student information or have students write their information in the appropriate places. This helps make your students feel an important part of your reading center.

√   **Book Clubs**

- Scholastic and Troll book clubs often send out magazines to teachers. If you do not receive any within the first month of school, go online to their websites and request the book orders magazine. There are book clubs for all age groups and often include books for all subject areas. Encourage your students to order.

> *"Don't forget about Public Library Sales and Garage Sales for low-cost books!"*

- **Free Books.** Oftentimes the book clubs will offer free books for every so many dollars spent. Let students help you choose some for the classroom library.

- **Bonus Points.** When students order, you get bonus points. You can use these bonus points to get books for your classroom library.

- **Teacher Specials.** Book clubs also offer teacher specials where you can get packages of books for lower prices. Take advantage of these deals!

- Usborne Books has some fantastic reference and other educational books available for students of all ages from pre-school to high school. Schools who host Usborne Book Fairs can get up to 60% in free books for their school! Their web address is usborne.com.

Finding Bookshelves

1. Ask the school custodian.

These school staff members can be a wealth of knowledge about furniture resources!

2. Ask the school librarian.

Sometimes the librarian may know where an extra bookshelf is, or may be able to order one for you.

3. Use old encyclopedia carts.

Old encyclopedia sets used to come on little carts. Use one of these to hold books.

"Try to think out of the box when looking for potential bookshelves!"

4. Use plastic crates.

They usually stack well and don't look bad in a reading corner.

Pillows, Beanbags, etc.

1. Salvation Army/ GoodWill

You can get lots of things at the Salvation Army or GoodWill store without spending a lot of money. Look there for a couch, stuffed animals, bean bags, pillows, etc. I once bought a couch for $35.00 and simply covered it with a clean sheet for my reading corner.

2. Fabric Store

If you know how to sew (or know someone who does), try buying some scrap material and stuffing. Also, the end of any bolt of fabric is cheaper than when it has to be cut to a specific size. This is great for pillows of all sizes. You may even be able to make a bean bag out of scrap cloth and packaging styrofoam chips.

3. Donations from Wal-Mart

Ask for torn or worn out pillows, end of season stuff, etc. If you tell them you are a teacher, they may help you out with donations.

4. Donations from Carpet stores

You can get old carpet samples from carpet stores. They are usually thrown away and sometimes the manager will give them to you for FREE.

Managing the Reading Area

Now that you have everything set up and ready to go, here are a few strategies for managing this very useful area:

Books

1. Set up a check-out system

- Use library check-out cards and folders. These can sometimes be found at Office Depot or your local office supply store. Some teacher supply stores carry these supplies. One last option is to check with your school librarian. Depending on your school, you might be able to ask her to order some for you and charge it to the Language Arts department or to your grade level budget.

- Write the title of the book, author's name, and cost to replace on each book check-out card. This helps at the end of the year with any books that have been permanently lost.

- When checking-out a book, have students fill out the card from the back of the book and place it in an index card box behind the letter of their last name.

- Appoint a student librarian to replace books in the shelves, or have students do it individually

- Make sure you put the price of the book on the card so that if a student loses a book, they can pay for you to replace it.

> *"Having a system in place for organizing and managing the reading area makes things easier."*

- Use a check-out log in a three-ring binder. Students write their name and the date when a book is checked out and then again when the book is checked back in. Be aware that this method is one of the easiest ways to permanently lose books. You may want a back-up accountability system where you initial when a student checks in a book.

2. Organize the books for easy reference

- Use color coded dots and write out a key where it can be clearly seen. For example, a red dot may mean science fiction, or a blue dot is a mystery book.

- Set aside each shelf for a different genre. However, if you do this, you must make sure that students are familiar with different genres.

- Keep a separate section of non-fiction books.

- Put books in alphabetical order by author's last name. Be warned - this is difficult to maintain unless you have a student librarian to help you.

Use of the Reading Area

1. Rotation

Have a rotation schedule for students to follow when deciding who gets to sit in the reading corner. Otherwise, you are going to have chaos on your hands with everybody fighting or racing to sit in the corner. (Even the big kids do this!) Alphabetical or table groups is the easiest way to arrange a schedule.

2. First come, first serve

This is a very dangerous way to decide who sits in the corner because everyone will race to get there first.

3. Reward system

Reward students who have good grades, good behavior, or who have improved by allowing them to sit in the reading corner. Be careful with this method and watch for inadequacies. Some students may never get to use the reading corner if you use it in this manner.

"I'm not a Reading teacher, so why should I have a reading corner?"

• Quiet time area   • Student research
• Access to books   • Enrichment of content

• A place for students who are finished early to read

Monitoring Students

1. Clipboard

Walk around and use the clipboard to help with observations. Keep notes on who is doing what during reading time. For more on this technique, see the Assessment and Classroom Management chapters.

Teacher Talk

"One way I use my reading corner is as a quiet place where angry or frustrated students can calm down. I start out the year by reading the book, Alexander and the Terrible, Horrible, No Good, Very Bad Day. Then I explain to my students that when we are having a horrible day, for whatever reason, it keeps us from learning properly. I encourage them to let me know when they need to cool down, and I send them to "Australia" which is my reading corner with a palm tree in it."

2. Reading Logs and Responses

Idea Share

Use Bloom's Keywords to help you develop reading responses on a variety of levels.

Have students keep a reading log with daily responses to their reading. Students should record the title of the book, author, and number of pages read each day before completing their response. A page of reading response questions is included in the back of this chapter.

Literature Circles/ Reading Groups

The Literature Circle, or Reading Group, is a strategy that can be used by any teacher. While Language Arts/Reading teachers may be using groups to read a novel, other subject area teachers may use this same strategy when reading a non-fiction source or textbook.

This strategy offers students a way to both read and discuss in a cooperative group setting. It allows students to work together and is very motivating. However, setting up literature groups can be very confusing and hard to manage. How can we effectively prepare to implement literature groups in our classroom? Below are several different strategies and tips:

1. Assign a group of 4 or 5 students to a particular book.

These groups are often heterogeneous, containing students at a variety of reading levels. You can have the students choose their own book to read as a group, or they can choose a book from several that you have picked out, or you can choose the book you expect them to read. The novel read in literature group can relate to a topic studied in Science or Social Studies, or might be a particular genre that you are studying.

- Each group either reads the book/text together aloud in class or assigns particular chapters/sections to be read each evening. Then, during class time, students discuss the chapter/section.

- It is important that you provide students with guiding questions to use during discussion. Each person should record the answers to discussion questions. Keywords from Bloom's Taxonomy of Thinking Skills can be used to help develop thought provoking discussion questions.

- Another option is to provide statements about characters or events within the story for students to either prove or disprove. Have students go around the circle and either agree or disagree with the statement. Require students to state their reasons and provide specific quotes or events from the story to support their position.

Example:	Charlotte is a nosey spider who should mind her own business. Do you agree or disagree with this statement? (Using Charlotte's Web) The Count of Monte Cristo is the true villian. Do you agree or disagree with this statement? (Using The Count of Monte Cristo)

- Groups can also create small products to show their comprehension of the story. These might include a storyboard of events, an illustration of the setting, a timeline, a pop-up book with information, etc.

As we stated earlier, it is vital that you remind students of class procedures, your expectations, and how to work together as a group every time. This should be done before students get together in their groups. When you begin to see student discussions that do not meet your expectations, model exactly what you want to see.

2. Teacher-led Literature Groups

Another option is to break students into smaller groups by ability level. Literature groups are a great way to practice decoding, comprehension, and other reading skills. Once again, each group should be assigned or allowed to choose a different book to read. Students are assigned chapter(s) to read and gather during class time to practice reading and to discuss the book with the teacher.

- Students keep books in a large plastic ziplock bag which can hold the book and any products, responses, etc. for discussion.

- Use an index card as a bookmark. Have the students write down the assigned chapter to read for that evening along with the date. This will keep a good log of reading assignments.

- Assign students either a guiding question for them to answer as they are reading a chapter, or a reading response of some sort to have ready for discussion. Sample responses can be found on pages 245 and 247.

189   190

> **Thank you to Carol Loper, 3rd grade teacher, Prosper ISD, for sharing these ideas with us!**

Managing Teacher-Led Literature Groups

How do I manage working with one group of kids while the rest are still there?

- **Train your students in classroom procedures and expectations.**
  All of your students should know exactly what to do each day during Literature Group time.

Generally you expect your other students to be working quietly on seatwork while you are reading with each group. This will not happen without training. In the beginning, you will find that you are interrupted frequently to quiet the class or get them focused on their assignment. You should get to a point where all you need is a look or to ring a small bell to remind students that they should be working quietly. This is not the time for groupwork activities for the rest of the class.

> **Idea Share**
>
> Assign meaningful seatwork for students not reading with you. This can include practice work for a specific skill/concept taught earlier, finishing other assignments, individual work in thinking/learning centers, individual research projects, etc.

What about the group I'm working with?

Determine how much time you want to spend with each group. Do you plan to work with 1 group each day for 20 or 30 minutes? Do you plan to work with 2 groups each day for 10 or 15 minutes? This decision is the first step towards preparing for how you will spend your time.

Next, break up the allotted time into 5 or 10 minute segments:

- 1 segment of the allotted time for students to read to you

- 1 segment for basic comprehension questions

- 1 segment for higher level thinking and discussion about the book

What activities can I use to jumpstart discussion or enrich student learning?

- Students create a storyboard that shows the major events happening within that chapter.

- Students create a timeline that shows the major events happening within that chapter

- Students keep an index card for each character. As they read, students are to write down different traits for each character. This could be extended to include relationships between that character and others as well as any changes that occur to the character over the course of the story.

- Use agree/disagree statements to jumpstart discussion. Students must support their opinion with reasons and with quotes or events from the story.

Internet application

When students come across a concept that is new and they have no prior knowledge about a concept (ex: sailing terms, rabbits vs. hares, a particular culture, etc.), utilize the internet to help extend their knowledge.

- Help students make a list of keywords related to the concept for an internet search (ex: schooner, rigging, etc.).

- The group can use the classroom computer to search for information.

- Students can print out information and share their new knowledge with the rest of the class (mini-research).

Idea Share

Two great search engines for kids are Google (www.google.com) and Ask Jeeves (www.askjeeves.com). Students can type in a variety of combinations of their keywords until they are able to locate relevant information.

Older students can do this on their own, but younger students will need to do this activity with the teacher.

Whole Class Reading Strategies

There are several different methods for reading a passage as a whole class. These can be used in any subject area.

Choral Reading

Students all read together out loud. A variation on this is to assign each student a different sentence. Have each student read their sentence in turn. Another way to do this is to break the students into groups and have assign each group a different passage to read aloud. Lastly, you could assign half the class to read every other paragraph.

Oral Reading

Students take turns reading aloud. The following techniques are fun to use:

- **Popcorn reading** requires students to read anywhere from two to 8 sentences aloud. When they are finished, they call on another student to pick up where they left off. If the student does not know where they are in the passage, they must stand up for their reading portion.

- **Pass the Ball** reading is where a student has a squishy ball or wadded up piece of paper. When they are through reading their paragraph, they "toss" the ball lightly to a student of their choice to continue the reading.

Reader's Theater

A technique where students sit in the front of the room and are each assigned a character. One student is the narrator. While reading a story, each student reads the dialogue spoken by their character and the narrator reads the rest of it. You could also assign several narrators.

- **Variation:** Break students into groups. Assign each group a section of the textbook chapter or novel chapter. Student groups take the text and turn it into a script to be read the following day. Make copies of the scripts, assign parts, and begin reading.

Reader's theater is just one way you can integrate the required curriculum element of theater into your classes.

Creating a script from a textbook chapter to read aloud in class is another way this skill can be integrated.

A third strategy is to have students act out the main events or main idea of the passage they are reading.

Once again, these ideas are not just for Language Arts classes. How can you integrate theater into other subject areas?

Primary Idea:

Get a class set of those plastic Halloween fingers from any party store or Oriental Trading Company. Have young children wear these "pointer fingers" to remind them to point to each word as they read.

Individual Reading Time

This may be called Silent Reading time, D.E.A.R. (Drop Everything and Read), or another name by your school and district. The idea is for students to quietly find a place in the room to read on their own to encourage the enjoyment of reading. Students often enjoy this time, especially if you dim the lights and play some soft piano or classical music. Allow your students to sit anywhere they want so that they will be comfortable and motivated to read.

Writing Activities with Reading Passages

Use writing activities to enhance reading. Whether you teach Language Arts or another subject area, reading and writing go hand in hand. We often write about the things we read and we read what someone has written. It is hard to keep the two separate. Here are some ways you can use writing activities to enhance student reading in your class.

Reading Logs

Have students keep a daily record of what they read in and out of class. You could also give students an easy to fill out log sheet to help you keep track of what they are reading and how much they are reading.

Dialectic Journals

A professor at Emory University in Atlanta, Georgia used to make her students keep dialectic journals to enforce "active" reading. Students fold their paper in half and draw a line down the middle. On one side they write any words or quotes from their book that captured their attention. On the other side, students write what they were thinking while they read that word or passage. This helps them track their train of thought through reading. A sample dialectic journal is provided on the next page.

You might use this with younger students using a combination of words and pictures. Perhaps the words they record from the story are their vocabulary words.

Genres

Teach students the different genres and have them write their own stories using the critical attributes of mystery, horror, science fiction, fantasy, fairy tales, adventure, fables, historical fiction, or biography.

> **Primary Idea:**
>
> *You could model the dialectic journal concept to students by using the whiteboard or chart paper while reading a fiction or non-fiction story. This helps model active reading for younger students.*

DIALECTIC JOURNAL

STUDENT RESPONSE

QUOTE FROM BOOK

I would be mad if my mom ignored me all the time. This woman sounds totally selfish! I guess as long as they could sew and talk, it didn't matter if they knew anything else. What a waste.

"To the education of her daughters, Lady Bertram paid not the smallest attention. She had no time for such cares." (*Mansfield Park*, p. 17)

She sounds like an 18th Century version of a couch potato. How boring to sit all day without TV. How did they do it? I don't think I could just sew all day long. I bet she gets fat because she sits all day.

"She was a woman who spent her days in sitting nicely dressed on a sofa, doing some long piece of needlework…" (*Mansfield Park*, p. 17)

I totally can't imagine sitting around basically doing nothing. Did all women do this?

"…of little use and no beauty…" (*Mansfield Park*, p. 17)

No brain and no beauty? How did she ever get married in the first place?

Reading Responses

Have a question ready for students to answer about their reading for the day. Students can record this in a journal of some sort. Collect these responses every week or every couple of weeks so that you can record participation grades for your individual reading time.

The reading response journal/log is also a perfect opportunity for students to practice various reading skills. Instead of always asking for a summary of the pages read, you could have students do one or more of the following:

> **Idea Share**
>
> Use the reading skills listed in the next couple of pages to create your own responses.
>
> Also, using Bloom's Keywords make creating reading responses a piece of cake!

- Create a storyboard showing at least 4 major events (events which impact the outcome of the story or impact other characters) from the pages read.

- Create an illustrated timeline showing at least 4 major events from the pages read.

- What were the pages mostly about? What are some specific details that support this main idea? Support the main idea with words, phrases, and actions from the story. Write down the page numbers where you found these details.

- Describe two or three different cause & effect patterns within the pages you read.

- Write down 2 fact statements and 2 opinion statements from your reading.

- What do you think will happen next in the story? Why? Support your reasons with quotes from the book. Include page numbers.

- What events in the story caused your character to react in an unusual manner? What events in this part of your reading have caused an unusual reaction? If none, why?

- What events are affecting your character, and in what way is the character affected?

- Compare and contrast the reactions of 2 different characters to the same event, or compare and contrast 2 characters from your story.

> *"This type of assessment helps prepare students for state tests such as the TAKS (Texas Assessment of Knowledge and Skills)."*

Reading Responses

- What made you like/dislike the main character?

- What animal is the main character mostly like? Why?

- Choose one of the characters to invite to a party. Which one did you choose and why?

- Would you be friends with the main character? Why or why not.

- Describe the tone of the story.

- Describe the mood of the story.

- How does the weather in the setting affect the story?

- What would happen to the story if the setting were 1000 years into the future?

- What would happen to the story if the setting were 250 years in the past?

- How might the setting be different if this were a different genre?

- If you were the main character's brother or sister, what advice would you give him/her?

- How might you describe the main character to a friend in a letter?

- What problem did the main character face? How would you have solved it differently?

- Which planet is the main character most like? Why?

- Which character would you like to be? Why?

- If you were one of the characters in this story, how would your life be different from the way it is now?

- Describe the relationship the main character has with the other characters in the book.

- Write about one funny thing that happens in the story.

- How would you end the book differently?

- What happened in the story that made you feel angry? Why?

- Write about one sad thing that happens in the story.

Reading Skills to be Taught and Practiced

The following are reading skills that should be taught in reading and practiced in every single class. If you do not specifically teach reading, it still should be relatively easy to integrate either a review or use of these skills in your class. The best way to help your students recognize that they use these skills on a daily basis is to use the vocabulary and point them out in your own lessons.

> **Examples:**
> *"What was the sequence of events that caused the Civil War?"*
> *"We just identified a cause and effect. That is an important reading skill."*

- Identify main idea
- Summarize a passage
- Distinguish fact from non-fact
- Sequence events
- Identify supporting details in a passage
- Determine word meaning (vocabulary)
- Determine cause & effect relationships
- Compare and contrast ideas
- Make observations and analyze issues within a passage
- Locate specific information in a passage
- Use graphic sources to help interpret reading
- Make generalizations and draw conclusions from a passage
- Identify purpose of a text
- Making predictions

As you read these objectives, ask yourself, how many of these am I already doing without being aware of it? How many Science and Social Studies teachers, for instance, require students to locate facts from the textbook? Sequencing is another commonly used skill in Math, Science, Social Studies, Music, Art, and PE classes.

"Well," you may ask, "since I'm already reinforcing many of these skills in the classroom, what more is there?" Awareness on the part of the teacher is the first step. However, we must also make our students aware that these skills are not just practiced in their Language Arts class, but that they can be applied in all areas - academic and real life.

> **Example:**
> *A Science teacher has a lesson on electricity. Before the textbook reading, the teacher introduces important vocabulary terms. At this time it would be very easy to incorporate a short discussion on how the prefix or suffix of a word gives a "clue" as to the meaning of the word. This little bit of "reading instruction" doesn't take long, but now two reading skills have been emphasized in a science class. To take it a step further, the teacher could also point out how using prefixes and suffixes help determine word meaning in everything they read from technical VCR manuals to advertisements. In the course of a few minutes within a lesson, the Science teacher has reinforced reading skills, applied it to their curriculum, and applied it to the real world!*

Ideas and Strategies

Below are some practical ways you can incorporate reading strategies into your classroom, no matter what subject you teach. Think about how you can use the different activities within your specific curriculum.

Vocabulary

Introduce vocabulary terms before beginning a unit or lesson. Discuss how the root word, prefix, or suffix offers a "clue" to the meaning of the word.

Activity:

Have students guess the meaning of a list of words on a sheet of paper. Next to their guess, ask them to write down the "clue" that helped them determine the meaning. Next, pass around a handout that gives students the correct definition of each word along with the "clue" or "clues." Allow students to share their meaning and "clue" for each word, then share the actual definitions. To add an element of fun to the activity, offer peppermints or red tickets (incentives) for students who get the definition correct. You could also offer a prize to the student with the most creative definition, logical reasoning, or creative "clues" for each word. This will encourage students to take risks in guessing the meaning and show them that you reward effort as much as correctness.

"If every teacher in the school makes an effort to point out and reinforce the reading skills used in their class, the effects will multiply and we will see a surge in fluent readers!"

Activity:

Create a word-wall for important terms. You can keep the word wall up all year, or change it for each unit of study. Another option is to create portable word walls for each unit using tri-fold display boards. These can be moved around the room easily or folded up and put away when not needed. Upper-level teachers may have one board for each class they teach. A permanent word wall might include terms that are needed all year while portable word walls would show the important terms for a specific unit.

A word wall is easy to create. Simply divide a section of your classroom wall or the display board into rows and columns to show each letter of the alphabet. You might need several rows to accommodate all 26 letters. Then, using Velcro or sticky-tape, place a laminated card with each letter in the appropriate column/row. As new terms are introduced, write them on laminated construction paper or cardstock and stick them under the appropriate letter. Older students could keep a vocabulary notebook with a "word-wall" of their own inside.

Activity:

Clap the syllables of each new word to help students remember it. Another way to help students remember a word is to either rap it or sing a song with it. A neat site that has more information about singing to remember words is Jazzles: http://phonics.jazzles.com/html/onehome.html

Reading a Textbook
    Use reading objectives to help focus the purpose of student reading.

Activity:
(Locating information from a non-fiction reading)

    Create a scavenger hunt of questions for students to answer when reading through a chapter or subchapter of a textbook. Students can work in groups or pairs, reading aloud (quietly) and helping each other locate the answers, or they can work individually. A scavenger hunt is also a fun homework assigment.

    An alternative for older students: Have students read through a subchapter or section of the chapter as a group. In pairs, or individually, students create their own scavenger hunt questions. Compile the questions for the entire class to complete. The Scavenger Hunt activity also works well for a take-home assessment activity.

> *"Use a variety of reading techniques. Students get bored doing the same thing every day."*

Activity: (Sequencing)

    There are several good sequencing activities that you can use in the classroom. We discussed a few earlier in this chapter in regards to reading groups. Additionally, when learning a scientific procedure or math equation, students can write out the steps to completing the procedure/solving the problem. Another idea is to then write a "How To" essay explaining the specific steps.

    When reading about a historical era or events, students can create an illustrated timeline to show the correct sequencing of events. Another fun way to present a sequence is through a storyboard.

    After students read a chapter about a scientific procedure, math equation, or historical time period, give students (or student groups) an envelope with the events, steps, etc. typed on slips of paper. Have students close their books and put the events/steps in correct order. Students can paste or tape their strips on colorful construction paper or on butcher paper as a class.

Idea Share

When presenting a new activity, have students do the work as a class the first time to model and answer any questions they may have. In the future, allow them to work in groups, then in pairs, and then individually.

This gives students the opportunity to help each other and learn from one another before applying what they have learned on their own.

Activity: (Fact/Non-fact)

    After students read a chapter or section in their textbook, have students create two to four statements. Two of the statements should be true and two should be false, but not outrageous. For example: a) Whales are mammals (T/F). b)Whales are related to fish (T/F). Students will have to have paid attention both to write the statements and to answer them correctly. Encourage students to try to "trip up" the rest of the class with their statements. This will motivate them to read and listen more carefully.

Graphic Organizers

After reading a passage, novel, or non-fiction book/textbook in class, have students fill in a graphic organizer. Graphic organizers are great to reinforce main idea, sequencing, compare/contrast, fact/non-fact, and many other skills.

Additionally, if you decide that you want to extend the reading into an essay or other written product, a graphic organizer is a great pre-writing activity. Several different types of graphic organizers are available in the back of this chapter to help you get started.

Webbing

Students draw a circle in the middle of their paper and write the title of the book in that circle. Then, they draw other circles off of the main one for each chapter, and write the main idea for one chapter in each of the smaller circles.

Venn Diagram

The Venn Diagram is a great way to organize compare/contrast information. Students draw two overlapping circles (a small portion is overlapping). In one circle write traits of one object. In the other circle write traits of the second object. In the overlapping section (middle), write traits that the two objects have in common.

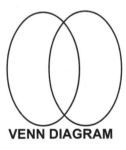

VENN DIAGRAM

Listing

Students can draw boxes down their paper, or number their paper 1-10. Have them put events from the book in order within the boxes.

Table

Students make a chart out of their paper by drawing a line across the top and one down the middle of their paper (forms a T-chart). Students can use this kind of a table for comparing/contrasting, advantages/disadvantages, pros/cons, or fact/non-fact.

Mind Mapping

This is exactly the same as webbing, except that students use pictures/illustrations instead of words.

Bloom's Taxonomy Keywords

We want to encourage higher level thinking skills in all areas of our classroom. What better way than to use the Bloom's keywords to help develop reading discussion questions, reading responses, and writing activities. Use the keywords below to create responses on a variety of reading responses.

KNOWLEDGE	COMPREHENSION	APPLICATION
define	explain	demonstrate
list	summarize	show
identify	interpret	operate
describe	rewrite	construct
match	convert	apply
located	give examples	illustrate

ANALYSIS	SYNTHESIS	EVALUATION
compare	create	judge
contrast	suppose	appraise
distinguish	design	debate
deduct	compose	criticize
infer	combine	support
categorize	rearrange	

Sample Questions: Charlotte's Web

"Increase critical thinking skills by utilizing higher levels of Bloom's Taxonomy when creating reading responses."

- Identify the main character(s).
- Describe the setting of the story.
- Explain why Charlotte is helping Wilbur.
- Give examples of how the other animals felt about Wilbur.
- Compare Charlotte with Templeton.
- Predict what you think will happen to Wilbur in the future.
- Compose your own message that Charlotte could use to help Wilbur.
- Design a web with a message for the farmer.
- Is Templeton a helpful character? In a paragraph, criticize his actions.
- Should Wilbur have taken Charlotte's egg sack back to the farm? Why or why not? Support your reasons.

Sample Questions: Count of Monte Cristo

- Describe the mood of the story.
- Explain why the Count is helping Morrel.
- Give examples of how Danglars betrayed Edmond Dantes.
- Predict what you think will happen to the Count now that his revenge has ended.
- Suppose Dantes escaped prison without knowing the events which led to his arrest. Create an outline of events that might have happened were this true.
- In a paragraph, criticize the actions of Faria in regards to Edmond Dantes.

Responding to Our Reading

   After reading the chosen fiction or non-fiction selection/ chapter, use the following discussion/question starters to further enhance student learning. Be sure that you use at least one starter from each level listed below to ensure the students are using higher level thinking skills. These starters can be written on a transparency for students to respond to their reading or for a group discussion.

KNOWLEDGE
Define words from the reading that were unfamiliar to you.
Identify three major events, concepts, or characters presented in the reading.
Describe the setting of the story or event, OR describe the concept from the reading selection.
Locate three facts/details from the passage read. Locate a place from the reading on a map.

COMPREHENSION
Retell the event/story/concept from the reading.
Summarize what you just read with the main idea and some supporting details.
Give examples of...
Explain how...

APPLICATION
Predict what will happen...
Demonstrate how...
Construct a model of..., character traits of...
Apply this reading to your own life.

ANALYSIS
Compare and Contrast ...
Make a T chart and categorize elements from the reading
What can we infer from this reading? about this character?
Distinguish one aspect of the character, event, concept from another

SYNTHESIS
Compose a letter...
Design your own...
Create a new product that solves a problem from the reading
Suppose you were in the situation we just read about, how would you react?

EVALUATION
Debate two sides of the issue/event in your reading
Appraise the usefulness of a concept/issue/event from your reading
Criticize a decision made by a historical figure or character from the reading
What is your opinion? Support it with details from the reading

Reading Novels in Class

It is very hard for students to sit still during an entire 50 or 90 minute class either reading or listening to someone else read. To keep students engaged during the entire class, alternate between reading, discussion, and written activities.

You may be tempted to either read the assigned novel every day or play a CD of the novel being read aloud. Not only is this incredibly boring, but it is not engaging students actively. It is important to stop at various times throughout the reading to check for understanding, discuss unfamiliar vocabulary, and relate the story to the students' lives.

Whenever teaching a novel, be sure to read it ahead of time and think about ways you can relate it to the students.

√ Look up information on the internet about the time period when the novel is set to look for fun or interesting facts.

√ Compare and contrast the life and times of the character with that of the students.

√ Bring in maps to integrate Geography skills and to help students determine location in relation to where they live.

√ Look up information on the author to help students understand why he/she may have written the book

√ How can you integrate information learned in other subject areas?

> **Example 1:** *Charles Dickens lived during the Industrial Revolution. He often wrote about the poor living conditions of the time through fictional stories. What kind of story plot might your students use for a story about today's society?*
>
> **Example 2:** *My Brother Sam is Dead is set during the American Revolution. This is a perfect opportunity for integrating a little history into the lesson.*

"Reading the novel before planning lessons helps us integrate our own experiences and knowledge into the discussion."

"Lesson planning for novel studies is more effective when the teacher has done some prior reading and research."

Ideas and Strategies

Activities done throughout the reading are more effective as teaching tools than when given after students finish reading the novel. Below are some different activities to use while reading.

Activity: Paper Bags

Use plain brown lunch sacks for this activity. Have students draw an image from the chapter or pages read that stood out in their mind (ex: the deep red brick house was imposing and seemed to Jack that it was frowning slightly at him). The image could also be a scene from the book, the setting, or a character from the novel or story. If you are reading a textbook, the image might be a famous person or event described in the passage, or a rendering of the concept being described in a textbook or non-fiction reading.

Students put other information inside the bag. Activities might include:

• main idea of the chapter/novel
• outline of the problem and solution
• timeline or storyboard of events
• explanation of skill or concept
• real world application of skill/concept

• vocabulary words
• drawing of plot events
• character cards with basic information
• description of the procedure or events

You can also create additional activities using the Bloom's Keywords in the back of this chapter.

Activity: Venn Diagram

Use this graphic organizer to compare/contrast different characters, events, etc. within the story. Require students to support this information from the text, referencing page numbers. (ex: Where exactly does the book say or show that Charlotte is generous? -using Charlotte's Web)

Activity: Letter Writing

Integrate two different skills with the letter writing activity. Have students write either an informal or formal letter to a character from the novel (or a person from the textbook) explaining his/her predictions about upcoming events or the outcome of the story. Students could also use the letter to draw conclusions about the novel or about characters within the novel. A letter is a fantastic forum for applying any of the reading skills mentioned earlier in this chapter.

> **Idea Share**
>
> Running out of ideas? Take a look at the Motivating Students chapter later in this book. Could you adapt any of those ideas to use as an activity with your reading assignment?

Activity: News Articles

Apply student comprehesion of the novel or textbook reading through a news article. Have students use the reporter's method of the 5 W's (who, what, where ,when, why) and 1 H (how) in analyzing the novel. Turn these "facts" into a news story complete with headline. This is a great activity for both novels and in-class textbook reading.

Beginning Book Study

Each six weeks you will be required to complete a book study. During this book study you will read a novel of at least 100 pages and complete the activities below. This project is due _____ . If you read more than one novel of 100 pages or more, you may choose one of the books to use when completing the activities below.

1) Illustrate a scene from your book on the front of a lunch sack (paper bag) with the title and author's name.

2) Write a summary of your book. Make sure you include the title, author's name, and the number of pages you read. The summary should be at least one page long. Remember, a summary includes the main idea with some details from the book.

3) If you could give this book a different title, what would it be? Write your title for the book and why you think it should be named that on a slip of paper and put it in your bag.

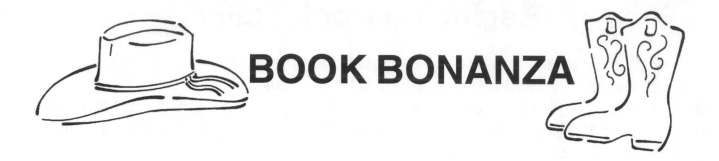

BOOK BONANZA

During this unit, you are to read a novel. After you have finished the novel, you will be responsible for completing the following activities.

This book study is due _____ .

1)   Write a summary of your book. Make sure you include the title, author's name, and the number of pages read. Remember, a summary is the main idea and some details. Focus on major events which affect the characters and/or story.

2)   Choose five new and interesting words from your book. Create a small vocabulary book. On each page, write the word in bold letter, the definition, your own sentence using the word correctly, and draw a picture of the word in a way that helps you visualize what it means. Try to think of creative ways to make your book!

3)   Create a map of the important locations in your novel. Use a key with symbols to explain your map.

4)   Project: Choose one of the following, or have your own idea approved by me.
      a.) create a game based on your novel
      b.) write a play script based on a scene in your novel
      c.) make a mobile depicting the characters and setting
      d.) act out a scene from your novel
      e.) write a song based on your novel
      f.) _____
          _____

Using Journals in All Classes

Journaling is not an activity set aside just for English teachers. The journal is one of the best ways to assess student learning after a lesson as well as a great way to provide one-on-one feedback for each student. Here are a few tips to help you implement journals in your classroom.

Provide Structure

Students need structure to feel comfortable with any assignment. This includes the journal. Simply asking students to "write down what you've learned today" won't work. An unstructured journal topic such as this leaves students feeling flustered and abandoned. They will spend the entire five minutes asking themselves and you, "what are you looking for? what should I write? How much is too much or too little? Where do I begin?" After a few seconds their brains overload and they go into self-preservation mode. This turns into the usual answer of "I don't know" or "Lots of stuff."

Instead, when planning your lessons, use your objectives or key elements to form your journal topic. The topic question or statement should directly relate to your lesson and should be easy to answer within a five minute time limit.

Examples:
- Explain briefly how you would figure the sales price of a $20 pair of jeans with a 15% discount. (used after a percentage lesson)
- What affect did the environment have on where early people settled and the type of home they built?
- What are the three branches of government and which is your favorite? Explain your reasons.

Have Expectations

Students also need to know what you expect of them. Have your expectations written out in detail for the journals. Think about the following questions as you decide.

- What is your goal for the journal each day?   What is the purpose?
- How much do you expect students to write?
- What kind of grade will they receive for their journal?
- What do you expect in terms of spelling, grammar, etc.?

Example:
I expect my students to write at least three sentences each day. Their journal entry must stay on topic and answer the question posed. I expect complete sentences and correct spelling. The journal is a way for me to check student learning each day and is also a way for me to talk with each student individually. If a student has something to say to me that they don't want to voice out loud, they may write it in their journal AFTER they have answered the question, OR before class the next day. Students will be given a participation grade for the journal once a week.

© 2005 McDonald and Hershman

Have a Procedure

It is important that you have a journaling procedure for your class. Students need to know exactly what to do for this type of assignment.

Example: (used at the end of class)
- Put away all materials
- Clean area around desk
- Take out journal
- Write journal entry silently until bell rings

You must get your journal from the table before class starts each day.

Grading

Let's face it, if we graded every journal on a subjective scale of 1-100, we'd be old and gray before ever getting through one year's worth of journals. Instead, it is important to hold students accountable for participating in this important activity. You can use the check system to give a quick grade that is easy to record. It shows students that you are reading their journal and that they are being held accountable.

Provide Feedback

Students really want to hear what you have to say. They look for your feedback every day. Be sure you have one or two things to say to each student in their journal. It doesn't need to be much, but at least once a week be sure that you offer detailed comments in their journal.

"Your attitude affects whether or not journals will be a valuable teaching tool in your classroom."

Don't be afraid to use your pen and correct mistakes. If no one ever corrects student mistakes, how will they learn? If you see a grammar or spelling error, correct that as well. The more students are held accountable for their writing skills, the more they will improve. An employer in the real world will judge every piece of writing received from an employee, even informal notes.

Use this as one-on-one time. Have you noticed something particular about one student? Take some time to write them a note and ask about the situation, or just let them know you are available to talk if they need it. The journal can serve more than just one purpose, and students really respond to the teachers who take time to learn more about them as a person.

Idea Share
I use spiral notebooks for my student journals and keep each class' in a plastic crate. At the beginning of each class period, I pull out the journals for students to grab as they enter the room. This is one way I check for student absences. I look to see which journals are still up front, check to see whether the students are actually in class, and mark the rest as absent. It works pretty well and takes less time than calling the roll.

Evaluating Student Reading

Now that you have your students reading and practicing vital reading skills, how are you going to evaluate what they know and don't know about the book/information they read? Whether your students read individually or as a class, you must determine three things:

1) Did they read? How much are they reading?
2) Did they understand what they read?
3) Can they think critically about their reading?

The following assessments will help you answer those three questions:

1. Book Study

Create a book study with several assignments designed to test various reading skills. For example, you might ask students to write a one page summary, create a diorama of the setting, make character trading cards, or write a poem about the main character. It is important to give students choice, so out of five activities, require students to complete three or four. It is also important that you give the book study to students up front so that they know what will be required of them when they finish reading the book. Two sample book study activities are included in this chapter. Also, using the Bloom's Keywords found in this chapter will help make Book Study activities easy to create.

Idea Share

Want to assess how much students are reading? Collect the reading logs to determine how much each student is reading during class and at home.

2. Dialectic Journals

Collect your students' dialectic journals and grade them. This is an excellent assessment tool since the students must write down their own thoughts and feelings about the story. It will give you a good indication of whether or not they understood what they were reading.

3.)\ Reading Responses

Collect the reading responses every two or three weeks for grading purposes. These will show you what your students are getting out of their reading time.

4. Formal Tests

You can give a formal test to see which reading skills students have mastered. Set up your formal tests so that they are similar to your State mandated test. This will provide your students with additional practice in that particular format. The more familiar students are with the format of a high-stakes test, the better they will perform.

"Help students become familiar with the format of your State's assessment tool. Format your formal tests to look and act like the real thing."

Writing In the Classroom

In this section, we are going to discuss the different writing modes and give you some ideas on how to use these modes in your class. For more detailed instruction on the Writing Workshop method, read Nancie Atwell's book *In The Middle*. It will give you a structured program for teaching writing. Our goal is not to teach you how to be a writing instructor, but to give you some more ideas on writing in your class.

The Writing Process

The writing process is the series of steps that a person uses when they write. Teaching children these steps can help them to think more about their writing rather than just slopping something on paper. It also teaches them that writing is a process that takes time!

Idea Share

Post the basic writing process steps on a poster where it can be clearly seen by all students.

STEPS

1. Pre-writing:
   Putting thoughts on paper informally. Students can use: jot list, brainstorming, webbing, journals, free-writing.

2. 1st Draft:
   This is also known as the rough draft. Students put earlier thoughts into paragraph form.

3. Peer Response:
   Students read their papers aloud to a partner. The partner makes notes on the following questions: What did you like about the paper? What questions do you have?

4. Revision:
   Students Add details, Remove extra words and phrases, Move words and phrases around and Substitute blah words for exciting ones (ARMS).

5. 2nd Draft:
   Students write a neat copy of their paper.

6. Proofread:
   Look for and correct grammar and spelling mistakes.

7. Final Copy:
   Write or type a neat draft to turn in.

PRE-WRITING NOTES

Pre-writing - the process of gathering ideas

There are 5 types of pre-writing:

Freewriting - write without stopping - don't worry about spelling or punctuation, just write!!!!

Jot list - list everything that comes to your mind about a topic

Webbing - use your topic and write down all ideas in a web

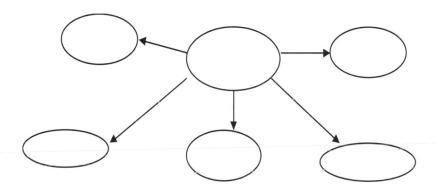

Mindmapping - just like a web except that you draw pictures instead of writing the ideas

Looping - after freewriting, pick ONE important idea, circle it and use it to start the next freewriting exercise

GLOBAL RESPONSE

WRITER/ READER

- Read your own story out loud to one or two partners.

- Speak clearly

- You may correct mistakes you see as you read your story.

- While you read your story, your partners should be taking notes by filling out the following form:

    I think this story is about _____.

    What I especially liked was _____.

    I was wondering _____.

- Write down ALL comments made by the listeners on the margins of your story.

- Underline things the listener especially liked.

- Write down all questions in the margins.

LISTENERS

- Listen to the story carefully

- While you are listening, jot down specific words, phrases, or other things that you liked or were confused about. Write down questions about the story.

- After the writer has finished reading the story, tell him/her your comments out loud. DO NOT simply GIVE the writer your sheet - tell him/her what you thought about the story.

When the first person is finished reading and all comments have been made and written down, it is the next person's turn.

(Adapted from Global Response presented duringSpring Branch Writing Project, 1993)

REVISING A STORY

A - Add details to your story — use a caret ^ to add stuff

R - Remove words, phrases, or sentences that are not needed
strike out words ~~words~~ you don't need

M - Move words, phrases, sentences, or paragraphs around —
circle (you want) words or phrases to move

S - Substitute exciting words for boring words—
Cross out the word and write the change on top
evil
ex: ~~bad~~

- Try to answer any questions asked by other
students or the teacher.

- You may need to revise your story more than once.

- A revised paper should look messy with arrows,
carets, circles, etc.

(Source: Spring Branch Writing Project, 1993)

© 2005 McDonald and Hershman

Idea

• Take each step of the writing process and write it out in bold letters on a thick paper plate (Dinnerware).

• Get a bag of clothespins and write a student name on each pin. Students can decorate these if you want them to be colorful.

• Post the plates in a circle around the words "Writing Workshop" on a bulletin board or classroom wall.

• As students work through the steps of the writing process, have them move their clip to the appropriate paper plate.

• Students move their own clips based on where they are in the writing process with their story or essay.

• Students may move between steps 2 through 4 several times before getting to the last step of Final Copy

• This offers the teacher a quick way to check on student progress as well as to redirect students who may be off task.

> Thank you to Michelle Vaughn, 4th grade teacher, Frisco ISD for sharing this idea with us!

The Writing Process

Pre-writing   Drafting   Peer Response   Revising   Final Copy

Writing Modes

•PERSUASIVE/DESCRIPTIVE - (a.k.a. persuasive essay)
Students must make a choice and convince an audience with reasons.

•INFORMATIVE/CLASSIFICATORY - (a.k.a. compare/contrast essay)
Students must discuss likenesses and differences between two objects, persons, or ideas.

•INFORMATIVE/DESCRIPTIVE - (a.k.a. descriptive essay)
Students must describe an object, picture, or event for an audience.

•INFORMATIVE/NARRATIVE - (a.k.a. how to essay)
Students must write a sequence of steps on how to do something for an audience.

COMPARE/CONTRAST MODE

Ideas for Practice Essays

- Tell how your shirt is different from your partner's.

- Tell how you and your mom think alike and how you think differently. (Let students choose another topic or suggest something like musical tastes — that should keep them going for a bit!)

- Tell how subtraction and division are alike and different.

- Tell how one problem solving technique is different from another.

- Tell how SimCity and SimAnt are alike and different.

- Tell how flowers and trees are alike and different.

- Compare and contrast the respiratory and circulatory systems.

- Compare and contrast sailboats with ocean cruisers.

- Compare and contrast the British soldiers and the Colonists soldiers.

- Tell how the hero and villain in your story are alike and different.

A fun way to organize a compare/ contrast essay is to use colored index cards. Use yellow, green and blue index cards. Write information about one object on the yellow cards. Write information about the other object on the blue cards. Write their shared characteristics on the green cards. This provides excellent visual organization.

Idea Share

When doing a Compare/Contrast essay with a novel or when using sources for information, be sure that your students support their statements with a citation of the page (page #) or source (book, page #).

We need to teach our students from the very beginning how to support their opinions with information from the story.

WHAT DO I LOOK FOR IN A COMPARISON/CONTRAST PAPER?

- Topic sentence that tells what is being compared and contrasted.

- Classificatory vocabulary (on one side, however, on the other side, unlike, like, similar to, different from)

- Transition words (first, second, third, instead)

- Expanded sentences (She was pretty and she was smart)

- Interesting adjectives (can you picture the difference between the two objects?)

- Advanced vocabulary (did the student think of using a thesaurus?)

- Adverbs (usually and especially are common here)

- Specific examples to support thoughts

Graphic Organizer for Comparison/ Contrast Essay

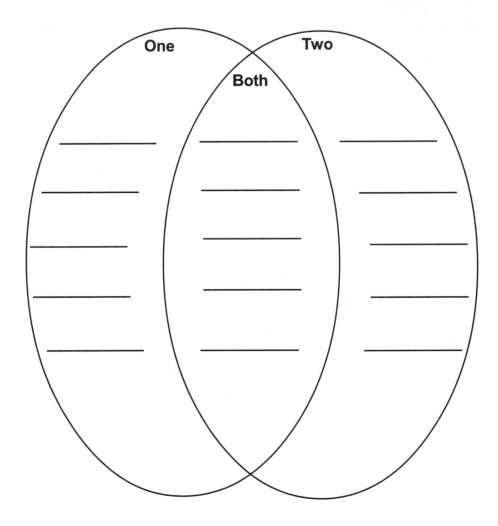

Be sure that you have an equal number of entries for each side so that your essay will not be lopsided. Also, don't forget to write in the page numbers from your text/story where you found words or events to support these characteristics.

GRADING CHECKLIST FOR COMPARISON/ CONTRAST ESSAY

Does the paper have:

_____ **Topic sentence that tells what is being compared and contrasted — specifically**

_____ **Classificatory vocabulary** (Merits, favorable, fitness, drawbacks, advisable, etc.)

_____ **Transition words** (one, second, third, instead, finally)

_____ **Expanded sentences** (complex or compound)

_____ **Interesting adjectives** (Can you picture the difference?)

_____ **Advanced vocabulary** (Did the student think of using a thesaurus?)

_____ **Adverbs** (Usually and especially are common here)

_____ **Specific examples to support thoughts** (Passing the test takes studying or great amounts of luck!)

Other comments:

PERSUASIVE MODE

Ideas for Practice Essays

- Should girls be allowed to play on the football team?

- Should students wear uniforms to school?

- Should students be allowed to use a calculator on math tests?

- Should students provide their own art supplies?

- Any concerns in the local or global community such as rainforests, oil spills, garbage dumps, cold war, etc.

- Any concerns in the school

- Mini-persuasive writings - Why I should be allowed to go to the bathroom, or, to see a principal or another teacher, or, why I shouldn't have to do homework.

This is the hardest purpose/mode for students and the one they are not given enough practice with. Mini-persuasive writings may help students be able to give solid reasons for choices.

> **Idea Share**
>
> Give a checklist to students that shows what elements you expect to see in their persuasive essay.
>
> Students need to know what is expected of them.
>
> Also, you can use the checklist to help you with the grading process.

WHAT DO I LOOK FOR IN A PERSUASIVE PAPER?

- Position Statement

- Introduction

- Three clearly stated reasons

- Specific examples under each reason

- Elaboration phrases (as well as, one example, for instance, additionally)

- Persuasive vocabulary (obviously, clearly, noticeably, stands to reason, unmistakably, evidently, glaringly, plainly, needs no explanation)

- Transition words (therefore, in conclusion, for example, nevertheless, another)

- Interesting adjectives

- Specific verbs

A graphic organizer and grading checklist are included in the back of this chapter.

Graphic Organizer for Persuasive Essay

Position Statement:	
Reason 1:	**Elaboration:**
Reason 2:	**Elaboration:**
Reason 3:	**Elaboration:**
Conclusion: (Restate your opinion and three reasons)	

ELABORATION: Each point should be elaborated with either:
-a story illustrating a specific example   -a quote   -statistics/data

GRADING CHECKLIST FOR PERSUASIVE ESSAY

Does the paper have:

_____ **Position statement**

_____ **Introduction**

_____ **Three clearly stated reasons**

_____ **Specific examples under each reason**

_____ **Elaborative phrases** (as well as, one example, for instance, additionally)

_____ **Persuasive vocabulary** (obviously, plead, visible, distinct, confidence, sincerely)

_____ **Transition words** (therefore, in conclusion, for example, nevertheless, another)

_____ **Interesting adjectives**

_____ **Specific verbs**

Other comments:

DESCRIPTIVE MODE

Ideas for Practice Essays

- Use objects from a particular time in history.

- Use objects from a particular area in science.

- Use geometric figures

- Historical or famous people

- Characters from a book

- A day in their life or in someone else's life

- An embarrassing event

- An alternative setting for a book

WHAT DO I LOOK FOR IN A DESCRIPTIVE PAPER?

- A topic sentence that tells the reader what is being described.

- Location words (up, down, below, above, next to, left, right, behind, in front of, beside, around)

- Time words (first, second, then, next, after that, finally)

- Interesting adjectives (radiant, sparkling, streaming, graceful, tinkling, delicate, gentle, ridged, cuddly, glistening)

- Interesting verbs

- Specific examples - elaboration

- Use of the 5 senses (touch, taste, smell, sight, sound)

- Comparisons to other objects (closer to, farther from, bigger than, smaller than, brighter than)

- Use of adverbs (slowly, quickly, intently, softly)

Fun Descriptive Activities

Give students peanuts or apples and have them describe theirs so that another person can pick it out. Take up the essays and pass them back randomly. Who can choose the correct peanut or apple from the description?

Put an unknown object in a bag and have students describe it by touch only. Who came the closest? Why?

Put students together. Students should be sitting with their backs to each other. One partner reads their description of an object and the other partner draws the picture of the object.

GRAPHIC ORGANIZER FOR DESCRIPTIVE ESSAY

Object 1:	Adjectives:	Location:

Object 2:	Adjectives:	Location:

Object 3:	Adjectives:	Location:

GRADING CHECKLIST FOR DESCRIPTIVE ESSAY

Does the paper have:

_____ **Topic sentence that tells what is being described**

_____ **Location words** (up, down, below, above, next to, left, right, behind, in front of, beside, around.)

_____ **Interesting adjectives** (radiant, sparkling, streaming, graceful, tinkling, delicate, gentle, ridged, cuddly, glistening)

_____ **Interesting verbs**

_____ **Specific examples – elaboration**

_____ **Use of the 5 senses** (Did they describe how it smells, looks, feels, tastes, sounds?)

_____ **Comparisons to other objects** (Is it larger or smaller, thinner or fatter than something?)

_____ **Use of adverbs**

Other comments:

© 2005 McDonald and Hershman

GRAPHIC ORGANIZER FOR
HOW TO ESSAY

INTRODUCTION

STEP ONE:

STEP TWO:

STEP THREE:

STEP FOUR:

STEP FIVE:

STEP SIX:

STEP SEVEN:

CONCLUSION:

GRADING CHECKLIST FOR HOW TO ESSAY

Does the paper have:

_____ **Topic sentence that tells what is being done or made**

_____ **Creative adverbs** (usually ends in –ly.)

_____ **Specific examples** (materials, techniques)

_____ **Interesting adjectives** (Describe persons, places or things — can you see it?)

_____ **Interesting verbs** (Not run — sprinted!)

_____ **Phrases and clauses** (Begin with which, that or who)

_____ **Other interesting vocabulary** (Use content specific vocabulary and avoid "baby talk")

_____ **Time order words** (First, second, next, then, last)

Other comments:

© 2005 McDonald and Hershman

Sample Lesson

The following is a sample lesson written by a P.E. teacher to integrate Reading and Writing skills into his class.

Objectives:

- Students will be able to use note-taking skills to read and research about Olympic Athletes.
- Students will be able to use reading strategies of selecting main idea, sequencing, and finding supporting details throughout note-taking.
- Students will be able to identify steps to becoming an Olympic athlete.
- Students will be able to write a formal business letter

Materials:

Video clips of Olympic Athletes, TV and VCR, Books and other print resources (magazines, etc.) on Olympic athletes and the Olympic games, Computers with Internet and CD-Rom Access, Encyclopedias, Paragraph on transparency to use to teach note-taking skills, clear transparencies to practice note-taking format, Index Cards, Transparency of proper business letter format for example of letter writing, paper and pencils (students)

Anticipatory Set/ Attention Getter:

1. Show the students video clip, "Highlights" of Olympic athletes. Most of the footage is of athletes participating in Olympic games. Some are performing their sport during the Games throughout the ages, some are in training, some are receiving medals, and others are in commercials for Nike, Gatorade, etc.

2. Discuss and brainstorm with students the following:
   "What does it take to become an Olympic Athlete?"

Begin a K-W-L chart to record "What we know" about becoming an Olympic athlete. examples (hard work, dedication, ability, money, etc.)

3. Review the KWL chart. Have students brainstorm questions to put in the "Want to Know" section. ***Examples:*** *How do they get to the game? How do they get the money to train?*

4. Explain objectives to students - to research information and take notes on how they might become an Olympic athlete, then to write a formal business letter requesting help in their steps to obtaining their goal - a Gold Medal!

5. Mini-lesson on Note-taking *(see pages 159-160)*
   -give specific notes on note-taking
   -practice with transparency of paragraph
   -show students how to use the index-card with title,
    author, and page number(s) of source at the top
    and notes in the middle.

> *Thank you to Juddson Smith, P.E. Coach, Plano ISD, for sharing this lesson plan with us!*

Continuing Instructional Procedures:

6. Students begin researching information individually and in groups on how a person becomes an Olympic athlete. Students should be recording the source information and taking notes on index cards.

Closure for Day: Have students tell me different steps for taking notes from a source. Ask students to tell one new thing they learned about the Olympics today.

Homework: Tonight think about which Olympic Sport you would like to participate in. Pretend you have mastered the sport and are ready to go to the Olympics. We will use this in tomorrow's lesson.

(continued lesson on Day 2)

Anticipatory Set (Day 2)

1. Read a silly (appropriate) letter from "Letters from a Nut" or a silly letter asking for donations. Ask students - How do you think a business would respond to this letter? If you were in charge of donating money, would you give this person any?

Procedures

2. Put transparency of proper letter on overhead. Discuss with students. Identify the parts of the letter (heading, body, closing) and go over expectations for activity (what I expect your letter to look like)

3. Students write 1st draft of letters.

Check for Understanding

-Monitor student work as they are researching and observe. Help as needed.
-Ask students to share their information periodically while monitoring.
-Monitor students while writing letters. Help as needed.
-Have students read letters aloud before writing final draft. Student correct errors as heard.

Closure

Have students each go to the chart and fill in one item they learned about becoming an Olympic Athlete. Read them and discuss.

Assessment of Learning:

-Collect notes taken during research -- did students follow the correct format? Evaluate student understanding of Main Idea and Supporting Details (TAKS skills) through notes.

-Use Rubric to grade the final draft of student letters. Grade content, correct knowledge, creativity, and neatness.

Conclusion

Reading and writing are not just skills that have importance in English and Literature courses. They are skills that impact student lives daily and must be practiced in ALL subject areas. The more students practice reading and writing, the more proficient they will become. This is especially true of those learning the English language. The more we encourage the use of reading and writing skills in all of our classes, the more our students will begin to see the importance of the written language in their lives. Many students feel that reading and formal writing are only important for their Language Arts classes. It is up to us to show them that even architects, scientists, and mathematicians must be able to write formal papers and understand what their colleagues have written in journal articles and other types of reading text. The best way we can do this is by pointing out how we use reading and writing in our course requirements. Just think what can be accomplished when students are actively reading and writing in each and every class!

Questions to Ponder

What is your philosophy of using and recognizing the use of reading and writing skills in your class? Is this something that is important to you? Why or why not?

Why do you think it is or is not important for specific reading and writing skills to be integrated in all curriculum areas?

What purposes can a reading area serve in other subject area classrooms?

Do you foresee e-books and/or the computer as part of your reading area in the future? Why or why not?

What are some ways you might ingetrate writing activities that encourage higher-level thinking skills into your lessons?

When reading a required textbook chapter, how might you incorporate various reading objectives?

Additional Resources

In the Middle: Writing, Reading, and Learning with Adolescents
by Nancie Atwell

Classrooms that Work: They can All Read and Write
by Patricia Cunningham and R.L. Allington

Primary Literacy Centers: Making Reading and Writing Stick
by Susan Nations and Mellissa Alonso

Never Too Early to Write: Adventures in the K-1 Writing Workshop
by Bea Johnson

Nonfiction Matters: Reading, Writing, and Research in Grades 3-8
by Stephanie Harvey

Recharging Your Math Lessons

How do you light the fire in students to want to learn math? Does this subject always have to be boring? Absolutely not! How can we make math interesting, fun, and integrated with other subject areas? These are questions that we all struggle with each year as we strive to light that fire of learning in our students..

When trying to rekindle your math lessons, first, think about the main math objectives you must teach each year. How can you integrate some of these skills into other subject areas? For example, both averaging and graphing skills can be used in both Science and Social Studies. We often taught these skills during math and then applied them in an appropriate Science or Social Studies unit. How might you do something similar with your teaching?

Next, tackle the math textbook, released standardized tests, and your other subject themes to develop a plan for teaching math concepts. Remember, you do not have to follow the textbook page by page! Teach math how it makes sense to you!

We would like to offer you some easy tips that you can try throughout the year to make teaching math more fun. This is just a small sampling of ideas. There is no way we could mention EVERYTHING that teachers can and are doing for math instruction within this chapter. The following are some key points to keep in mind when teaching math:

- Integrate Math with other subject areas
- Use practical/real world applications

In this chapter, we have outlined a step-by-step strategy for teaching math concepts as well as several different ideas for integrating math with other subject areas. We hope you will find it helpful to refresh your teaching of math.

Integrating Math Concepts with Other Academic Areas

Integrate math concepts into other subject areas through maps, tables, graphs, measurement, cooking, banking, logical thinking, etc... Many math concepts can be taught during history, economics, science, language arts, music, and geography. The possibilities are endless!

- Have students calculate distances on a map using the scale and a ruler. This is a great exercise in fractions, as well as multiplication, division, addition, and subtraction skills.

- Have students work with music notes, rhythms, and scales to practice counting and patterns.

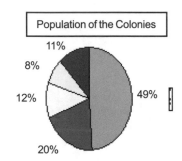

Population of the Colonies

- Creating bar graphs, pie charts, and line graphs is a good way to connect math skills to social studies and science.

- You could have students make a line graph and chart the growth of their plant in a science experiment.

- Students could use a pie chart to represent any number of historical trends, such as the percentages of national origins of the people living in the first Thirteen Colonies.

- Tables are a great way to organize information for research projects.

- Teach coordinate graphing while studying latitude and longitude on maps.

- In Health, students study and compare health statistics. Teachers can write to any number of organizations to get statistics: government offices, American Heart Association, National Cancer Society, etc.

- Have students calculate their weights on different planets while studying space.

- While studying different countries, have students exchange currency. This is a fun, but tricky way to practice multiplication, decimals, and working with money.

"Creating bar graphs, pie charts, and line graphs is a fun way to connect math skills to social studies and science!"

Using Children's Literature

Use children's literature as a springboard to teach math. Bob Krech, author of Meeting the Math Standards with Favorite Picture Books, offers some fantastic ideas for teaching math in motivating ways.

Some examples of good books to teach math shared by Krech include:
- How Much is a Million?
- Counting on Frank
- Sir Cumference and the First Round Table

Use Games to Teach Math Skills

Teach math through fun activities and games. Don't be afraid to let the students play and have fun. They are still learning and practicing!

- Cooking teaches measurement and fractions. Ask the students to *double* or *half* a recipe. This can teach equivalent fractions.

- When teaching measurement, have a "Scavenger Hunt" for objects of different sizes around the classroom. You could do this in metric or standard units of measurement, or both, if you were comparing the two.

- When it is time to teach coordinate graphing, the students could practice with various kinds of art projects that require grids, such as cross stitching. You could also play "Location Race" by using maps with grids or latitude and longitude.

- Have students go shopping at their favorite store and pick out items for purchase. They can write down the amount of the item, any sales (25% off), and ask the salesperson about tax. Students can bring this information back to class where you can use it to teach percentages, adding or subtracting decimals, estimating, etc.

- Have students plan a fun trip to the destination of their choice, including keeping a budget, finding distances on a map, determining the time it takes to travel certain distances, currency exchanges, etc..

"Many board games, such as Monopoly, use math skills."

- There are many games that require math skills including card games, dice games, Dominoes, Monopoly, Life, and others. Also, games such as MasterMind teach logical thinking skills which help with math concepts.

"How can you use different board games in your lessons?"

Math with Holidays and Special Events

Create math problems and projects that relate to holidays and special events throughout the year!

> Word problems are a great way to do this! Again, only your imagination and creativity can limit you! The possibilities are numerous!

Examples of Word Problems Using Holidays and Special Events:

*During Halloween, pumpkins are usually marked up in price at least 50% due to the demand for them. If in August a pumpkin that weighed 15 pounds costs $8.00, how much would that pumpkin cost on October 31st?

*Last month Julie attended 4 Professional football games. The tickets cost $44.75 each. She even got to see the Green Bay Packers play the Dallas Cowboys! How much did she spend on game tickets?

*At the grocery store in which Bobby shops, turkeys for Thanksgiving cost $1.89 a pound. If Bobby buys a 10 pound turkey, what will it cost?

*Kelly loves to make new friends. She has made 4 new friends a year for 5 years in a row. If Kelly received two flowers on Valentine's Day for every new friend, how many flowers did Kelly receive?

> Notice: Some of these word problems have extraneous information. (Information not needed to solve the problem!) This is an important lesson to teach students, as these types of problems often occur on standardized tests.

Fun day-long math projects centered around a holiday theme can spark interest!

> *Example:*
>
> **Spend the day studying the mathematics of a pumpkin.**
>
> - Measure the circumference and diameter
> - Estimate how many seeds will be inside
> - Bake pumpkin pies for the whole class
>   In making the pies, the measuring cups are a great way to explore fractions, and then the pies themselves can be utilized for a fractions lesson!

Tip: Make sure to plan in advance with the Cafeteria Staff and your principal before you plan this "pie making" adventure!

Relating Math to Students

Use Familiar Names and Funny Stories in Word Problems

When giving math notes and word problems, add excitement to your lessons by using:

- Students' names
- Making up funny stories/situations
- Including objects, famous people, and ideas that motivate the students.

Ideas:
Sports and Sports Celebrities
Popular Toys
"In-style" Clothes and Trends
Popular Celebrities
TV Shows and Cartoons
Cars
Candy
Music

> **Idea Share**
>
> Many students love hearing their name, or better yet, your name, in math word problems. This simple little act can make boring word problems turn into fun activities. Do you have a favorite hobby that would work well in a math word problem? Use real-life events to make word problems meaningful for students.

Use "Pop Culture" to Stimulate Math Lessons

Sports -- Sports Illustrated for Kids often includes statistics and other data that can easily be used to introduce, apply, or enhance a lesson. Students can also compare and contrast different scoring methods? How are these methods implemented? What different kinds of math are needed to compute the scores or statistics?

Olympics -- Have student graph medals won by different countries.

Racing -- This is the perfect sport for learning about time, distance, velocity, speed, and other math skills.

Celebrity Magazines -- What is the net worth of different celebrities? Introducing place value when looking at celebrity salaries would be fun. How would you plot the place value for Oprah's yearly income? Compare and contrast different salaries to show range, mean, median.

Television ratings -- Average and compare /contrast ratings for different TV shows. Movies can also be compared as to their gross opening earnings. This information can also be graphed or shown in other types of data charts.

Fashion -- Measurement skills, circumference, and other geometry skills can be studied through fashion. How do designers actually design their clothes? What are some common shapes used for different types of outfits? How do tailors take three dimensional measurements, two dimensional fabric and create clothes for us to wear?

Math Teaching Strategy

We would like to share with you the way we taught math concepts which takes various theories on the best ways to teach math and combines them. This strategy has several stages where the teacher guides the students with the end result being student learning. We love using this strategy because it teaches to several different learning styles found in the classroom.

Step 1: Visual and Tactile Learning - Concrete Models

This is the first stage of teaching a math concept. The teacher introduces the new concept using manipulatives, models, diagrams, patterns, games and/or student movement and involvement. This stage encompasses the "hands-on" approach to teaching math.

Concrete models let children understand abstract ideas. We need to teach students to understand how numbers and relationships work – not just throw rules of mathematics at them! Models allow students to have a visual picture, which can enhance comprehension.

- It is important that in this stage you are consistently asking the students questions, and guiding them in their learning.

"Students need to understand each concept learned so they can build their knowledge of basic math skills."

Examples of "guiding" questions to ask:

- What observations can you make?

- Compare and contrast these models.

- That is a good way to show this problem, try to find another solution. There is more than one way to solve a problem.

- Can you explain how you solved that problem?

- Explain your reasoning.

- What were your thought processes while you were working on that?

- What will you do next?

More tips to use during the "hands-on" phase:

This is a very thought provoking stage where students need to use their brains in a way they may have never done before. Asking probing questions and having students make observations is the key to this stage. It will not feel comfortable for some students at first, as some prefer paper/pencil activities, but all students benefit from concrete models.

Don't rush to correct students if they are not solving or demonstrating something correctly. Wait a few minutes to see if they can figure it out on their own. If you see that they are not anywhere near the correct answer, help them get back on track.

"Encourage curiosity, logical thinking, and expression of ideas."

Encourage curiosity, logical thinking and reasoning, and expression of ideas. Allow students to verbalize their ideas and share with the class.

Encourage students to share what they discover with each other. Students often learn more from their peers than from the teacher!

Manipulatives, and/or concrete modeling does not have to be expensive or fancy. Use common household items and things found in school such as:

egg cartons	fruit	M&M's
beans	straws	plastic animals
coffee stirrers	cheerios	popcorn
Lego's	students	blocks

Be sure to allow time for reflection of the student learning experiences before leaving this stage of teaching a math concept. If using rotating centers with math manipulatives, give students two or three minutes before switching to write their findings, describe what they did, etc., in their math journal.

"Concrete models do not have to be expensive, use what you can find at home or in the school. Food always works well to motivate."

Here are some examples of how you can use concrete modeling in your classroom:

If you are introducing decimals, let children work with play money. Ask them probing questions about the value of a dollar in comparison to 20 cents, 7 cents, one dollar and 50 cents.

For example: Have students demonstrate equal values, using different money pieces (3 dimes = 30 pennies = 6 nickles)

"Play money is a great way to introduce and discuss concepts such as decimals and reasonableness."

When teaching greater than and less than signs, have students participate in the lesson by having several students stand at the front of the room. More students should be standing on one side than on the other. Either the teacher or another student is a "hungry alligator" in the middle. Which side would the alligator want to eat? The most people of course! So the big open alligator mouth always faces the biggest number.

Teacher Talk

"As a Kindergarten teacher, I used the "alligator" idea to help my little ones understand the concept of greater than/ less than. Each one loved to be the alligator and wanted to "gobble up" as many people as possible. I would stand back and count each side of the room. Then I would ask the "alligator" which side do you want to eat? They, of course, would always pick the bigger side. "Yes," I say, "when we have two groups of numbers, the alligator always wants to eat the larger number." Then we would practice on paper what we did as a class. I think the parents were really impressed that their little ones learned this concept so easily!"

If you are teaching multiplication principles to younger students, use color tiles, rainbow cubes, dried kidney beans, or anything that can be used to count in large numbers.

Lead the students to discover that 3 x 5 = three groups of five. Count (or add) them all up and they equal 15! Practice this concept many times before moving on to the mathematical symbols.

3 groups of 5 equal 15 total pieces
5 groups of 3 equal 15 total pieces

Students can actually see how multiplication works to support the facts they must learn.

If you are introducing equivalent fractions, bring in egg cartons and cotton balls. Have the students show you 6 out of 12, and then have them tell you *how much of the egg carton is full?* They should say *half*! This will prompt you into a discussion of how 1/2 = 6/12! You can then ask the students to divide the carton up into 3 equal parts using yarn or markers. This allows you to discuss thirds.

Think about using oranges when teaching fractions. Peel the orange and talk about how the whole orange is broken into sections. As you separate the segments, have students count them aloud and then record the total number of segments. Give students different segments and talk about how the students have two-tenths, four-tenths, and five-tenths. Which student has more of the orange?

Another way to help introduce and/or conceptualize fractions is by cutting up drinking straws into equal parts. Oranges, egg cartons, straws, and any type of candy is a fun way to teach division as well. What other types of food can you use to teach math concepts?

Don't just stop using manipulatives with older students. You can still introduce math concepts with models or manipulatives. If you are teaching geometry, you can use pattern blocks (different colored and sized blocks that form varying geometric shapes). Have students explore the many different sides and angles, teach perimeter with them, find equivalent shapes, etc.

Tips for Using Manipulatives in the Classroom

- Monitor student behavior by walking around the room the entire time they are exploring and figuring with manipulatives.

- While monitoring, ask probing questions to check for understanding.

- Let students explore with the manipulatives prior to starting your lesson. Let them play before you expect them to listen. Otherwise you will find that they are still playing, and not listening. Actually, allowing students to explore is a learning experience in itself.

- Listen to students and how they discuss and interact with one another regarding their observations of the manipulatives. This can be a great springboard for your discussions.

- Provide a time for students to record their thoughts into a journal.

> **Idea Share**
>
> Set clear directions and expectations for students when working with manipulatives, or any time students work in groups. Review these expectations before you start the lesson or activity every time!

Primary Ideas

- When looking at attributes of shapes, colors, etc., use plastic hoops or baskets to sort items with similar attributes.

- For each shape, ask students to find as many of that shape in the classroom as possible. For example, with rectangles students can find them in the windows, whiteboard or teacher's desk. Squares would be student desks or a book perhaps. Have a "treasure hunt" to find different shapes in the room. You could also do a scavenger hunt that asks for one of each type of shape.

- Have a mystery bag as a learning center. Inside different bags are mystery shapes. Students must feel the shape without looking at it, guess the shape and draw what they felt. This is a great tactile activity for kids who learn kinesthetically.

- Play games such as snap to match shapes or fruit salad with shapes instead of pieces of fruit.

- Use bread and shape cutters to have them make different shapes. You could also do this with cookie dough and let the students decorate before baking them. Edible shapes are fun! You could also do this with playdough - but please don't let them eat it!

- Surround your students with literature about shapes. Make a book about shapes with them involving their own photos, drawings, and writing.

- Go for a walk around the school to find shapes, colors, etc. The real world provides so many wonderful aspects of math in things to count and observe.

- Use beads and blocks to help them understand the concepts of units, tens, hundreds, etc. Montessori schools use these types of manipulatives and they are quite successful.

Idea Share

A fun way to teach time is through literature. There are several books available for young children to help them learn about time. Additionally, you can find manipulative clocks where young children can actually move the hour and minute hands to create a specific time. Use these clocks in conjunction with reading one of the following stories:

Bunny Day: Telling Time from Breakfast to Bedtime by Rick Walton and Paige Miglio

Pooh's First Clock inspired by A.A. Milne

Time for Tom by Phil Vischer

Thank you to Tracy Paul, Kindergarten Teacher, for sharing these ideas with us.

Step 2: The Math Notebook

This is the second step in teaching math concepts. In this stage, the teacher moves from concrete models to the more abstract method of teaching math using symbols. This can be used from 2nd or 3rd grade and up.

This is the more traditional way of teaching math by giving notes on how to solve a problem, and allowing the students to practice in abundance.This method has been used for decades, and the children will continue to be exposed to this type of teaching for the rest of their school career.

Yes, we believe that giving notes and practice, through paper and pencil activities, is still important! As long as this method is used in conjunction with the visual tools and real-life applications of math, the notes and practice part of teaching is vital.

The Math Notebook Details:

• The Math Notebook or Math Spiral is the center focus of this stage. Each student will have their own math notebook, which is to be separate from their student binder.

• Set this up at the very beginning of the year, and be consistent in using it all year long. You may choose to have the students use a thick spiral notebook, or a three-hole pocket folder with notebook paper inside.

• This notebook is for math notes and practice only.

• Encourage your students to take these math notebooks home with them every night to use as a guide in solving homework problems. Often your notes will be more helpful to them than the textbook.

• This notebook is also an excellent reference for parents. By seeing how you have taught the skills, they will be better able to help their child with homework, if given.

Teacher Talk

"After using the math notebook idea for a couple of years, I was so pleased when a few of my students from the previous year came by to thank me. They told me that they were still using the notes I gave them in 5th grade to help them with their homework. It turned out to be a resource that they kept and continued to use!"

Sample Notes Page for Math Notebook

Adding Whole Numbers

Step 1	**Step 1**
Add the Ones/Units. If total equals ten or more, write the "tens" unit at the top of the Tens block *(Regroup)*	Th H T O ① 1 3 4 **2** + 7 8 **9** **1**
Step 2	**Step 2**
Add the Tens. If total equals ten or more, write the "tens" unit at the top of the Hundreds block *(Regroup)*.	Th H T O ①**1** 1 3 **4** 2 + 7 **8** 9 **3** 1
Step 3	**Step 3**
Add the Hundreds. If total equals ten or more, write the "tens" unit at the top of the Thousands block *(Regroup)*.	Th H T O ①**1** 1 1 **3** 4 2 + **7** 8 9 **1** 3 1
Step 4	**Step 4**
Add the Thousands. Write the total number under the Thousands, and if necessary the Ten-Thousands block.	Th H T O **1** 1 1 **1** 3 4 2 + 7 8 9 **2,**1 3 1
Step 5	**Step 5**
Rewrite the total.	Answer is 2,131

- Once you have introduced a math concept with concrete models and exploration, the students are now ready to move into solving problems using symbols.

- For some students this will come as a relief, as they are more accustomed to being given the steps in how to solve a problem and working out math problems on paper. Other students find this method boring and not as easily understandable.

> **Students need to understand that both of these stages in teaching math are equally important.**

- Give step-by-step instructions in the notes on how to solve each math problem. Use abundant examples of problems solved correctly.

- Provide opportunities for independent practice problems in their notebook, after you have given notes and done several sample problems as a class. Always correct practice problems in their notebook as a class before moving on! This way they are not mislead and use incorrect information when doing homework.

- The students should have a table of contents at the beginning of their notebook, and they should make an entry into this every time a new concept is taught.

- Monitor the students and insist that they copy everything down into their notebook. This is not a selective exercise, where the students copy down what they want to. They copy everything, so you know that they have all the steps and notes.

- The math notebook is much more successful in teaching a concept than just using the textbook, even if you get your notes from the text. You can always add information and steps to help your students learn, because you know what your students need more than anyone!

- When giving math notes, using an overhead projector is easier than writing them on a chalkboard. Often times, I would prepare the notes ahead of time and then reveal the transparency to the students a little bit at a time.

> *"Provide any mathematical rules they need to be aware of in the math notebook for easy reference."*

Step 3: Practical/ Real World Applications

Once you have taught the students the concept and skills necessary to solve a type of math problem, you must make that skill meaningful for them! The students need to be capable of applying that skill in real life. This sounds harder than it really is. The key to this section is "word problems!" Word problems offer real life situations, and the students must be able to solve the problem using the skills and concepts you taught them. This keeps your math instruction from dealing with rote memory and actually forces the students to use reasoning and their newly acquired skills.

"Use real world scenarios such as grocery shopping, cooking, figuring the tip for dinner, sales tax, etc. to apply math skills and motivate students."

Tips for Real World Math

• Bring grocery store ads, department store ads, sales catalogs and mail order catalogs to class. Make up questions or word problems so that the students have to use these items to solve your problem.

Examples:

•   Applyling multiplication with decimals and practicing working with percentages - Find something that you would like to buy and pretend that the store is having a 25% off sale. Calculate the new sales price of your item. Now add 8.25% sales tax. What is the total price? How much money, in whole dollars, will you have to take to the store in order to buy this item? (25, 30, etc.)

•   Applying addition and subtraction -- If you buy five apples for your teacher, on sale for 25 cents each in the grocer's ad, how much will your total price be? How much change will you have if you pay with a $10.00 bill?

•   Have students plan a fun trip to the destination of their choice and figure the costs, mileage, etc. Older students can plan a trip to Europe to visit World War II battlefields/ monuments or for a summer trip. This can include exchanging money as well as calculating mileage, etc.

•   Let older students plan a class party given a certain budget.

•   Have students design and build an invention or object using a variety of materials. They will need to use correct measurements in their design and apply those measurements when building their object.

•   Many different careers including architects, construction, engineers (mechanical, construction, chemical, etc.), caterers, and any small business, must use math on a daily basis. Explore some of these different careers and the math associated with them.

Solving Math Word Problems

These days standardized tests are going more and more towards real life types of word problems. Many of our students can solve math equations, but have so much difficulty in reading and decoding what they are supposed to do in a word problem. Below is a short refresher on teaching students how to solve word problems.

When solving a word problem, it is important to follow the steps needed to find the correct answer:

- Read the question - Make sure to read the whole question from beginning to end. Don't assume you know how to solve the problem without reading the entire question.

1. Re-read the question and Box key words. Some key words are:

Total	**Product**	**Sum**
Difference	**More or Less**	**Each**
How much	**How many**	**Altogether**

2. Underline the question part of the problem. Think: What are they asking for?

3. Determine the operation needed to solve the problem and write it next to the question. *the operation*

4. Cross out extraneous information - this is information that is not needed! Don't let them fool you!

5. Circle the numbers needed to solve the problem.

6. Write a number sentence next to the problem.

   Example: 58 - 9

7. Solve the problem showing all your work.

8. Write the solution sentence.

   Example: 58 - 9 = 49
   There are 49 white doves left in the sky.

9. Check it! Is it reasonable? Does it make sense?

If Multiple choice test:
- Locate the answer in the answer choices.

- Determine why the other answer choices are Not Correct.

- Circle the correct answer. Bubble on the answer sheet.

Idea Share

Integrate a common LA strategy into your math classroom - the Word Wall! Take the math vocabulary commonly used in Word Problems and post them on a portable Word Wall. This can simply be a poster of terms. The Word Wall works as a great reminder for students.

Sample Problems

1) Josie went to a bird watching festival on Sunday. There were 200 people at the festival. The music started and 58 white doves flew into the sky. Nine of the doves flew into a nest in the tree. How many doves were left flying in the sky?

      258 people   67 doves altogether

      49 doves were left   209 doves were in the sky

2) The teacher received flowers for her birthday. She got 64 yellow flowers, 21 white flowers, and 17 red flowers. How many more yellow flowers did she have than white flowers?

     102   85   60   43

3) The zoo had 2 beautiful peacocks and 6 zebras. Each peacock weighs 21 pounds. What is the total weight of the two peacocks?

     8 pounds   11 pounds   42 pounds   19 pounds

4) It took Chad and his mom 4 weeks and 2 days to sew some shirts. How many total days is this?

     28 days   30 days   8 days   22 days

5) A teacher had 22 students in her class. Five students made the honor roll. The teacher wanted to give each honor roll student the same amount of bonus points. She had 55 bonus points to share equally among her the honor students. How many will each student get?

     110   275   11   5

6) Sea World opened in Houston, Texas in 1989. Today, Sea World has 45 dolphins, 18 sea lions, and 2 killer whales. How many sea mammals does Sea World have altogether?

     63   65   47   20

7) It takes Jill and her mom one hour to water the plants in their garden. Each day of the week for 7 days they water the garden. How many minutes does Jill water the garden in 1 week?

     420 minutes   60 minutes   49 minutes   7 minutes

Sample Math Lesson

The following is a short example of how to teach a math concept, using all three steps of our math strategy.

Graphing Lesson

OBJECTIVES: To teach students the concept of a graph
To teach students the four main types of graphs
To teach students how to read and interpret different kinds of graphs
To teach students how to create their own graphs.

This lesson should be taught over several days. You cannot cram the whole lesson into one hour!

Step 1: The Concrete Model

Birthday Graph

- Have every month of the year written neatly on 12 separate, rather large, sheets of paper. Have this done before the lesson.

- **Do not tell the students what you are doing before you begin your lesson.**

- Lay out all of the months of the year in order with some space between them, about 6-12 inches, on the ground in the front of the classroom, in the hallway, outside or on the parking lots.

- Have the students get in a line in front of the month their birthday falls. When they are in straight lines, have them remove their shoes and leave them in their place. Have all students stand back behind the pictograph and observe.

- Ask them if they know what they are looking at? (A pictograph)

- Have students draw the pictograph neatly on a piece of paper. They will need to sit on the floor where they can see it and they will not be able to put their shoes on yet.

- Have the students put on their shoes, clean up the papers, and have students return to their seats.

- Once all students are in their seats and have their drawn pictographs in front of them, have all students look at their graphs to discuss:

    - What does each pair of shoes represent?
    - What observations can we make by looking at this pictograph.**Make them give specifics!**
        - Which month has the most birthdays in our class?
        - Which month has the least?
        - How many months have no class birthdays? How can you tell?

Step 2: Math Notebook Notes

Teaching the Concept of Graphing

- Give general information about graphs (Notes):
- Discuss, show samples, and give notes on different kinds of graphs
  ~ Bar graphs, pie graphs, line graphs, pictographs.

Sample Notes:

Graphs

Graphs represent data that has been collected.
Definition of a Graph – A visual tool that makes it easier for us to see information.

4 Kinds of Graphs:

- Pictograph – uses pictures instead of numbers and it uses a key
  *Example: 1 pair of shoes = 1 person
- Bar Graph – shows us information by the height or length of the bars
  *Show a sample! Draw a quick sketch of one with the students for their notes.
- Pie Graph – also known as a circle graph. Shows how information is divided into parts of a whole.
  *Show a sample and draw a pie graph with the students in their notes.
- Line Graph – uses dots and lines to show how things change and compare.
  *Show a sample and draw a line graph with the students in their notes.

- Compare the different kinds of graphs and how they represent information   differently. Are some graphs easier to read? Why? Would some types of graphs be better for representing certain types of data? Talk about specific examples.

- There is an excellent book on maps, charts and graphs that would be helpful in teaching this graphing unit. The book is: Maps, Charts, Graphs, and Diagrams: 1990 Teacher Created Materials, Inc.

- You can make sample graphs on the computer using a spreadsheet program (like Microsoft Excel), or you can find graphs in newspapers, magazines, social studies and science texts. Show these graphs to the students and discuss them during your note giving.

- Demonstrate how to use graph paper and make a sample graph as a class.

- Assign Homework: To transfer the pictograph of class birthdays into a bar graph on graph paper.

Step 3: Practical Application

Studying graphs and their use in real life.

- Collect graphs from newspapers, magazines, and books. Copy them and give samples to students to examine and discuss.

- Ask the students to interpret and/or compare the information shown in the graph.

- Finally, have the students gather information of some sort and create their own graphs. Give a choice of graphs to create, but explain to the students that the kind of graph they choose must match with the type of information they are trying to represent.

Make sure the students consult their notes and samples for help in creating their own graphs.

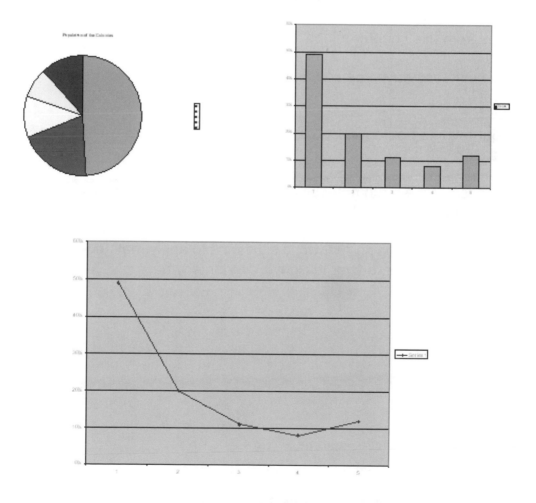

> *Have students compare the birthday results in different graphs. Which graph best represents the information so that we can understand it?*

CONCLUSION:

Teaching math is much more than just skill and drill. If we want our students to thoroughly understand and be able to apply these skills, it is vital that they know the "whys" behind different concepts. Using manipulatives helps students begin with concrete visual examples that can be applied to the abstract number equations. A math notebook will help keep students organized and offer an easy reference manual throughout the year. Lastly, we need to help students understand how they will apply these skills to their lives in the real world. These types of real world activities are not only motivating, but also vital to completing the learning process.

Questions to Ponder

What math strategies have worked for you in the past? Why were these so successful?

What math strategies have not been successful in motivating students to learn math skills? Why were they less successful than others? What could you have done differently?

What strategies from this chapter might you use to refresh your math lessons?

What are some different ways you can incorporate math skills into other academic areas for your grade level?

What were your favorite board games growing up? How might you utilize these fun activities in your math class?

What is the purpose of the math notebook? Would this activity be appropriate for your grade level? Why or why not?

What are some reasons for using real world situations to apply math concepts? Do you ever incorporate real world math into your lessons? Why or why not?

Additional Resources

Maps, Charts, Graphs, and Diagrams
by Teacher Created Materials

Meeting the Math Standards with Favorite Picture Books
by Bob Krech

Writing in Math Class: A Resource for Grades 2-8
by Marilyn Burns and Susan Ohanian

Fanning
the Flames

"To waken interest and kindle enthusiasm is the sure way to teach easily and successfully."

--- Tyron Edwards

"If what you're doing isn't working, try something else!"

--- NLP adage

Snap, Crackle, Pop:

Quick Tips for Motivating Students A-Z

What do you do when the flames of your fire are burning low? This can happen quite frequently throughout the school year. The answer? Fan the flames! Give them more oxygen. You need to add some life to your fire. This can be tricky in the classroom, though. One of the most difficult aspects of teaching is motivating students. In fact, William Glasser, in his book entitled *Choice Theory in the Classroom*, states that trying to teach students who do not want to learn is impossible.

When we think about motivating students, it is important for us to first consider, what is motivating to us? I know that for myself, I am motivated when a topic interests me or relates to me personally. For example, when my son was small, he didn't speak for the longest time. This was a big concern for me. I hooked up to the Internet and did quite a bit of research on language acquisition. I also learned a lot about different speech disorders which led me to the topic of learning disabilities. My son's issues prompted me to learn new ideas.

What else motivates people to learn new things? Survival is a definite motivation. Think about our international students who are thrown into an English speaking classroom or even an ESL classroom where the teacher speaks only English. Their survival instinct kicks in and they learn English in order to live in their new environment.

What about waiting? Think about the times in your life when you were waiting in line, for that new job, to be accepted into a school, for an answer to question, etc. To sit and do nothing is very unmotivating. We get restless, bored, stifled. This is part of our human nature.

Now apply those thoughts to your classroom. Are your students given a purpose each day? Do they have a meaningful purpose in each lesson? Or are they just warming a chair/desk day after day?

Listening to others, unless we are motivated to do so, is boring, boring, boring. We all feel it. Think about any conversations you've had with people who were uninteresting or who were talking way over your head. If you're like me, you probably felt like Charlie Brown listening to the teacher, "Wangh, Wangh, Waa, Waa, Waa." Do your students feel that way about you? Are you talking over their head? Are you going on and on and on about concepts that your students would rather be experiencing?

Take a look at your lessons. How much talking on your part is involved? How much are students actively engaged in an activity that applies the concept? Take a look at your lecture and ask yourself, "Could I pull some of this information out and let the students learn it for themselves?", "Could I replace this part of the lecture with an activity that demonstrates the topic/concept instead?"

Also, look at your activites. Do they relate to the real world? For example, are your students just practicing their understanding of percentages or are they applying it? A worksheet is easier for us, but using store flyers to figure sales prices (or original prices) of favorite clothes, toys, electronics, etc. is both more practical and motivational. Based on each student's allowance, how long would it take them to save for the item they chose? These activities require students to apply their knowledge (and can be used as an assessment), relate the concept to theim personally, and are motivating.

Remember, the more engaged your students are, the more they will be motivated to learn. Engaging activities are ones where students must manipulate the information, skill, or concept in a variety of ways. This can include working in teams, discussion, projects, research, or creating a product of some sort.

Take a few minutes to think about classes that you've attended throughout your lifetime. Which ones do you remember as positive and motivating experiences? Which ones were so boring that you spent every minute counting the seconds until it was time to leave? Generally classes where the teacher or professor lectured at students or required students to do meaningless work, busy-work, or repetitive tasks are the most boring. Classes which get students actively involved in discovering their own learning, interacting with each other, and encourage respect between the teacher and students are the most motivating.

So what can you do? Come to class prepared with a variety of activities that will engage students in their own learning. If a lesson seems to be faltering or you notice a glazed-over look in the eyes of your students, smile a big smile, do a little dance, and pull out something different to capture their attention. Have you been doing all of the talking and action for the lesson? Think quickly how you can get students involved instead.

Our goal with this chapter is to share a few easy-to-implement strategies to help you engage and motivate students. These can be referenced when planning lessons, or in many instances, used at the spur-of-the moment when you see that glazed-over look. Remember, the more actively involved your students are in the lesson, the more excited they will be and won't want to leave your classroom! Not only that, but students who are engaged and excited about their learning also cause fewer discipline problems. So take a look at the following strategies and think about different ways you could make your students motivated and engaged each and every day!

 *is for Atlas*

Having students research using a world atlas is a great way to teach them about Geography and other fun facts of countries around the world.

- Pick out a different latitude and longitude for each student to locate. Have them look up information about that city/town/country including average temperature, precipitation, foods, dwellings, customs, etc..

- When reading a story or novel, have students find the city/town/country of the setting on a map. Discuss where it is located in relation to where the school is located. Older students can determine the latitude and longitude to practice Geography skills.

  - Discuss the culture, environment, and weather of the area. How does this affect the story, if at all? Is the setting a true representation of this actual city/town/country?

  - If the story has a make-believe setting, where is the author from? Does the story reflect the culture and weather of the author's hometown?

- Identify historical events on the map.
- Identify place of birth/residence of different Scientists, Mathematicians, Artists, Musicians, Sports Figures, Famous People, etc.
  - How did the culture, history, geography, weather of where they live(d) affect them?

- Have students create their own city/town/country. Students exhibit Geography skills by drawing a map. Be sure they include important elements such as the Legend/Key, landforms, a grid system, etc.

Teacher Talk

"One fun activity our students enjoy is our Volcano Island unit. First we study about volcanoes and how they often form islands. Then we make volcanoes in class and do the fun "explosion" with vinegar and baking soda. Then students create a "foot island" by tracing their foot on white paper. Students turn their footprint into their very own island country complete with cities, a capitol, different landforms, roads and railroads, and any other element they've studied in Geography and mapping. We have our students create their own legend and grid system for their map."

Atlas Race - Have students race against one another to locate various places on the earth using an atlas. Start with the entire class. Play five games as a class to get five different semi-finalists. These students then play two rounds to determine the finalists. The last two players play one round to determine the Champion for this game.

A is for Alien

After teaching students a concept, checking for understanding can be fun when you have them write out an explanation to an alien from outer space. You might even use a fun picture on the computer presentation station or overhead to give them a picture of their alien. This is also a great way to review a previous skill and can be used across the curriculum.

Examples: Explain to your alien how to multiply two-digit numbers.
Explain the Scientific Method to your alien.
Explain how flowers grow to your alien.

 **is for Books**

Children's books are an excellent way to introduce units and lessons. Everyone loves to be read to, even if older students won't admit it! If you're not sure how you can introduce a particular concept or skill, see if you can find a children's book that can be used as a jumping off point for your lesson. Amazon.com and other online bookstores are a great way to search for books. With their search engines, all you need to do is type in the keywords in the children's books section and many titles should pop up for you to browse. Here are a few ideas:

Dem Bones - Skeleton/ Body Unit
My Body - Body Unit
The Real Story of the 3 Little Pigs - Point of View
Once Upon a Time - How to write a Narrative
Sidewalk Math - Real Life Math
Brown Bear, Brown Bear - Patterns
The Great One and The Pain - Point of View

UFO - Point of View
Thumb, Thumb, Fingers, Drum - Ryhming
Mr. Brown Can Moo - Onomatopoeia
Math Curse - Real Life Math
Stellaluna - Bats
Magic School Bus - Science

B is for Brainstorming

Brainstorming provides students an opportunity for input in class decisions and class discussions. It also offers a way for students to voice out loud what they already know (or think they know) and generates ideas for everyone to think about. Brainstorming is an excellent pre-writing strategy as well as a way to stimulate thinking when beginning a new concept. Jot lists can be done independently and then shared with the group. Be sure that each and every idea is valued and none ridiculed. It does not matter how impossible an idea might be, during brainstorming everything is to be included. We want to encourage our students to think "out of the box" rather than all conform to one way of thinking. You can use brainstorming to:

- Generate writing topics
- K-W-L
- Generate questions for interviews or research projects
- Generate questions to ask guest speakers
- Generate a list of items to look for when on a field trip

 **is for Concept Boards**

Students love to share and displaying their work is vital. A fun way to encourage this is by allowing them to create tri-fold concept boards. They are great when you are working on experiments in science or doing book reports. Concept boards also come in handy when reviewing previous skills, and parents love seeing them displayed for curriculum fairs and parent nights.

Concept Boards do not have to be huge. Students can create mini tri-fold boards out of 1/2 or even 1/3 of poster board. Once they've cut the posterboard in half or one-third, students need to fold the remaining portion into three sections. Now you have a ready-to-use mini concept-board!

Create mini-centers using the same concept outlined above. These can be easily sorted and taken to a student's desk when they are ready to work on it. Use a plastic crate and hanging folders to organize the centers by category for easy student access.

 **is for Dioramas**

After reading or learning about a new concept, have students show what they've learned by making a diorama, or shoe-box scene. Using a shoe box, have students create a 3-D scene using construction paper and other materials such as grass, twigs, plastic figures, fishing wire, etc.. On the outside, students should write a short paragraph telling about the scene or explaining the concept.

D is for Drawing

Have students draw about a topic before reading or writing about it. This helps focus students on what they are about to learn. It is also a great way to encourage students who do not feel successful when reading or writing.

Utilize the mind-map strategy. The mind-map is very similar to webbing except that students draw pictures instead of only using words. Each thought or idea branches off of the main topic. This can be used in all subject areas to show relationships between ideas, events, people, etc.

Utilize the story board strategy. Have students fold their paper into four to six squares, depending on age level. They then illustrate the sequence of events on the story board. This could be used to show the sequence of a story, historical events, steps to solve an equation or steps in a particular skill. The story board is also a great way to pre-write for a "How To" essay.

is for Everybody

When students work together in teams, they are motivated to learn. Student talking becomes more meaningful as they discuss what must be accomplished. Additionally, working in teams gives students some time in class to socialize which means they will be less likely to disrupt your lesson. If they know there will be time later when they can talk, they will be quiet and pay attention when necessary.

Get everybody involved by using pass-along stories, or round-robin stories. Each student will write one beginning sentence on their paper. They then pass their paper on to the next student who adds another sentence or two continuing the same thought. The paper is passed around the table or down the row until everyone has had a turn adding to each story. This is an excellent way to teach the importance of staying on a topic and learning about fluent story lines.

The round robin concept can also be used when solving equations. Have each student solve step one of an equation and pass it along to the next student. The paper continue to rotate until each problem is solved.

Another use for the round robin concept is with a sequence of events.

Involve everyone in a class discussion by writing a question or thought-provoking statement on the board. Have each student write their example/thought/answer/idea on the board under and around what you have written. Have different colors of chalk available for students to choose. This is a great way to jump-start a discussion. This idea also works well with graphic organizers. Have students write their answer inside a graphic organizer posted on the board or large butcher paper.

is for Fun

Don't be afraid to have fun and laugh with your students. Fun is an important need of all human beings. Once you have established work time vs. play time, enjoy humor in your classroom. Share a joke or funny story with your students and encourage them to share some with you.

F is for Freedom of Expression

Provide your students with lots of options. Every child, just like every adult, is better at one medium than another. Let them try their hand at writing music lyrics, poems, raps, and plays. Set up an area with odds and ends, paint, posters, etc. so that they can create puppets, collages, and other artisitic endeavors. They will love the chance to explore their creative side.

G is for Games

Using games is a great way to teach teamwork. There are many new and old games that involve skills we teach in school. Monopoly and Backgammon involve the problem-solving skills we like to encourage, while Scrabble promotes vocabulary and spelling. There are even junior versions of games for primary and elementary students. Many board games designed for young children are available and help teach skills such as taking turns and being good sports when winning and losing as well as academic skills. Other fun games that also stimulate the brain are Scatergories and Mastermind.

You can become a game creator as well. Our students love to review for tests by playing bingo, overhead football, and jeopardy.

FunBrain.com is a great way to introduce online games to your students that challenge their thinking. It has a great resource for teachers as well.

Students also love to create their own game. This type of activity really forces them to use higher level thinking, although they never realize it! Have students make up a game using information they've learned. How will they teach others the skill and/ or knowledge they've learned through their game? Is this a review type game or a teaching type game. Stress the importance of clear and precise instructions.

G is for Getting to Know your Students

The more you know your students as persons, the better you will be able to relate to them. Each child in your class is a unique individual with their own personality, their own wants, needs, likes, and dislikes. Do you really know them as a person or are they just another face to you? Our students are often motivated to work harder for the teachers who take time to get to know them on a personal level and show that they care. This is often done in primary grades, but as students get older, it happens less frequently.

H is for Happy Sack

Whenever a student practices a random act of kindness, the recipient of the kindness writes the deed down on paper and puts it in the happy sack. Every week on a designated day the teacher reads all of the kind acts collected in the happy sack. This really encourages consideration and friendship among the students. A variation of this for older students is to use a Warm Fuzzy box or a Kool Kids box.

H is for Helping

Helping others can be motivating to students. It provides them with a chance to show what they know and to be appreciated. Students can help one another when partnered together in class for activities and projects. Have students create study groups within the class to develop the skill of networking with others.

is for The Important Book

The Important Book written by Margaret Wise Brown follows a fun pattern. This pattern can be used by students to explore any concept or problem. It is a circle book where the ending is the same as the beginning. It follows this pattern:

_____ is important because...
It is...
It is true that...
It is true that...
It is true that...
It is also true that...
_____ is important because...

How could you use this pattern to explore or assess a concept in your class?

Begin by reading the book aloud to students and have them use the pattern to write about colors, shapes, or some other simple concept. You can also use this pattern to write about any concept learned in class such as atoms or algebra.

is for Jobs

Have older students apply and interview for any class jobs you might have available. This will help students practice for the real world and will motivate them to do an extra good job when they know they might get "fired." Change your jobs each semester so that other students have a chance to apply and interview. Having class jobs is extremely motivating because students love to be valued as a helper.

Do you have a particularly challenging student? Often our worst troublemakers are actually our best leaders. Capitalize on those leadership qualities and put them to work for you. This student may simply need someone to believe they are more than what *they* believe themselves to be.

> *"I noticed that many of the students in this class look up to you. That shows good leadership qualities. I could use a leader like you to help me..."*

Being asked to help with an important and meaningful job can often turn these students into your biggest allies.

J is for Journals

Writing out information often helps students conceptualize information and place it in their long term memory. For example, think about how you would write out an explanation of "3 x 5." Journals can be utilized in all classrooms. In fact, the Olympic Gold Medal Gymnast, Kurt Thomas, when teaching his students, has them keep a journal of their work-out to solidify in their minds what has been done and what needs to be done. Journals can also be done in fun shape books that relate to a particular unit. We discuss additional ideas for using Journals in all subject areas in the Making Connections chapter.

is for K-W-L

KWL stands for Know-, Want to Know-, Learned-, and is written across the top of a chart, chalkboard, or paper. Students fill in the first two sections as a class before a new unit or concept is learned. The last section is completed at the end of the unit or lesson. With primary students this can be done orally or as a class using large sheets of butcher paper.

K is for Kush Ball

Reading aloud from a textbook can be fun when you use a kush ball or other type of soft ball. Have students choose who is next to read by lightly tossing the ball to another student. It is VITAL that you go over your expectations and consequences for off task behavior before you begin this activity.

A variation on Kush Ball is to have students stop in the middle of a sentence or paragraph. The next student must start at the EXACT place the last student left off. This should be approached as a game, not a punishment-based issue.

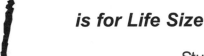

is for Life Size

Students love anything different from paper and pencil activities, so give them a large piece of butcher paper and markers and let them make life sized timelines in History, graphs in Science and Math, solve problems, create storyboards, or brainstorm ideas. Another fun activity is to trace their body when studying Health. Hang them around the room to create stimulation for your visual learners.

L is for Letter Writing

Writing letters to the President, Governor, local Congressman or Senator, or to other famous figures, is extremely motivating to students. Many addresses for government officials and businesses can be found in the almanac and on the internet. This is an excellent way for reviewing both friendly and business letter formats with students. Not only do they have a real audience, but also have a variety of topics to write about. This can also be used as a tool for assessment since students have to know the subject in order to make a coherent letter. Everyone will be excited when they receive a reply letter in the mail.

For older students, there is an excellent book called "Letters from a Nut" (you will have to edit some of the material for appropriateness), that uses letters written in a serious format to poke fun at the world. The author has written letters to actual businesses with either a compliment or a complaint and has published the return letter. This book is a fun way to introduce writing letters to businesses to either compliment or complain about a particular product or service.

 **is for Mobiles**

Mobiles are a fun way to display information. Students can make mobiles of atoms, story settings, and timelines. Require written explanations of the mobile. This is great for visual learners and can be used as an assessment tool. We've used everything from coat hangers to dowel rods to make mobiles. Students can be creative in what they decide to hang when representing a concept.

M is for M&M's

The M&M game can be used not only as an ice breaker, but also to review or test knowledge in various areas. Pass around a jar of M&M's and instruct students to take some. After everyone has taken some, have students tell you a fact, or give a math problem for each M&M they take. This is also a great way to review for a test or as a unit culmination. AIMES, a teaching tool, also has a great math activity using M&M's as part of a graphing lesson.

 **is for Note Writing**

We are forever picking up notes in class, so why not use this time worthy tradition by encouraging students to write informal letters for information, send birthday notes to a classmate, or even write notes to their parents about their day.

With computers and specialty paper, it is easy to create personalized note cards to give to students. At the beginning of the year you could use Microsoft Publisher or any Card Maker program to create a variety of cards with different messages on them. Then, throughout the year, pick a card and personalize it for the student.

Everyone likes to get a card that shows someone is thinking of them. If a student seems sad all day, give them a "Cheer Up" or "Hang in There" card. Don't just make cards to show appreciation for hard work and improvement, but think of other situations where a personal card would make a difference to a student. If you make up a wide variety of cards with different messages, then you can just write in, "Dear_____," jot a quick note, and sign your name. If you have a few minutes, then write more.

Don't get so caught up in the day to day business of teaching that you forget your students are people with feelings and needs.

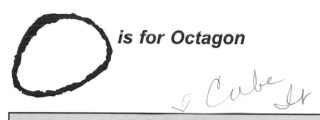

O *is for Octagon*

Cube It

> In one of our Gifted/Talented training seminars, the presenter gave us all smal 4"x4" boxes and asked us to decorate each side with different colors of construction paper. Then we placed one Bloom's Taxonomy level along with the keywords on each side. When working with students, we can toss the box on each table and ask them to "Cube It". After a lesson or unit, students complete one task using each level found on the cube. All of our kids really enjoy this activity, not just the gifted ones.
>
> *-Emma and Dyan*

Octagon, squares, stars, and other shapes make learning fun. Use various shapes to help students see similarities and differences, categorize items, or order concepts. For example, a triangle is an excellent way for students to visualize hierarchies.

A variation on this activity is to make these objects 3-D and place instructions or questions on each surface.

O is for Open Sharing

Allowing students to share in class helps create a positive learning environment and makes students feel important. Have them share what they have written or learned. Encourage students to relate their learning to their life. Have they ever been in a particular situation described in the story or event? Have them share relevant experiences. Younger children especially love to share their own stories as a way of making learning meaningful for themselves.

P *is for Poems*

Poems can be written about seasons, historical events, and even math. The more they write, the better writers they will become. A Bio-Poem is a fun way to show knowledge about a historical figure or concept.

The pattern is:
Line 1: Person's name/ Concept
Line 2: 2 adjectives to describe
Line 3: An action phrase with an -ing word
Line 4: An action phrase with an -ing word
Line 5: An action phrase with an -ing word
Line 6: Wrap up word or phrase that is a
         synonym for line one

A Name poem, or anacronym poem, is another type of poem that works well in describing concepts or famous figures.

Examples:
Abraham Lincoln
Honest and just,
Fighting a bitter war,
Leading a broken nation,
Living on through time,
A Man for the Ages.

Volcanoes
Hot and Fierce,
Spitting out ash and rocks,
Spilling out lava,
Covering everything in sight,
New land is formed.

P is for Paper Bags

Students can use paper bags as an alternative to routine paper/pencil tasks. Fill the bags with flash cards, sequence strips, or character traits. Decorate the outside of the bag and put in exciting events from history, a script for a skit, events of a novel, etc. Students can complete the activity found within the bag.

This is a great way to jump start an activity with student groups. Have them predict what the activity will be based on the outside of the bag. Encourage student cooperation with paper bags. If each group has one or more items another group needs to complete their task, they will need to cooperate with one another in sharing and exchaging needed information.

Students can also put their work inside a paper bag and illustrate the outside. The possibilities are endless! When using paper bags as part of a project, be sure to use a checklist so that students know exactly what is expected of them.

P is for Pop-Up Books

Pop-up books are such a fun way to publish student writing. When students are writing one or two paragraphs to answer a research question, have them publish their information in an illustrated pop-up book. Students simply fold a piece of construction paper in half for their book. The title should be written on the front and an "About the Author" on the back along with illustrations. Inside, have students write their paragraph(s) on the bottom half of each side and illustrate the top. A pop-up image can be created by folding a small piece of cardstock or construction paper in an "L" shape and pasting it on the page. You might also ask your art teacher to help you with other ideas for creating pop-up images.

 **is for Quotes**

As students make profound, or humorous statements, have them write these down and display them on a bulletin board or walls of your classroom. What a great way to let students know that what they say is important!

A variation to this activity is to have a quote of the day or a quote of the week from different famous figures. Use the quote as a springboard for your discussion that day or week.

> **For example**, a music teacher might use, "We are the music makers
> and we are the dreamers of the dream," by William Shakespeare.
> Students can interpret what they think this quote means.

Another variation for quotes is to have students finish the quote. Provide students with the beginning of a famous quote or saying and have them finish it in their own words. You'll enjoy reading the results as will the parents! Afterwards, discuss each quote and its meaning with students.

The internet is an excellent source to find books of quotes or even websites full of quotes ready to be used.

 **is for Remembering**

Students are motivated to work for people who care about them. Remembering their name after the first day of school is one way to show that you care. Play the Name Game or another type of game that will help you remember each child's face and name together. You'll see their face light up, no matter what age, when on the second day you say good morning to each along with their name.

Birthdays is another area where students want to be remembered. Celebrating another year, another milestone is important in our students' lives and for some of them it may be the only time that they get any personalized attention. Celebrate birthdays as often as you can. A birthday card, a cupcake with a candle, or any other simple act goes a long way with students.

Another fun way to celebrate is with a birthday bag. During the first week of school have students each decorate a paper bag. They should not write their names on the bag. Then, throughout the year, pull out a bag at random and have the other students write short, fun, positive birthday messages to the birthday boy or girl. Place the messages, some candy, a bookmark or sticker page into the bag. At lunch, everyone can sing "Happy Birthday" and you can present the birthday bag to the student. This can be extremely motivating since many of our students may not get a formal birthday party and in some instances their birthdays go completely unnoticed by everyone else.

R is for Research

Have students research more often and less formally to establish a love of searching out answers. Research does not have to be massive, but can be an easy quest for knowledge. Assign mini-research topics using a variety of resources. Let students research information to answer questions they may have on a particular topic. Make it as non-threatening as possible so that students will enjoy seeking information and reveling in the success of finding it.

Remember, research can be as simple as finding the answer to a question. When a student asks, "Mrs. ....., why does a hummingbird move so fast?" encourage that student to discover the answer through books, pictures, videos, and the internet. A great answer to the question above would be, "I don't know, why don't we find out?" Then help the child learn how to find answers. Don't make them wait, if you can. Immediately satisfy that need for information and you'll be teaching a life-long learning skill!

Most States now require that even our primary students engage in some type of research!

Have students make books cut into shapes that fit the current theme or topic of study. Shape books are lots of fun to make and easy too! Just punch holes in the tops or sides and thread with brightly dyed year or O-rings.

Shape books can be used as journals, to hold illustrations, timelines, or even to complete daily assignments.

S is for Shape Books

S is for Spelling Games

Review for spelling and vocabulary using fun games. One is Spelling Bee Basketball. Have all of the spelling words on little strips of paper in a cup or basket. Break the students into two teams. One student picks a word out of the basket and reads it to the next student who must spell it. If they spell the word correctly, then that student gets to try and make a "basket" with the basketball and a trashcan. The team with the most points at the end wins.

Another fun game is the Spelling Bee Race. Group students into four or five lines. Call out the word and have students race to the board to spell it. Whoever spells the word correctly first wins that round. A variation on this is a spelling relay where each student writes one letter of the word for their team. The first team to correctly spell the word wins that round.

S is for Sentence Strips

Sentence strips have a variety of uses. Write different sentence parts on various strips and cut them to size. Have several different nouns, verbs, connecting words, prepositions and/or prepositional phrases. Mix them all up and have students create their own sentences using the different parts.

For younger students you might want to color code each part of the sentence so that they can self-check to see if they have a correct sentence.

You can use this same concept in just about any class. Use strips of paper to organize or categorize information into a T-chart, timeline, Venn Diagram, or any other graphic organizer. Type out statements, words, ideas, etc. and cut them into strips. Have an envelope or baggie with the strips ready for each student group. Students then work together to put information in correct order or correct category. They can paste their final product onto construction paper or a large sheet of colored butcher paper. This activity helps students mainpulate information in a variety of ways.

 **is for Transparencies**

To add enthusiasm to your class, divide students into teams and let them solve problems or answer questions on an overhead transparency. Students can then share or explain this information to the class.

During a class discussion, allow students to come to the overhead and write their answer or idea using colored Vis á Vis pens.

T is for True or False

Reviewing facts in class can be fun using the game True or False. Have student groups work together to create three to five statements regarding a recent lesson that are either true or false. Have the groups go to the front of the room to share their statements. The other students in the room then decide whether each statement is true or false. Students really enjoy this game because they have a chance to "trick" other students with their statements. It works great as a review because you can stop after each statement and discuss why it was or was not true.

U is for Underlining

Give students special colored pens, pencils, or highlighters when they have to underline a reading passage. Another fun way to use underlining is in teaching the parts of speech. Have students use a different colored pen or pencil to underline each part of speech in a sentence. This is a great group activity where each team member has a different colored pen. They must work together to identify the parts of speech in a sentence.

 **is for Unwrapping**

Students describe a famous person, place, or concept on a sheet of paper. Encourage creativity with illustrations and/ or objects that help represent the information. Have students put their information in a box, wrap it up, and exchange their "gift" of knowledge with another student.

This can also be used for sensory activities where the student unwraps the "gift" blindfolded and tries to predict what it is by using their five senses.

V *is for Learning Vine*

Make a vine of butcher paper or construction paper and string it across the room or down a wall. Have students add "flowers" or "leaves" to the vine with facts from your unit. At the beginning of a new unit, take down the old leaves and flowers to make room for new ones. You could also use the vine as your word wall or to teach parts of speech.

V is for Vacation Brochure

A brochure is a great way for students to show their creativity. They can use it to market a "time travel" vacation. Students design the brochure to convince people to travel back to a specific time period in history. Who will they see? Where will they go? What will they experience?

Have students plan a trip to anywhere in the United States or the world. What will they see? What route will they drive? How many miles is it? Will they need to fly? What is the cost? Where will they stay? Math concepts are integrated by figuring the cost of gas/travel, and setting a budget for food, lodging and attractions. How much will the total trip cost? For older students, how long will each leg of the trip take when traveling *x* miles an hour? Also, if they were able to save x dollars each month, how long would it take them to save up for the trip?

When students are studying a new math concept, have them make a travel brochure to "Problem Solving Land" with tips on how to solve this type of math problem.

When studying world cultures, have students make travel brochures to convince people to travel to different countries.

When studying any concept, have students create a travel brochure to visit the "Land of ..." (atoms, volcanoes, baseball, etc.) in which they explain information about that particular concept.

 **is for Walkabout**

The Walkabout is a type of research adapted from a traditional practice of Aboriginal Australian tribes in which adolescents are sent alone into the outback for several months to prove their readiness for adulthood. Dr. Maurice Gibbons, in his book, *The Walkabout, Searching for the Rite of Passage from Childhood and School*, adapted this practice into a form of real-life teaching to help students want to learn.

The Walkabout is a year-long project in which students explore one topic of interest to them. Students must go on an adventure, create something unique, research one aspect of the topic, do a community service, and show professional skills attained. Pictures, journals, and information gathered for each section are organized into a 3-ring binder and presented to a panel of teachers, peers, and parents at the end of the year.

Teacher Talk

"I've done the walkabout project with my sixth, seventh, and eighth grade students and it has been a huge success! One student decided to do her walkabout on being a veternarian. She volunteered in a Veternarian clinic, interviewed the Veternarians, researched information about stray animals, worked in a pet shop, and learned how to properly bathe and dip animals . She used a journal and pictures to present her efforts and during the presentation demonstrated how to wash and dip a cat. All of my students were excited to show the new skills they had learned through this project!"

 **is for X-tra Small or Large**

Have students do their assignments on extra large or extra small pieces of paper. This makes boring, repetitive type tasks more fun. Another way to spruce up their work is by providing them with brightly colored paper or index cards.

X is for "Excellent"

Praising students is an excellent way to motivate them. When they share an answer with the class, thank them. Say, "Excellent answer!" or "Excellent effort!" You will be surprised at how many more hands will begin to go up when you do this.

Y *is for Yarn*

Younger students can use yarn to practice letters and match objects. Older students can match terms and definitions. Yarn is also a handy way to measure circumference and to compare fractions. Yarn can be a miracle motivator!

Y is for Yard

We're talking about the school-yard here! Take students out and about on beautiful days. Walk around and pick up different kinds of leaves, look at trees and roots, pick up rocks to identify, or notice different cloud shapes. There is so much for us to learn from our world that we should take advantage of it and spend some time outdoors. Who says that all learning must occur inside buildings?

Take some time to play team-building games outside or use chalk to do sidewalk math. Have students make butter, bricks, or other objects that reinforce your topic of discussion. Measure the distance from the sun to each planet with chalk, or have student groups use their bodies create "live" mini solar systems with "planets" rotating around the "sun."

Go outside to write poetry or stories and let the great outdoors inspire your young writers and artists. There are so many different ways that you and your students can enjoy the outside world and learn at the same time!

Doing a unit on birds? Have students go outside and pick things up like grass and leaves, etc. with a clothespin.

Z *is for Zooming In*

Have students take a broad topic and "zoom in" on one tiny detail to explore fully. For example, when studying a culture, focus on hairstyles or clothing. It is also easy to "zoom in" in science by using microscopes and magnifying glasses to write about what students see.

Z is for Zest

Add zest to your classroom by participating in the activities you require of your students. They will love to see your product and will be more motivated to put time and effort into it when they see how much effort you put into yours. This is an excellent way to model your expectations as well as a way for you to enjoy being with your students.

Working with Special Needs Students

This section is in the this chapter because oftentimes these are the hardest students to motivate. Mainstreamed students include Special Education and ESL (English as a Second Language) students. As teachers we know that our job is to teach ALL students regardless of their inherent ability. However, we also know that there are some students who are harder to reach for whatever reason. This section contains tips and reminders to help you cope with the varying abilities of your students.

Special Education Students

Remember...

- Do not treat these students any differently than the others.

- Pair them with someone in your class who is patient and willing to help.

- Read each I.E.P. (Individualized Education Plan). There are times when the I.E.P. is confusing. Go ahead and ask the Special Education teacher to explain what that particular student needs. **It never hurts to ask for help!**

- Remember, you are required by law to follow each I.E.P. exactly when modifying for the student.

- Get textbooks that you can highlight. Some I.E.P.'s request this. Your Special Education teacher will know where to get them or may have some you can use.

- Modify tests BEFORE you hand them out. It only takes a few minutes to cross out or highlight sections for the student to complete. Don't embarrass the student by making them wait while you modify the test or assignment right at their desk.

- Do not tolerate jibes or funny remarks about Special Education students by others – even other teachers!

- Read to and with these students every day, even if it is only for a few minutes. That extra time reinforces that they are worth your attention.

- Do not make a big deal about Special Education students leaving your class if they go to a resource classroom.

- Try not to lose your temper and if you do, apologize. Kids understand that everyone has bad days.

- Be Patient!

- Find out what that student is interested in and use it!

- Be prepared to explain the concept or lesson in a different way for them.

Remember...

- Some students need to move to learn. Allow an active student to sit in the back and move around a little, as long as he/she doesn't disturb anybody.

- Find out how that student works and be flexible! If a student needs to draw to listen, then let him/her draw.

- If you don't feel comfortable with modifying tests and assignments, you also have the option of modifying grades for Special Education students. (See the back of the Assessment chapter)

- Trust your gut instinct!

- Don't get discouraged! It is hard when you know a student needs help, but they don't qualify according to the state requirements. Do what you can.

- Keep your eyes open for students who need help and are not getting it. Not everyone needs Special Education resources. Check it out first to make sure that the student is not just goofing off..

- Ask about other programs, such as tutoring and Big Brother/ Big Sister, that might help your student.

- Have documentation of any behavior and/or academic problems the student has exhibited in your classroom.

- If your student does not qualify for special education services, but you still feel they need extra help, discuss a 504 plan or speech referral with your special education teacher.

- Remember that parents are not always happy about their child being referred for Special Education services. Many times parents feel that you are simply trying to label their student as "dumb". Reassure them that you are trying to find a way for them to be successful in the classroom.

> *"Keep your eyes open for students who need special help.*
>
> *Do you see a discrepancy between their intelligence and their abilities?"*

Working with ESL Students

It is frustrating to have someone in our class who can't understand anything we're saying. How do we know that they are learning anything or that they are being successful? This is often the case with our ESL students. Many times students arrive in our class having just entered the country. Others, however, have been here for some time, but do not have a good grasp on the English language. Whatever the case, we need to be prepared to offer these students a good education. Here are a few tips used by effective ESL teachers that you can use with ESL students in the classroom.

Students with no English language skills

"Respect an ESL student's need for silence when faced with a new language."

- Provide ample listening opportunities

- Use mixed ability groups

- Create high context for shared reading

- Use physical movement

- Use art, mime, and music

- Put yourself in their shoes to gain perspective and understanding

- Demonstrate

- Restate/ paraphrase

- Use Gestures

- Explain or define any and all terms used in class.

- Use illustrations and photographs; label items in the room

- Remember, these students are scared and confused and do not understand anything that is going on in the classroom.

- Do not force them to talk until they are ready. Respect their silence.

- Pair with a student who can fluently speak their language and can help translate.

Students with extremely limited language skills

- Ask *yes/no* and *who? what? where?* questions.

- Continue to provide listening opportunities.

- Have students label pictures and objects.

- Have students complete sentences with 1 or 2 word phrases.

- Use pattern books and picture dictionaries.

- Try to help them understand what is going on in your classroom.

- Pair them with a student who is fluent in English as well as in their home language, if you can.

- Build vocabulary in the content areas using visuals and meaningful experiences.

Students with less limited language skills

- Ask open-ended questions.

- Model, expand, restate, and enrich student language.

- Have students describe personal experiences.

- Use predictable and patterned books for shared and guided reading.

- Use role-play and retelling of content area text.

- Have students create books.

- Do not assume that the students have the appropriate academic skills.

- Teach students academic language – what is a noun, subtraction, etc.

- Help students by modeling thinking aloud. Encourage students to only use English at school.

Students with fluent language skills

- Pair them with another student who needs help.

- Use group discussions to help them continue practicing their language skills.

- Guide them in the use of reference materials such as dictionaries, almanacs, atlases, and encyclopedias

- Provide higher level reading materials.

- Have students write their own stories.

- Provide realistic writing opportunities.

- Provide visuals to help with comprehension.

- Publish student writings.

- Encourage them to use both of their languages as a translator.

All ESL students

- Do not let them use their lack of language skills as a crutch!

- Be understanding and flexible with the ESL teachers. Ask for strategies and ideas to help you in the classroom.

- If you see that a student needs help and you do not feel that you do an adequate job, send them to their ESL teacher for extra help.

- Begin with shortened assignments and gradually increase them as they gain fluency.

- Do not make a big deal of students leaving your classroom for their ESL classes.

- Keep them as involved as you can in your classroom. They need to do everything the other students are doing!

- Have students do the regular assignment and then modify their grade if necessary.

Idea Share

Have students create understanding thermometers to help them show you their level of comfort and understanding. Use heavy cardstock paper for the thermometer. Cut the page into three sections approximately 4" by 7". Label the top "Understanding Thermometer" and draw a line down the middle. On the right side of the line write "No Clue," then "Confused," then "Questions," then "I get it." On the left side of the line draw faces to represent these statements. Cut a hole at the top and bottom of the line. Thread a piece of yarn with a bead. Next, thread the yarn through the holes so that the bead is on the front of the card. Tie the yarn in back. Students can move the bead up and down the thermometer to show you how they are doing.

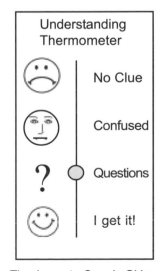

Thank you to Connie Skipper, ESL teacher, Garland ISD for sharing this idea with us!

Conclusion

Remember, the more motivated your students are, the more learning will take place. When students are energized and engaged, their minds are like sponges absorbing new information and storing it. This happens so easily when they have a fun activity to connect with concepts learned. Additionally, many of these activities help our Special Needs and ESL students to feel success and enjoy the learning process. Thus, planning motivating lessons is not such a difficult task when you use simple activities like the ones in this chapter to add zest!

Questions to Ponder

If you could use one word to sum up how to motivate students to want to learn, what word would you use? Why?

Why is it helpful to have quick and easy ways to make learning fun? Is this something you strive to do for your students? Why or why not?

What is your attitude towards your Special Education students? Is this helpful or hurtful for them? What might you change to create a positive learning experience for these students in your class?

What are some ways you currently help ESL students at different levels in your classroom? What are some other strategies you might implement?

Additional Resources

Reading, Writing, and Learning in ESL (2nd Edition) by Suzanne Peregoy and Owen Boyle

Exceptional Lives: Special Education in Today's Schools (3rd Edition)
by Ann Turnbull, et. al.

Motivating Your Students: Before You Can Teach Them, You Have to Reach Them
by Hanoch McCarty and Frank Siccone

Choice Theory in the Classroom
by William Glasser

Moving into the 21st Century:

Technology in the Classroom

Another way we can fan the flames is by incorporating technology into our classroom. While the computer is becoming a major tool within the classroom, technology comes in all shapes and sizes. Not every school is fully equipped with computers and other types of high-tech hardware. This can be frustrating to tech savvy teachers. Even more frustrating is the fact that many teachers across the United States are equipped with computer presentation stations and other hardware/ software options that they rarely or never use. These are missed opportunities for rekindling the flame of learning in our students!

There are lots of different, helpful, and motivating ways you can use technology in your classroom to enhance student learning. However, we must stress the importance of attending training provided by your school or district in how to use these tools. Remember, if we are not familiar with the technology, we will not use it in the classroom. This hurts our students who need that exposure to help prepare them for life in the new millennium.

Computers

Computers have so many different uses in the classroom. Whether you have a presentation station, one computer for the whole class, or several workstations, computers can be used in a variety of ways to enhance your learning environment. We are going to discuss both teacher use and student use of equipment and software programs for the computer in this section.

Teacher Use of the Computer

Presentation Station

A presentation station includes a Television Set, a computer, and sometimes a VCR and internet connection. All of these items are hooked up together so that the teacher can present information from the computer/internet for students to view on the TV. Schools across the country are moving towards this type of setup for teachers to make technology more accessible as a teaching tool. Below are a few examples of how you might use the Presentation Station

- Notes for lecture
- Class presentations
- Post focus or warm-up

- Teach editing/Word Processing skills
- Demonstrate a particular computer program
- Post Vocabulary or other assignments

Computer/TV Hookup Cables

These days computers can easily hook up to the TV through a series of cables which your librarian may have available. If not, Radio Shack and other Computer stores will be able to help you find the correct cables to use.

LCD Panel

These panels will also project information from the computer to a screen, usually the overhead screen. Some schools may have an LCD panel available for check-out through the library. However, the LCD panel does not provide as crisp of a picture and can be hard to see clearly.

Projector Unit

Some schools have projector units that connect to a computer and project the information directly to a screen. These are clear projections, unlike the LCD panel, and can often be used to project other images as well.

Of course, the ideal is that every teacher would have their own presentation station to be able to present lessons using a variety of technology and media.

Cameras/Digital Camera

- Take or bring pictures to class to enhance your lessons. Often your life experiences with travel can bring learning to life for students! Many students have never traveled out of their own city, and have never been to an art museum, arboretum, or any historical monument!

- Have students take pictures for special projects.

- Pictures can easily be integrated into documents on the computer with the digital camera or scanner.

- Integrate pictures into parent newsletters, student projects, etc.

I have the equipment, but what do I do with it?

There are a plethora of fantastic software programs that will help you with lesson presentations, creating forms, developing web pages, contacting students and parents, and more! On the next couple of pages we are going to review some of the different programs you might find useful.

Power Point

Power Point is a program that is used to present information. The pages can be changed manually with the click of a mouse, or automatically through the slide show mode. You choose how many seconds or minutes you want to pause in-between each slide.

Power Point can replace the overhead transparency when presenting notes, pictures, or information. Simply type your notes, information, or insert pictures onto each page (called a slide). When teaching, either time the slides to automatically switch or use the mouse to click over to the next slide of information. This is a great way to integrate pictures along with information. You can use digital camera images or clipart. The program includes a nice little collection of clipart that is easy to insert.

Other Uses include:

- Post class objectives, the date, homework assignments, or your focus assignment (warm-up, sponge, bell-ringer, etc.). This helps keep your whiteboard or chalkboard open for other teaching needs.

- Post Vocabulary or Spelling words for students to copy or look up in the dictionary.

- Post your Word(s) of the Day or Quote of the Day

- Print the outline version of the slides to use as notes when presenting the lesson. You could also give these to students who were absent or special needs students who cannot copy as quickly.

- Review for a test. Create one slide for each review question. Set the time between each slide to give ample opportunity for answering the question before it switches to the next slide. This keeps you free to monitor students while they work and to help answer questions. This method saves on copies and is a great alternative when the copier is broken or the school is out of paper.

- Post directions for assignments, lab rotations, or group work.

- Have you run out of room on the overhead or whiteboard? Think about posting some of the information using Power Point.

274 Technology

Word Perfect or Microsoft Word

You can use Word for the same reasons as Power Point. The difference is that multiple pages will not change automatically. Also, you must remember that students can only see what is visible on the screen. With Power Point, once you start the slide show, each slide will adjust itself to fit perfectly to the screen.

Use Word to:

- Create and save letters to parents
- Create note cards or post cards to give to students
- Create tests
- Create welcoming letters for parents and/or students
- Create forms to use in the classroom
- Create checklists for assignments
- Create assignment handouts
- Create lesson plans
- Create lesson handouts
- Teach editing skills -- Have students point out mistakes in a typed paragraph. You can correct the mistakes on the computer while students are watching. You might use a different color to fix the problems in order for the changes to stand out.

EXCEL

Excel is a spreadsheet program and has many different uses. We highly recommend that you take a course in using Excel to learn all of the different ways it can be used in the classroom. Here are a few examples:

Graph data or information to encourage higher level thinking with students.

Keep and average grades if your school/district does not have an electronic gradebook. The spreadsheet will actually calculate the averages for you if you set up the equations correctly.

Make a spreadsheet to keep track of student work, absences, etc., or to use for the Clipboard Management techniques we discussed earlier in the book.

Create databases to use for mailing labels

Also, you can use your presentation station to teach students how to use any program through demonstration.

© 2005 McDonald and Hershman

Microsoft Publisher

With this program you can create multiple text boxes to hold typed information and place them anywhere on the page. You can also insert and place graphics much easier than with Word. Publisher is a much more versatile program. You can use it to create note-cards, postcards, newsletters, flyers, labels, coupons, brochures, websites, and more with their ready-to-use templates.

Additionally, any document you create can be saved as HTML to upload as a webpage. Publisher is a WYSIWYG (What you see is What you Get) type of HTML editor. Your web pages will look exactly as you create them on the page. You can make text and graphics into hyperlinks to make your site as interactive as you wish. There is even an option for creating response forms and adding your own HTML code, if you know it.

Here are a few ideas:

- Post class information/ newsletters as a website for parents and students to view
- Post tests and assignments for students to complete online
- Post student work for parents to view
- Post your professional portfolio

Can you think of any other ways you could use a classroom website?

Idea Share

Students can use software programs such as Publisher, Word, and Power Point to create presentations for the class, write research reports or essays, create brochures, flyers, class newsletters, or websites exhibiting information they've learned. Excel can be used to create their own charts and graphs as a way of organizing and intepreting data.

Give students meaningful uses of computer programs as part of their learning and watch them blow you away with their abilities!

Student Use of the Computer

- Use the computer(s) you have in the classroom as a Learning Center for student enrichment.

- Computer games are a fun way to teach valuable skills, and they won't even know they are learning!

- Teach word processing skills for writing pieces and projects.

- Students can practice or learn to type on the computer.

- Use the internet to research information (closely monitored by the teacher).

- Email famous figures, experts, and government officials to ask questions related to units of study.

CD Programs can extend lessons and units, and can be used creatively for all kinds of research projects.

Educational CD programs are now widely available through Office Supply stores, Computer stores, Teacher Supply stores, Bookstores, and places like Wal-Mart and Target. Most programs cost between three and thirty dollars although some are considerably more costly.

A few good programs for classroom use are:

> The Animals – San Diego Zoo
> Atlas Pack
> Grolier's Encyclopedia
> Guinness Records
> Compton's Encyclopedia
> Magazine Article Summaries
> Time Almanac
> Magic School Bus
> News Lines
> American Journey – Exploring American History
> Where in the World/US is Carmen Sandiego
> Reader Rabbit Series
> Jump Start Series

More Ideas

Math

- Create spreadsheets using mathematical equations
- Study and draw geometric figures using Draw or Paint programs
- Create graphs, charts, tables and diagrams to represent information
- Practice math skills using the variety of math programs available Example: *Speedway Math*
- Create a website to help other students practice or learn more

Science

- Use CD Roms, Software, Internet and Email for research
- Create data bases of information
- Write research reports and science projects
- Use pictures/images from CD Rom and Software programs to enhance science projects, especially for the Science Fair!
- Create spreadsheets, graphs, tables, and diagrams for representing data
- Create a website to teach others

Social Studies

- Use CD Roms, Software, Internet and Email for research
  Example: *Take a "Tour of the White House" over the Internet!*

- Write research reports and complete projects
  *The computer has different fonts and images that can make historical reports look authentic!

- Create graphs and charts showing information

- Create Maps and Travel Brochures for geography

- Create slide show presentations for lessons and/or student projects

- Create a website to help other students practice or learn more

Language Arts

- Write compositions

- Create 'About the Author' Pages using the digital camera to place a picture of the student on the page with their biographical sketch

- Use the computer for Final Drafts or to Publish students' works
  *Poetry can look beautiful when using the variety of fonts and illustrations from the computer!

- Use *Print Shop*, Draw and Paint programs to illustrate stories and projects

- Create cards for classmates and family

- Create invitations for parents to come to events like open house

- Students can practice grammar and reading skills using programs in your school.

- Create a website to share information or publish written works

---

Teacher Talk

"As a Kindergarten teacher, I sometimes have trouble figuring out how to incorporate technology into my lessons. However, one activity I did after a field trip, as closure, was to have my students each make up one sentence about the trip. I typed out each sentence on half of a page using the presentation station. I did this as a whole class so that my students could see me writing the sentences in correct format. Next, I printed off each sentence (two per page) and asked students to illustrate their own. Lastly, we gathered each half page together and created a class book about our field trip. It was a fun closing activity that incorporated technology and ended with a product my students were proud to show to everyone!"

Scheduling Computer Time

It is important that each of your students has a chance to work and practice on the computer. Sometimes teachers tend to only allow their top students to use the computer, because they are usually finished with their work first and already know how to use computer technology. Your goal should be for every student in your class, no matter what learning level, to have a certain amount of time on the computer each week or month…whatever you decide.

Organizing Computer Time in Your Classroom

If you have only one or two computers in your classroom, you probably utilize your computer(s) daily as learning and practice centers, and often as research centers for projects. For daily use, teachers might let students take turns on the computer instead of their silent reading time or other daily events. You will want to create a schedule or a method of keeping track, so you ensure each student has their fair share of time on a computer.

Notebook method

Each student's name is written along the side of the paper with days or weeks in a month written at the top. The students must record their time on the computer in the appropriate section. The teacher checks the notebook weekly to verify that all students are taking their turn. Once a student has used their time, they may not work on the computer unless it is approved by the teacher.

Posting a schedule

Each week or each month the teacher posts a large schedule above the computer table, which displays each student's time slot.

Tips of the Trade: Effectively utilizing school computers

➔ When working on special projects that need computers for research, consult with your librarian. Libraries often have extra computers and printers that can be rolled down to your classroom, or the librarian may allow students to come to the library and work. Your librarian is an excellent resource!

➔ Many school districts issue laptop computers to teachers. When planning special projects, coordinate and reserve the use of teacher laptops to add to the number of computers in your classroom. Many of your colleagues would probably be willing to help out in lending their laptop for a good cause.

➔ Don't hesitate to use the computer lab if your campus has one. Teach word processing/editing skills, how to create databases, spreadsheets, graphs… Sign up in advance if you want to use the lab for special projects, as this will often require more time than the standard 30 minutes.

Internet Web Sites

There are many interactive internet sites which offer free services for students. These can include review of facts/concepts, games, and other online type programs that are educational. However, be very careful that you personally review any website before allowing students to view them. In the last few years we have seen an increase in unacceptable adult websites buying expired education domain names. This practice is horrific and can cause major problems. For example, we had a link to a site for lesson plans which at one time hosted fantastic teacher lesson plans. Just recently we checked our links and found that this domain name now leads to an adult-only website. Needless to say, we took that link off immediately. This story is just to caution you to preview all sites before letting students view them.

In the next few pages we have listed some internet sites that you might find helpful in the classroom. We have checked all of these links and updated them. However, as with everything on the internet, there is no telling when site names will change or disappear. Your best bet is to spend some time previewing and investigating these and other sites to be sure of what you will find.

Teacher Resources:

Beginning Teacher's Tool Box http://www.inspiringteachers.com
TeacherNet http://www.teachers.net/
Teachers Helping Teachers http://www.pacificnet.net/~mandel/
Tenet Halls of Academia   http://www.tenet.edu
Education World   http://www.education-world.com/
Classroom Connect   http://www.classroom.net/
Busy Teacher's Web Site   http://www.ceismc.gatech.edu/BusyT/

Content Resources:

Color Landform Atlas of the United States
http://fermi.jhuapl.edu/states/states.html

National Geographic
http://www.nationalgeographic.com/main.html

Presidents of the United States
http://ipl.sils.umich.edu/ref/POTUS/

"Remember, always preview web sites before students look at them."

"It is important to closely monitor internet use by students."

Content Resources Continued:

This Day in History
http://www.historychannel.com/thisday/

The History Channel
http://www.historychannel.com

Yahoo! Countries
http://www.yahooligans.com/

World Cultures
http://www.kent.wednet.edu/curriculum/soc_studies/text gr7.html#top

U.S. Government
http://www.vote-smart.org/index.html

White House for Kids
http://www.whitehouse.gov/kids/l

The Exploratorium
http://www.exploratorium.edu/

National Park Service
http://www.nps.gov/parks.html

American Museum of Natural History
http://www.amnh.org

Ask Dr. Math
http://forum.swarthmore.edu/dr.math/dr-math.html

Math Forum
http://forum.swarthmore.edu/

Mrs. Glosser's Math Goodes
http://www.mathgoodies.com/

Mathematics Archives
http://archives.math.utk.edu/k12.html

Eisenhower National Clearinghouse for Mathematics
http://www.enc.org/about/nf_index.html

Content Resources Continued:

Bill Nye - The Science Guy
http://billnye.com

The Nine Planets
http://seds.lpl.arizona.edu/nineplanets/nineplanets/nineplanets.html

Science Hobbyist
http://www.eskimo.com/~billb/

How Things Work
http://howthingswork.virginia.edu

NASA
http://www.nasa.gov/

Magic School Bus
http://scholastic.com/MagicSchoolBus/

Weather Channel
http://www.weather.com/twc/homepage.twc

Cells Alive
http://www.cellsalive.com

San Diego Zoo
http://www.sandiegozoo.org/

VolcanoWorld
http://volcanoworld.org

Books

Looking for a particular book or books on a particular topic? Try Amazon.com or any other large online bookstore. They have a great database that is easy to search. Once you've found the book you are looking for, you can buy it or try to find it at the local libarary.

Amazon.com   http://www.amazon.com

Searches

Do searches for information, interactive sites for students, or websites for teachers using keywords for your topic. String several keywords together for results that will meet your needs. We recommend the following Search Engines:

Google   http://www.google.com
Ask Jeeves   http://www.askjeeves.com

Conclusion

Technology is an excellent way to fan the flames of learning in your classroom. Technology is now an integral part of our society, and therefore should be an integral part of our classrooms as well. There are so many different ways to incorporate technology into our daily lessons that we really have no excuse not to. The computer offers a doorway into a world where we can easily find answers to our questions and implement mini-research into our classroom on a daily basis. Presentation stations help us with an extra format to present lesson information or post assignments. And there are so many quality educational software programs available now that help even our most challenging students learn! What fabulous tools we modern teachers have available to help us inspire our students to become life-long learners.

Questions to Ponder

What is your philosophy of student computer use in the classroom? How should it be different for primary versus secondary students? Do you see any difference?

How comfortable do you feel with using technology in preparing for lessons or in your classroom? What are some ways you could become more comfortable, if you are not already?

Why is it important to attend training for different hardware and software programs and then use those programs frequently? Do you keep yourself up to date on the different programs available through your district?

What are some different ways you incorporate technology in your classroom if computers and other high-tech hardware tools are not available?

Do you utilize the internet in your classroom? What are some different ways you use the internet as a teaching tool? If you are not currently using the internet, how might you use it in the future?

Additional Resources

Best Lesson Plan Websites
by Karla Spencer

The Busy Educator's Guide to the World Wide Web
by Marjan Glavac

Teaching with Technology: Creating Student Centered Classrooms
by Judith Haymore Sandholtz, Cathy Ringstaff, David C. Dwyer

Earobics
Computer software game designed to help students improve listening skills.

Parents as Partners

Developing a relationship with parents is one way we can help fan the flames of learning in our classroom. How? Parents have the greatest impact on their child's life, whether positive or negative. We may not want to admit this, but we really and truly need parents to be actively involved in their child's school life. We need to develop a partnership that ultimately becomes a support system for the student.

It is difficult to know when and how a positive partnership can begin with parents. Many of us may feel insecure or awkward when communicating with parents and try to get away with as little interaction as possible. However, this attitude of minimal contact is one that will ultimately hurt the student.

We must remember that the parents are their child's first teacher. As the child reaches school age, the parent passes the bulk of teaching and learning responsibilities to the professional teacher. So, in essence, we are "in locos parentis," or are taking the place of the parent for the time that the child is in our classroom. Therefore, it is vital that we become partners with the parents because of the dramatic roles we both hold in each child's life.

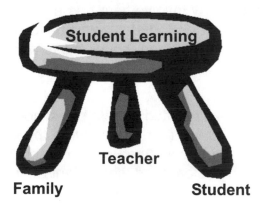

Webster's Dictionary defines **partner** as *two or more people working together towards the same goal....* This requires participation from both the teacher and the parent. Neither party can do all that is needed and so, instead, we must work together to accomplish the goal of educating our children.

Not only must the teacher and parent work together as partners, but the student should be included as well. After all, our common goal is student achievement and success. Where would we be without the student? We can think of this partnership as a three-legged stool. Each leg must be of equal length in order for the stool to work properly. If one leg is unequal, the stool will be unbalanced. It is the same with the student - teacher - parent partnership. Each part must work together in unison with equal knowledge, involvement, and accountability in order for students to be successful.

What can cause this partnership to become unbalanced?

- When parents are not involved enough or even too involved (i.e. - making decisions for both the student and the teacher), the partnership can become unbalanced. This kind of lopsided partnership can ultimately cause problems for their child.

- When teachers do not strive to involve parents, but rather make decisions without knowing the whole picture of the student's circumstances, the partnership can become unbalanced. Such decisions may not be appropriate and may even be detrimental to the student's well-being.

- When a student makes no effort in taking on the responsibility of learning for himself, and continually points his finger at the parents or teachers, there is a pattern of dependence and lack of personal responsibility which can seriously affect his future.

Why involve parents?

Not only do parents know more about their child than any other person, but they are the ones who are ultimately responsible for that child's well-being. Just because they are required by law to send their children to school doesn't mean they have relinquished their responsibility. It is vital that we involve parents in all aspects of their child's life, including their school life.

As educators, we have a responsibility to involve parents because of their fundamental rights. However, it is also to our great advantage as well as the student's to involve parents. Recent research documented by Fuller and Olsen in their book, *Home-School Relations: Working Successfully with Parents and Families* (1998), shows that family involvement has a profound effect on student success in both academic achievement and behavior. Students who have highly involved parents are more likely to be well-adjusted and successful than those whose parents are not involved in their school life.

These studies began with the Head Start program which was created to help pre-schoolers. After extensive evaluations, it was determined that the most effective programs were the ones where both the parent and child participated, and were regularly contacted by the teacher. In programs where parents and teachers were not involved with one another, the students lost any gains made after a few years (McConkey, 1985).

Urie Brofenbrenner in his study of the Head Start program showed that children in these programs who were supported by active family involvement had:

- fewer instances of failing a grade level
- fewer referrals to special education classes
- higher levels of elementary and high school completion

The benefits of informing and involving parents in your classroom include:

Students strive for a higher level of academics such as:
- earning better grades
- completing enriched course work
- enrolling in honors classes
- setting long term goals for themselves
- participating in extra-curricular activities that enhance learning

Students tend to avoid negative behavior trends such as:
- taking drugs
- running with a gang
- bullying other students
- giving in to peer pressure
- committing criminal activity
- leading classroom disruptions

Students have a higher level of participation in school and community activities such as:
- clubs
- athletics
- music
- church/religious activities
- community service

Teachers experience more support and appreciation from parents.

Parents feel a new appreciation for the commitment and skill of teachers.

Schools are able to access a variety of resources from parents.
(Swap, 1987)

The barriers to a positive parent partnership:

Even though the effects of parent involvement are obvious, teachers and parents often run into obstacles and attitudes that keep them from being true partners. Some of these impediments include:

Lack of family resources to complete required school activities/projects.
Some families will not have the monetary and time resources necessary to participate fully in school and classroom functions.

Lack of information from the teacher to the parent.
If teachers do not inform parents about classroom and school events, a lack of involvement will result. Most parents do not have the time to initiate requests for information, therefore teachers must make the effort. When teachers do not make the effort, parents assume that no news is good news which is not always the case.

Fear on the part of the teacher.
Many times new teachers find it difficult to initiate parent contact. This "fear" can stunt the growth of a positive partnership between the parent and teacher and leave both feeling frustrated.

Fear on the part of the parent.
Sometimes parents come to the classroom with prior anxieties about school. These may be due to previous negative encounters with teachers, or from their own unpleasant school experiences.

Lack of a supportive school environment.
If teachers and parents do not feel welcomed or supported within the school building, they will refrain from communicating with one another. It is vital for administrators to encourage both their teachers and the parents to interact freely.

Teacher assumptions about family life.
If a teacher assumes that each student has access to every day items such as a television or newspaper, then some families/students will feel alienated. Some families will not be vocal in communicating their situation due to embarrassment which may come across to the teacher as hostility or indifference.

Variables that Affect Parent Communication and Involvement

In order to have an equal working partnership between two individuals, there must be some level of understanding. This comes from finding out more about the person's background, attitudes, and relationships with others. By better understanding parents, we can work with them to ensure a successful learning experience for their child. Similarly, when parents understand us as people as well as our teaching philosophy and strategies, their level of trust will increase. When this happens, parents are more likely to work with us as equal partners rather than as silent partners.

As teachers we must deal with a wide diversity of family characteristics. Each of these characteristics influences the attitude of the parent and, in many cases, our attitudes as well. Additionally, each family is individual and consists of both observable and unobservable traits including traditions and a heritage unique to them. This can make communicating with parents very difficult at times. It is important to take into consideration both the general variables that affect families and the characteristics of human behavior when meeting with parents.

The variables that most affect parents and families include:

- Availability of Resources
- Parenting Styles
- Parental Beliefs about School
- Family Structures
- Cultural Background

© 2005 McDonald and Hershman

Availability of Resources: Money and Time

Every family we encounter has a different level of financial security and available time that affects how much they are able to support their student and be involved in the classroom. This can range from profound poverty where survival issues dominate family life to working parents who are financially secure, but do not have the time to volunteer in the classroom. Take some time to learn about the financial and time issues facing your students' families. This will help you to better understand the attitudes of the parents you encounter.

Parenting Styles

Each family has its own set of values and beliefs which determine how parents discipline and interact with their children. Baumrind (1967), in an article found in *Genetic Psychology Monographs*, identifies three parenting styles: Authoritarian, Authoritative, and Permissive. Our classroom leadership styles are also based on these different behaviors. If our leadership style and a parent's parenting style clash, we may have some issues in communication.

However, as teachers we must acknowledge each parent's right to raise their children according to their own values and beliefs even if we do not agree with it. It is not our place to judge. We can offer suggestions and model positive strategies for parents and we can encourage. If the situation is one that is harmful to the child, then we can take steps to protect that child, but we must remember that we are not that child's parent. It is a tough dilemma at times, but having a better understanding of each style will help us to better understand each parent.

- **Authoritarian** - Parents are in absolute control and uses mainly punishment strategies to improve behavior.

- **Authoritative** - Parents create a balance between setting limits and offering personal freedoms. Children are held accountable for their actions, but the focus is more on encouraging positive behaviors.

- **Permissive** - Parents have little or no control over the child. Limits are not set and children are often not held accountable for their actions.

Parental Beliefs about School

Each parent you face has had their own experiences with school. Those experiences may have had a positive or negative impact on their life. This previous experience colors their perception of school and will affect your relationship with this parent. You may encounter parents who are fearful or insecure, angry, or positive and encouraging. The best advice is to remember that no matter what the parent's attitude may be towards you and the school, your attitude should always be positive and helpful. When we consistently serve others in a positive manner, we can overcome even the greatest obstacles. Parents who are fearful or angry may come to trust you and to eventually trust the school. Parents who are positive will have their beliefs confirmed and will go on to be advocates for the schools as well as for their children.

Family Structures

Although society generally labels a "family" as being a mom, dad, two kids and a pet or two, in today's world this is frequently not the case. There are many different types of families and these differing structures may affect the individual student. Since you are dealing with a variety of family structures in your classroom, it is important to gather information about each student's family. This will help you interact with both the child and parents in a positive manner. What are some of the different family structures represented in the classroom?

Traditional Families - Most teachers assume their students come from this type of a family which includes a mother, father and children. Be very careful about making assumptions when you see what looks like a traditional family when in actuality it may not be one.

Single Mom - This family consists of the mother and the child/children. The burden of providing basic needs plus other parenting responsibilities lies with one person rather than two. This means that the single mom's time and energy is extremely limited.

Divorced/Single Parent - This family consists of one parent (either mother or father) and a child/children. This family has all of the time and energy struggles faced by the single mom plus the emotional devastation that occurs when parents break up or a spouse dies. These students may be operating in crisis mode which will affect how they act in your classroom.

Stepfamilies - This family consists of two single parent families joined together. While this family looks like the traditional family, there are extra concerns. Often the children are jealous of each other and the attention of their parent. Everyone may feel awkward in relation to the children that are not theirs by birth, and there may be other complications.

Guardian Parents - This family consists of a child/children being reared by someone other than his or her parent. This could include grandparents, aunts, uncles, guardians, or foster parents. The variables with this type of family are so widely ranged that it is very important for you to get a general understanding of how each particular family operates so that you can better meet their needs.

Cultural Backgrounds

Our students and their families come from a wide range of cultures. It is important to learn as much as you can either from the parents themselves or from other books about the basic customs and values from each culture. Remember, that within each cultural group, individual families are affected differently by the traditions and values passed down from their ancestors. These customs vary from country to country or state to state. Some of the different cultures we may see in our classroom include:

- African Americans
- Anglo-European Americans
- Asian Americans
- Hispanic Americans
- Multi-ethnic Americans
- Native Americans

The back of this chapter lists several excellent resources for further reading.

Tips for working with different family variables

- Before failing a student for not turning in homework, first consider whether or not you are punishing the student for his or her poverty situation.

- Do not assume that basic supplies such as scissors, markers, paper, or glue are in the home.

- Parents in poverty, while they love their children, are limited in the amount of support they can offer. The more you acknowledge their efforts, the more they will do for you and their child.

- Don't assume that parents don't care. Some parents may not show up for teacher conferences because they have no way to get to the school.

- Make the effort to welcome parents into your classroom whenever they can drop by. This shows them you are willing to work with their schedule.

- Offer flexible conference times for parents who work long hours or several jobs.

- Parents may arrive at conferences feeling exhausted and overburdened. Offer to be a listener before you begin the official conference.

- A positive attitude and willingness to work with the parent to help the child will help deflate angry parents. Always keep the focus of your conversations on the welfare of the student.

- Put defensive parents at ease by starting with positive comments about the student.

- Be careful about the way you phrase concerns to authoritarian parents. Punishment at home can take many different forms, some of them abusive.

- Authoritarian parents may transfer their feelings of anger caused by frustration or embarrassment toward the teacher. Let the parent vent. Then express a genuine interest in working together to solve the problem.

- Before making any major decisions regarding a student, solicit informaiton from the parent regarding their child. It could be that they have already dealt with the problem at home. Be sure to take their advice seriously.

- If you have a student who is exhibiting disruptive behaviors and/or is not making any effort in school, call the parents. You may find that the student or family has gone through a serious life change which is affecting his or her behavior and schoolwork.

- Try to use a translator as often as possible when working with parents who speak a different language. There are now online translation services that can sometimes help. Language can often be a barrier to both communication and involvement on the part of the parent.

Making First Contact

There are several things a teacher can do to get off to a great start with students and their families. The initial contact can set the tone for the remainder of the year whether good or bad and should occur before school starts.

Generally schools give out class lists along with other demographic information including phone numbers and addresses anywhere from two weeks to two days before school begins. Once you have your class list for the year, you can begin the communication process. This initial contact can be accomplished in a variety of ways even before school starts.

- home visits
- introductory postcard/letter
- welcome package
- phone calls

Home Visits

Some principals require their teachers to conduct home visits before school begins. The thought behind this action is that it gives teachers a greater understanding of their students' background and special needs. It also paves the road towards two-way communication between parents and teachers.

When visiting the home, the teacher becomes the guest whereas the parent has a position of control. This is a reversal of the usual parent/teacher meeting where the parent is the invited guest into the teacher's territory. By allowing the parent to feel that same sense of control, a more equal partnership can begin from the start.

Other teachers like to conduct home visits, although not required by the principal, in order to meet his or her students and their parents in a more relaxed and non-threatening environment. The first day of school is nerve-wracking enough for everyone without adding the extra stress of conducting an initial meeting. By making a home visit, teachers can avoid this stress for both themselves, their students, and their parents. An extra bonus is that students often come to class with much more enthusiasm than when the teacher is a complete stranger.

This is also a good time to meet additional family members, and observe parent-child interactions within a comfortable setting for the family. A home visit helps the teacher gain a more realistic picture of the student and his or her home life.

"Visiting families in person help us to better understand our students and make good decisions in the classroom."

Tips for Home Visits

Call first to schedule a time

- Remember, some parents may not want you to come to their home.

- Be flexible.

- Offer to meet them for coffee, lunch, or dinner in a neutral place.

- Another option would be to meet in front of the school or in the school's library.

- Some parents may be embarrassed about their home situation and it is important to respect their feelings on this issue.

- Don't force the issue. If the parents can't meet with you, then ask for a current address so that you can send them a welcome packet.

Think Safety

- Be sure that at least one other person knows where you are and how to get in touch with you.

- If you have a mobile phone or pager, be sure to take it with you.

- Don't go into questionable neighborhoods at night alone.

- Consider pairing up with your teaching partner or another school staff member when making home visits.

Bring something to give the parents when you visit

- A welcome packet which can include a welcome letter, a map of the school, a picture of yourself, classroom procedures & rules, school forms, a list of books & supplies, a survey, and a fun activity for parents and students to do together before school starts.

- A small token gift such as a gift bag or basket with fruit or snacks, pencils, school paraphernalia or other cute buttons. You might also want to create a calling card with your name and contact information to leave with parents.

- Ask the principal or PTA if you can have some school spirit items to use in gift baskets for parents.
  For example, A school cup or mug filled with pencils, a button, and peppermints.

Keep your visits brief and to the point

- Keep your conversation light and informal. You are not here to discuss everything about the upcoming school year. There will be other times for that during Open House, etc.

- Stick to topics that allow parents to either lead or participate in the conversation.

- Be aware of the comments you make. You don't want to accidentally upset the parents with a flippant remark that may be offensive.

- Stay away from gossip. You are there to get to know your student and his/her parents better.

- Go with an agenda in mind. Know ahead of time what you want to tell them about yourself and have some questions ready to get to know them better as well.

- Be prepared with conversation starters. Some parents may not be as adept at starting and continuing a conversation. It may be up to you to keep things going.

- This is the perfect time to find out what the parents expect from their child and the school year. By understanding what they expect, you won't be caught off guard later in the year.

- Don't feel that you need to stay there all night long. A brief 15 to 30 minute visit is acceptable.

- Pull out your resources, or search the internet on different cultures to prepare for meeting different families.

- Remember, a wrong comment or action could jepordize a positive relationship.

- Be professional and appropriate at all times when meeting with students and parents.

- Not all families will want to invite you into their home. Offer to meet at a local restaurant, library, or park near the school for your initial visit.

> *"Always be aware of cultural differences when meeting with families."*

Introductory Postcard/Letter

Many of us send home a brief postcard or letter before school starts. This is one of the easiest ways to get the year off to a great start. Below are a few reminders of what you might include in this type of communication.

Your welcome message should include:

- An introduction of who you are

- A little bit about your educational/training background.

- A little bit about your previous teaching experience.

- The name of your class and your room number

- A statement expressing your excitement/interest in meeting the student

- A statement about the upcoming year

Options:

- postcards

- fold-over note cards

- colored paper/stationary

> **Idea Share**
>
> Type up the letter, save it, and print it out on colorful paper rather than handwriting each student a letter. This is especially helpful for secondary teachers who may have up to 150 students.

Other Tips for Communicating with Students and Parents

- Create a web site complete with a picture of you that explains more about who you are, your educational training background, and your previous teaching experience.

- Put your web site address on your postcard/ welcome letter so that students and parents with computers can get to know you better!

> **Idea Share**
>
> If you work in an area with a high population of non-English speaking families, it is vital that they receive this information in their own language. Ask around the school, public library, churches or other community services to find a translator for each language spoken. You may want to consider sending a copy of the letter in both English and their native language.

Parent Survey/ Response Sheet

It is a good idea to send home some sort of a survey or parent response sheet to gather information about individual students within your class. Some teachers like to include this response sheet with their welcome letter. Other options include placing it in the welcome package, or sending it home the first day of school.

Sample Survey Questions to include in a Parent Response form

- Name of child
- Parent names (in full - first & last) - mother, father, guardian
- Parent address(s)
- Parent e-mail
- Parent fax number
- Is it okay to fax you notices and letters at this number?
- Student e-mail
- Daytime and Evening phone numbers for both parents
- Special Interests (sports, hobbies, etc) of student
- List any allergies student has
- List any medication student is currently taking
- List special needs of student (both academic & medical)
- Special Notes or comments?
- What are your goals and expectations for your child this year?
- What motivates your student?
- Any special family circumstances?
- Do you have any areas of expertise that you feel would be helpful for the school or this particular class?
- Circle 3 things you would be willing to do as a volunteer
  - -library   -field trips   - guest speakers   - class parties/event
  - -booster clubs   -carnival   -student clubs   -lunchroom
  - -reading to students   -tutoring   -monitoring the school grounds
- Would you be willing to help translate? If so, what language(s)? Do you need a translator yourself?

Welcome Packet

Take some time before school starts to create a packet of information for parents. You can use colored pocket-folders for this.

Create a label on the computer with the school name, class name (i.e.-English), your name, and grade level (if appropriate). We suggest that you use a shipping label so that it will look nice. Most office supply stores carry pre-made sticky labels that can be used with either a desk-jet or laser printer.

Put forms that need to be returned on one side, and information pages on the other. Be sure to label each side as "Keep" or "Return".

The packet should include:

- A note of welcome
- Parent response sheet/survey form
- Classroom procedures
- Rules
- Discipline system
- Homework/grading policy
- Supply list
- Recommended book list for your grade level
- A general outline of your classroom curriculum
        (including year-long and six weeks themes).
- School forms that need to be completed and returned.
- Map of school with a star next to your room.
- Names of the school administrators and office staff

> **Idea Share**
>
> Make several extra of these packets and keep them handy for when a new student enters your class during the school year. Parents will be impressed at how efficient you are!
>
> If you work in a school with a high mobility rate, be sure to have plenty of extras ready!

Phone Calls

Some teachers prefer a more personal type of contact with students and parents before school starts. A phone call is a very nice way to welcome students and parents to the new school year and doesn't have to take a lot of time in the process.

When making a welcome phone call, you might want to:

- Talk to the student first.

- Introduce yourself.

- Tell the grade/subject area you teach (if secondary).

- Let the student know when to report to school.

- Let the student know your room number.

- Ask to talk to his or her parent(s) or guardian.

- Introduce yourself to the parents.

- Tell the parent about your teaching style/ background and teaching philosophy.

- Ask the parents if they have any questions for you.

- Answer any questions.

- Encourage parents to be active in the school this year.

- Encourage parents to help with their children's school work when appropriate.

Once School Starts

As we stated earlier, the first contact home is always the most important. It begins the relationship between you and the parents. Do you want the relationship to be one-sided or two-sided? Are you interested in a true partnership with the parents or are you only giving lip-service to parent communication and involvement? Your tone of voice and the way you handle the conversation will communicate your attitudes and expectations to the parents.

We are not always able to make a call home before school starts. If that is the case, then a phone call needs to be made within the first few weeks of school. The parents need to hear your voice and know that there is a competent professional teacher in charge of their child's education. Yes, even the parents of the middle and high school students want to receive this phone call from you!

Since this call is being made after school has started, you have already had a chance to get to know the students a little bit. This is a great opportunity to offer the parents specific comments about their child and even begin working on issues before they have a chance to develop into real problems. Below is a sample conversation you might find useful:

Hello, Mr./Mrs. _____

I am glad to have __(student name)__ in my class this year. He/She seems to be very ___(positive comment)___.

witty	bright	attentive	vivacious	personable
talented	cheerful	friendly	cooperative	punctual
a class leader	spontaneous	hard-worker	helpful	energetic

This is going to be a busy year for us. We will be studying [insert areas of study here]. I am really looking forward to a great year and I hope you are too! Are there any areas of concern you'd like to discuss with me at this time? Is there anything I need to know about?

If the student is already exhibiting negative behavior, this is the prime place to mention it.

[I want to share with you that I have noticed _____'s tendency to _____.

talk too much	interrupt others	disturb the class
disrupt instruction	use time ineffectively	have difficulty working with others

Have you had experience with this in previous years or do you have anything to add about this type of behavior from your child? What strategies have you used in the past? I know that together we will be able to solve this problem and make this a successful year for _____.]

I wanted to let you know that I am hoping for open lines of communication between us, so if you have any questions or concerns, please do not hesitate to call me right away. My planning/team time is from _____ to _____ everyday.

It was great talking with you and I look forward to working with you and ___(student's name)___ this year.

Grade Level Meetings

Your school may want you to have a grade level or team meeting with all of the parents. This is a great time to inform your parents about the policies, procedures, and expectations of the teachers in the grade level/department. This is for parents only and is more formal than the open house. Here are some tips to running a smooth meeting.

Have an agenda prepared

This can be a simple outline of the topics you will be discussing. An agenda will help keep you organized in your thoughts and will keep parents from changing the subject. A good way to keep from making unnecessary copies is to make a transparency of the agenda so that everyone can see it.

Grade Level Meeting Agenda

I.   Welcome and Introductions
II.   Discipline Program
          rewards
          absence policy
III. Field Trips
          Planetarium   Symphony
IV.   Schedule
          Daily Activities   Math   L.A.   Science
V.   Organization
          Procedures - homework/calendar
          Student binders
VI.   Grading
          Types of grades
          Progress reports
VIII. Volunteers
          Field Trips
          Room Parents
          Supplies needed

It is important for your parents to understand EXACTLY what you expect from their child. For example, you might say, "I expect all of my students to do their personal best on ALL assignments. If I see that a student has turned in a poorly done assignment, it will be returned ungraded. This means that the assignment when turned in correctly will be counted as late."

This type of meeting is the perfect place to garner parent volunteers for guest speakers, chaperones, tutoring, or other classroom events. Create a notebook of parent data that you can draw from when you need a helping hand. Use the form we have provided, and make enough copies for each family. Have the parents fill out this form during your meetings and leave it with you before they go. Take a 3-ring notebook, and place the forms inside sorted alphabetically or by your class schedule. Tabbed dividers help keep this information organized when you have several different courses.

Parent Information Sheet

Student Name: _____

Mother's Name (first, last):_____

Occupation: _____

Work Phone:_____

Home Phone:_____

Special abilities/ Interests:

How would you like to help our class this year?

_____ Tutoring   _____ Field Trips   _____ Guest Speaker
_____ Reading   _____ Classroom Events   _____ Other

Father's Name (first, last) _____

Occupation: _____

Work phone:_____

Home phone:_____

Special abilities/ Interests:

How would you like to help our class this year?

_____ Tutoring   _____ Field Trips   _____ Guest Speaker
_____ Reading   _____ Classroom Events   _____ Other

Keeping Parents Up-to-Speed

In order to help their child, parents need to have the whole picture of what is going on in school. Their only reliable link to this information is you, the teacher. Here are a few ideas for relating this information to parents:

- Warm Fuzzies
- Progress Reports
- Academic Calendars
- Newsletters

Warm Fuzzies

Send short notes of praise or "job well done" home with the student. This only takes a few seconds on the part of the teacher, but can make a world of difference for the student and parent. Students feel appreciated and rewarded. Parents feel proud, happy, and thankful that the teacher is dedicated and paying attention to their child.

Even older students benefit from this type of attention. Many businesses have started using this type of praise and motivation with their employees to raise morale and satisfaction with their job. It is well-known that people like to be appreciated. Our students are no different.

> **Teacher Tip:**
> Work up a half sheet form with a graphic of a "thumbs up" or smiley face that you can use for your Warm Fuzzies. Put a general statement of "Job Well Done" or "Good Going" at the top. Copy this form on brightly colored card stock paper. Put a stack of forms in several places around the room where they are easily accessible. Now all you have to do is pull one out and write on it.

Progress Reports

We all have to send out progress reports every three weeks, but do you ever send out a report more than that? Progress reports really help keep parents on top of what is happening with their students. These days many of us have electronic grade books that make reporting easy!

> **Idea Share**
>
> Take some time and brainstorm several different positive feedback statements. Type them up and keep the list in a handy spot near your desk or podium. That way you'll have a "cheat sheet" when you want to jot a quick note to send home with students. Make sure your statements are specific and not just, "Good job" or "Great work."

Take a look at the program you use to see if you can generate reports of missing work and/or average grades. These types of reports are easy to print and send home with the students. Of course, if you think they aren't making it home, mail it "return receipt." This will ensure that someone signs for the letter.

What if you don't have an electronic grade program? Parents still need to be kept on top of what is happening with their child in class. Make up a generic form with each student's name at the top. Make enough copies for the year and keep them in the student's folder. A checklist form takes a few minutes to complete, but still keeps parents up to date.

Weekly Progress Report

Student Name _____   Date _____

WORK HABITS	E.E.	M.E.	N.I.	COMMENTS
Completes assignments on time				
Follows directions readily				
Uses time wisely				
Contributes to activities/ discussion				
Works neatly and carefully				
Works Independently				
BEHAVIOR				
Follows school/ class rules				
Respects authority				
Considerate of peers				
Cares for school property				
Is self-disciplined				
ACADEMICS				
Reading				
Writing				
Social Studies				
Math				
Science				
Extra-curricular				

EE = Exceeds Expectations   ME = Meets Expectations   NI = Needs Improvement   *(Developed by Spring Branch ISD Summer Program)*

MISSING ASSIGNMENTS:

Parent Signature _____   Date _____

If you have any questions, feel free to call me at _____ .

© 2005 McDonald and Hershman   This page may be reproduced for classroom use only.

Mid-Term Progress Report

The grades below reflect your child's grade mid-way through the current grading period.

Student's Name _____

Reading _____   **Language Arts** _____   **Art** _____

Math _____   **Science** _____   **P.E.** _____

Social Studies _____   **Foreign Language** _____   **Behavior** _____

══ CONCERNS ══

_____ **Low grades on homework**

_____ **Does not complete assigned work**

_____ **Poor homework/ study habits**

_____ **Does not pay attention in class**

_____ **Does not make up missed work**

══ COMMENTS: ══

- -

I have seen my child's mid-term grades.

Student _____

Parent _____

Missing Assignments

Name: _____

Assignments: **Original Due Date:**

_____

_____

_____

_____

_____

_____

_____

_____

_____

_____

_____

_____

Parent Signature: _____

Academic Calendars

An academic/homework calendar can work as a wonderful two-way communication between you and the parents. Having the students fill out their own calendar each day is also an excellent way for them to be held accountable for their class and homework assignments. This calendar should be kept in the front of each student's binder.

- Plan class time each day to write in homework assignments, upcoming events, etc. into the calendar.

- Be consistent in your use of the calendar. This will be helpful during parent conferences.

> **For example,** *a parent may be upset because he/she "wasn't aware" of the assignments due, simply say, "Did you check the academic calendar? All of our assignments are written there and initialed by me each day for accuracy."*

- This is a life-skill you are teaching. Be systematic about it.

- Leave 5 minutes at the start of class or before the end of class for students to copy assignments.

- Require parents to read and sign the calendar at least once a week. Check that they have signed it.

- Encourage parents to make their own comments in the calendar as a way to communicate with you.

- Check calendars at the start of each class. Be sure you read the comments so that you can respond appropriately and in a timely manner.

- Assist special needs students with filling in the calendar. You might assign a "buddy" to help them copy the information as needed.

- Remind parents that the academic calendar is a tool to help them monitor their student's homework and other assignments such as projects and tests. There is no excuse for either parents or students to say they were not aware of an assignment/test when the calendar is used properly.

Idea Share

Initialing each student's academic calendar while they are doing the focus assignment is a great way to say hello to each student AND make sure they've copied down the assignments correctly.

This also provides you an opportunity to read any comments made by parents in the calendar. Encourage this type of two-way communication between you and the parents!

Newsletters

In our classrooms, we send home a weekly newsletter. If you are extremely busy with other duties maybe a bi-monthly or monthly newsletter would be more manageable for you. A newsletter is an excellent way of keeping your parents informed of:

- Classroom activities
- Units/themes of study
- Upcoming events and field trips
- Important due dates for projects and tests
- Keep them up-to-speed on the latest learning strategies
- Give parents tips on creating a good learning/study environment at home

Tips for Helping Parents Create Good Study Habits at Home

A few of our families come from backgrounds where they did not learn good study skills, and don't know how to help their children establish them. As educators, we can help parents. By giving tips, advice, and strategies in quick increments that are not too overwhelming for parents to absorb and enact into their daily lives, we are educating parents and making our jobs as teachers easier.

Here are some tips you can include in your newsletters to "train" parents on how to create good and effective study habits for their child.

> **Idea Share**
>
> Create a newsletter template on the computer that you can use over and over. Simply cut out the parts that no longer apply and insert the new events and information.
>
> Use the information you receive at staff developments to keep parents up-to-date on the latest teaching and learning strategies. Explain in plain language to help parents better understand *why* you are using these "new-fangled" ways of teaching.
>
> Send a copy to your principal, assistant principal, counselor, and department/grade-level chair so that everyone is on the same page.

Be sure to only put one or two tips per newsletter in order to keep parents from being overwhelmed. Feel free to rephrase these in your own style.

Stress to your child/ teen that you are a team player in their school life. Your role is to help them be better students. It is important for your children that you create an environment where they can study and do homework with few interruptions and distractions.

Schedule a time to complete homework when it is appropriate for both your teen and the rest of the family. Routines are important as adolescents feel more balanced and comfortable when they know what to do each day. Don't expect them to sit and work quietly on homework during a chaotic time in the house.

Plan a "calm," "settle down," or "quiet time" for the family every day. Parents can be reading, folding laundry, working on the computer, etc., but the TV and phone should be off limits during this time. This will send the message that we all need time in a quiet environment.

Tips for Parents

Help your child/ teen set up an area where he/she can study. This does not necessarily have to be their bedroom. Most kids do better when Mom or Dad are nearby and would work well at the kitchen table. If younger siblings offer too much distraction, send them to their room or another room for "quiet time". Decide upon one location and consistently use it as a place to work and study.

Don't complain about homework in front of the student. If you have a comment or concern about homework or academic requirements, please call the teacher later. You have a huge impact on how your child views school and the teacher; don't let it be a negative one. You may be undermining the ability of the teacher to do his/her job.

Parents need to keep in mind the goal of homework. It is an opportunity for older students to have additional practice in skills learned throughout the day as well as a discipline building activity. Homework gives your teenagers the opportunity to work independently, develop responsibility and self-discipline.

Don't do the homework for your child/teen. Some parents may get carried away and want to do the project so that it is "done right." Doing the work for your child may hamper their comprehension of the material and interfere in the teacher's reasoning behind the assignment. Offer your help as a guide and advisor. Ask questions that will help the student come to their own conclusions about the assignment. If your child/teen is having extreme difficulties, call the teacher and ask for extra tutoring before or after school.

Make sure that your family is eating well. Just like our cars cannot run without fuel, the human brain cannot run without food. Even just one missed meal can affect an student's behavior and learning. Please make sure that everyone comes to school well-fed and fueled up for the day.

Other Study Tips:

• Parents should check each evening that the homework listed in the calendar has been completed.

• Help student put completed work into appropriate section of binder or "finished" side of folder.

• Check off each assignment in the calendar as it is completed.

• Have snacks readily available to help keep the brain going during work time.

PARENT NEWSLETTER (Elementary)
September 1, 20__

THIS WEEK

In math this week we are practicing word problems using division and learning the steps in long division by two digits. In Social Studies/Science we are studying the layers of the earth as well as history of the earth as a planet. Students will be illustrating a timeline of the earth's history and will choose one event to write a story about. In Language Arts we are exploring figurative language through poetry. Near the end of the week students will create their own poetry anthology of favorites.

BIRTHDAYS THIS WEEK

John B. Student - September 3, 20__
Julie R. Student - September 4, 20__

THANK YOU'S

Thank you to all the parents who volunteered to go on our field trip to the planetarium. We appreciate your support. Thank you to Mrs. Jones for reading with several of our students.

MAJOR DUE DATES

September 22, 20__	Poetry Theater Presentations
September 29, 20__	Long Division Math Test

LEARNING/TESTING STRATEGIES

Sequencing is an important skill. We are focusing on sequencing over the next three weeks. To help your child practice their sequencing skills, read with them each night. Have your child tell you what happened first, second, third, etc. in the story. Another way to practice sequencing is to follow the directions in a recipe.

PARENT NEWSLETTER (Secondary)
September 1, 20__

THIS MONTH

We begin our economics unit this month and will be studying different money systems, the exchange rate, the stock exchange, and real life finances including balancing a check book and keeping a budget.

THANK YOU'S

Thank you to all the parents who volunteered to go on our field trip to the Museum of Natural Science and History. We appreciate your support.

MAJOR DUE DATES

September 22, 20__	Life Finance Project Due
September 29, 20__	Economics Test

WISH LIST

If anyone has experience with the stock market, budgeting, accounting, or economics itself, we are in need of several guest speakers and/or materials to enhance student learning during this unit. Please contact me at 555-456-7890 as soon as possible to discuss ways you can help us learn about world economics! Thanks!

LEARNING/ TESTING STRATEGIES

Recent research shows us that real world experiences help students retain information and skills better than lectures and rote drill. Take time this month to share how you handle your budget and checking account with your teen. This might also be a great time to open a bank account in the student's name so that they can begin to learn the skills of balancing an account and setting a budget for their own extra expenses. Another real world experience that will enrich your teen's learning this month is to check out the stock reports in the newspaper. Pick one or two favorite stocks and follow them each day.

Building the Relationship

Building a relationship takes time and effort. However, it is these relationships that help everyone. They are the lifeblood of the school. Although many times we'd rather parents just stay out of our business and let us do our job, that is not the best attitude to foster a partnership. We need the cooperation and the help of parents to help make our job easier in teaching our students.

Keeping parents informed of what is happening in school is one way to begin the relationship, but it cannot grow without personal interaction. We need that two-way communication where we can each hear the other person's voice or see the other person's face. This means phone calls and parent conferences.

The problem is that most of us wait until there is a major problem before we ever pick up the phone or meet face to face. By that time it is too late. More often than not we end up facing frustrated and defensive parents who would rather blame us for their child's problems than work with us to solve those problems. So rather than waiting until the last minute, go ahead and pick up the phone.

Tips for Calling Parents:

- Decide in advance what is to be discussed.

- Rehearse in your mind what you plan to say. Jot down a few notes or a short outline to help you remember your points and stay on topic. If you are approaching a sensitive topic, rehearse out loud to see how it will sound to parents. You don't want to start the conversation by offending parents accidentally.

- Pick a time and place that will allow you to be calm and relaxed in your conversation. Calling a parent in the office two minutes before the bell rings will add an extra element of stress and can cause tension between you.

- Gather information and documentation to support your purpose for calling. (i.e. - grades, behavior records, health records, notes from the parents, student work) All of this information can be helpful to your discussion. It is helpful to already have a folder for each student with this information included in it.

- Begin with a positive comment before stating anything else.

- Always tell the parent that you and the family need to work together as a team for the best interests of their child. Tell the parent that he/she is the most important person in that child's life, and it is in the child's best interest if the parent and teacher work together as partners.

- State your reason for calling in specific terms:
  - I need your help to...
  - Let's work together to solve this problem I am seeing which is...

- When appropriate, offer the parent assistance in disciplining their child and/or helping their child.

  For example: *"You might want to start checking the homework calendar every night to monitor your child's homework assignments and check for completed assignments."*

- Offer a consequence when possible for the behavior if not improved.
  If your child does not _____ , he/she will have _____ as a consequence. Please let's see if we can't try to solve this problem as soon as possible so we can move on with a terrific year.

- Before hanging up, summarize the conversation and reiterate any agreement that you came to. End the conversation on a positive note by trying to mention something the student did well that week.

- Always follow up a parent phone call with a note acknowledging your conversation, reiterating any solution strategies, and thanking them for their time and support.

- Keep diligent records of every parent phone call.

- You may want to keep a copy of the phone record in your student information folder, OR you can keep index cards on each student.

  - **Index cards** - Set up a 5 x 7 index card for each student. Include the student's name, address, birthdate, parent's names, and phone numbers. Under this information, keep a record of parent contacts with dates and comments. Whenever you are ready to make a phone call, simply pull the index card and take it with you.

Don't forget the importance of calling home for students who are doing well in your class. These phone calls are generally quick in nature and go a long way to building a relationship with parents.

> **Teacher Tip:** *Schedule some time once a week to make positive phone calls home. Jot down the name of several students to call for each appointment.*

Simmons, Paul 2211 St. Andrews Place Wonderful, CA 34598	5th period 11/07/86
Martha Simmons (H) 456-9089(W) 329-0897	
Peter Simmons (H) 456-9089(W) 289-7658	

2/1/97   called re: no homework -- spoke with mom, she will begin
              checking academic calendar and will sign every night. I will
              check in the morning that it was signed.	

Parent Phone Record

Student's Name _____

Date Call Completed _____

Subject (s) _____

Parent's Name _____

Telephone Numbers (Home) _____ **(Work)** _____

Purpose of Call _____

_____

Matters Discussed: _____

_____

_____

_____

_____

Plan of Action:

_____

_____

_____

_____

_____

Communicating with Parents

There are times when we must speak with parents and assert ourselves in asking for help. How can we phrase our concerns and our requests in a way that is both polite and firmly lets the parents know we need their cooperation? Check out the ideas below:

- I am very concerned for your child's well being, and I thought that you should be aware of what I am noticing.

- I understand your point and/or feelings, how can we work together to solve this problem?

- It is in your child's best interest that we work together to solve this problem.

- Your child needs your help.

- I need your support.

- You are an important influence on your child. Your involvement is crucial for his or her success.

- When students do not follow the rules/expectations, it is their responsibility to be held accountable for their actions.

- If this problem isn't solved now, it could lead to greater problems later on.

- I need you to take stronger disciplinary action at home.

- I want to help your child improve, but we need to work together, not against each other!

- We need to talk together face to face in order to determine the best way to help your child. When can we meet?

Idea Share

When talking with angry or frustrated parents, the best course of action is to let them vent their emotions at the beginning of the conversation. Take notes so that you can verify their concerns after they are finished. Next, explain that you want what is best for the child/teen and that your job is to help this person do well in school, not fail. Ask the parent if that is their goal as well. If they answer yes, then say, "We want the same thing for (the student), so how can we work together to help him/her?

Remember, your goal is not to get into a battle with the parent, to make them angry, or to sound superior to them. You just want them to realize that you need their help and support.

There are some words and phrases that will not elicit a good response from parents – Try using statements that are less threatening instead.

Before using a strong or harsh word, rethink that expression and state your case in a more pleasant way.

Remember, not only are you trying to help the student, but you are also a representative of your school and district. It is imperative that you be professional in all communications with parents and other community members.

Negative Phrases	**More appropriate Phrases**
Poor study habits	Not meeting her potential
Dirty/ Smelly	Is not using proper hygiene
Irresponsible	Can learn to make better choices
Wastes time	Needs to use time wisely
Rude or mean	Inconsiderate of others
Lazy	Capable of more when he tries
	Not meeting his potential
Troublemaker	Disturbs the class
Cheats	Depends on others to do his work
Sloppy	Should try to be neater
Selfish	Does not like to share
Steals	Takes objects without permission
Stubborn	Insists on having her own way
Uncooperative	Difficulty in working with others
Obnoxious	Tries to get constant attention

Reminder

Each student you have in your class is the special pride and joy of their parents. Using diplomacy at all times goes a long way towards building a positive relationship with parents!

Using the wrong phrase with parents can really bomb!

Parent Communication

DATE: _____

SUBJECT: _____

Today, _____

        _____ was tardy to class.

        _____ was unprepared for class.

           _____ no pen/pencil

           _____ no notebook

           _____ no textbook

      _____ did not have his/her assignment or homework

           _____ ASSIGNMENT/HOMEWORK _____

           _____

           _____ Other _____

           _____

This is the second occurrence of this problem. If the problem persists, I will call you. Please sign this note and return it to school tomorrow. Thanks for your cooperation.

Sincerely,

Teacher

PARENT SIGNATURE: _____

The Parent-Teacher Conference

Many teachers and parents worry about conferences. This shows in the fact that so many parents never show up for a scheduled parent-teacher conference.

- Teaches may feel nervous or fearful. This is normal, no matter how effective of a teacher you are!

- Parents often feel uncertain and have mixed emotions about meeting with their child's teacher.

- Parents may want to please the teacher and make a good impression, but also want to express their concerns or frustrations.

- Many parents have a hard time saying what they really think and are timid, but some parents are extremely defensive and overbearing.

- A good start to every conference is a warm and welcoming greeting along with a smile!

"Always start a parent meeting with an open smile and welcoming attitude."

- Whatever the type of parent that a teacher may be dealing with, teachers should always have the same goal in mind.

- The objective of every conference should be to develop a working partnership with the parents, so that the student's best interests and learning is everyone's focus.

- You want to put the parents at ease by letting them know that your only goal for the conference is to build a positive relationship with them in order to benefit their child.

- Keep in mind the variables that cause each family to be unique and come to the conference with a positive attitude and willingness to compromise.

- If you anticipate an explosive situation with a parent, let them know that a principal, counselor, team leader, etc. will be present. It is always better to have a support system in the room when working in this type of situation.

"Remember that some parents are fearful of the school because of their own past experiences.

How can you help them overcome their fears?"

Preparing for the Conference

- Decide in advance the purpose of the conference. Make notes to yourself of what is to be discussed.

- Learn about the home environment as much as possible to avoid uncomfortable topics or saying the wrong thing. If the student's father is dead, you don't want to ask, "Where is Suzy's dad today?"

- Collect information and documentation on the student, such as grades, your grade book, student work, behavior records, tardy slips, absent notes, and health records. You should have a student folder with all of this information together, but you may not want to bring everything you have compiled on this student over the year. Be selective, only bring what is necessary and could be helpful during the conference. Planning is a huge part of preparing for a conference!

- Be organized with materials ready before the parents arrive.

- Prepare a plan or agenda for the parents to follow along. It takes pressure off of the parents if they know what to expect. The parents and teacher can make notations on the agenda. Write down any plans that were decided upon. See the sample agenda prepared for you on the next few pages.

- Some teachers meet in their own classrooms, others arrange to meet in the library, principal's office, or school conference room.

- Parents have busy lives, too! Send home a reminder note to parents with the date, time and location of the conference. You may want to have a tear-off portion of the note where parents can jot down questions and concerns they'd like to discuss with you, and send it back to school with their child, so that you can be even more prepared!

> *"Teachers look professional and organized when ready with student records and an agenda for the conference."*

10 Hints for a Successful Conference:

Having a successful conference can be an obtainable goal. Here are some suggestions for after the parent arrives.

1. Stand when the parents enter the room. Start with a friendly greeting and a smile. Thank the parents for making the effort to come, and show a pleasant relaxed attitude. Try to put them at ease and make them feel welcome.

2. Ask how the parents/family is doing and give them a few minutes to tell you about their day. It will give them a chance to vent a few feelings and will give you an insight into their life.

3. Begin your comments with a positive statement about their child.
   For example:
   "Bobby always keeps our class in stitches! He is a born comedian."

4. Share observations about the student. Ask for parent observations and compare with yours.

5. Ask how the parent is feeling about their child's behavior, progress, and/or grades. It helps the teacher to understand the student's behavior if the parents' attitudes are known.

6. Listen to what the parents say and respond to their comments. You do not necessarily have to control every discussion.

7. Do not interrupt the parents while they are speaking. This often makes them feel defensive. Wait until they are finished speaking before you begin.

8. Discuss ways both you and the parents can help the student improve.

9. Make sure to have documentation in order to demonstrate your concerns. If the child has been having problems with grades, show the parent some of the student's work (or lack thereof), or maybe show them a negative pattern that is forming in your grade book. Do not make generalized statements, but instead "State the facts, Ma'am!"

10. If conferencing through an interpreter, before hand discuss with the translator that you only want a literal translation. Some interpreters take liberties and you, the teacher, need to know exactly what is being said.

Teacher Agenda for meeting with Parents

The following is a suggested agenda for conducting a student/parent conference:

1. Greeting - Smile and welcome the parents. Introduce yourself if this is your first meeting. Thank the parents for coming.

2. Start with a positive or encouraging comment about their child.

3. Explain the objective and purposes of the conference, and why you feel it is necessary to meet in person. (i.e. - you can better share work samples, can meet with student and parents together, etc.) Provide the parents with their own copy of the conference schedule/ agenda.

4. Ask the parent for their observations and/or feelings about their child.

5. Provide your observations and concerns. Be specific on how you feel the student could make improvements.

6. Review the documentation that you have gathered for the conference.

    - Student work samples
    - Grade book
    - Discipline/ Behavioral Reports
    - Any special education forms or referrals
    - Scores and reports from standardized testing
    - Any input provided by other teachers that work with this student

7. Ask for parental input, questions, and/or concerns.

8. Discuss ideas and develop a strategy for student improvement. Write down any plans on the agenda. Also, be sure to include a way to monitor student behavior and goals.

9. Plan a timetable for expectations of improvements made, and plan for a follow-up conference to discuss the results of the first conference.

10. Closure - Summarize the conversation and reiterate any agreement that you came to.

11. Thank the parents again for their cooperation and try to end on a positive note.

Conference Request Form

Date _____

Student's Name _____

Teacher(s) _____

Dear Parent(s): _____

It is important that we have a conference regarding your child's:

_____ ATTENDANCE   _____ WORK HABITS

_____ BEHAVIOR   _____ OTHER

This conference has been scheduled for :

Date: _____ Time: _____

Location: _____

If you have any questions, or need to schedule for a different time, please call me at

_____

_____ I will be at the conference. My questions and/ or concerns are:

_____

_____

_____ I cannot make this scheduled conference. A better time would be:

_____

Parent Name: _____

© 2005 McDonald and Hershman

Parent Notification of Student Conference

Date_____

Dear_____ ,

     This note is to let you know that my teacher and I have had a conference and we have decided that I need to improve in the areas checked below. If I improve my behavior, it will not be necessary to schedule a parent conference at this time.

_____ Poor attitude

_____ Showing respect for other students

_____ Showing respect for adults

_____ Knowing when to talk and when to listen

_____ Staying in my seat

_____ Behavior in the halls

_____ Behavior in the restroom

_____ Courtesy when teacher is talking with a visitor

_____ Good manners in the cafeteria

_____ Following guidelines of lunchroom behavior

_____ Getting assignments in on time

_____ Using time wisely

_____ Good sportsmanship
                              _____Playground   _____P.E.   _____Classroom

Please sign to show that we have discussed this note. This will be in your classroom file.

Student_____

Teacher_____   Parent _____

Parent-Teacher Conference Plan

Please feel free to make any notations on the agenda.

1. Objective and/or purposes of conference

2. Parents share any observations of the student they feel are important and that relate to student work and behavior at school.

3. Teachers provide observations, review documentation and share any concerns.

4. Parents and teachers discuss possible strategies for improvement.

5. Parents and teachers decide on a plan of action.

6. Closure

© 2005 McDonald and Hershman

Middle School Teachers and Student Conferences

Often Middle Schools work in teams who will use their team planning time to conduct student or parent/student conferences. These steps for conferencing will work well for students as well as parents. Also, the previous agenda will work for student conferences.

It is important when working with older students to give them input in a parent/teacher conference. This builds their self-esteem and will motivate them to change their behavior. Simple threats of conferencing with parents do not always motivate older students.

Working up a Behavior Plan

It may be helpful to bring a behavior plan with you to a student or parent conference. It may be completed when deciding upon a course of action with the student. You and the student/parent can brainstorm both the goals and rewards to be used with the plan.

Remember, behavior plans are a means to correcting student behavior, not punishment. Also, students and parents will be motivated to follow this plan if they are allowed to participate in the creation of it.

Be sure to use rewards that are motivational to that particular student. Also, encourage the parents to use the plan at home as well. If the student realizes that he will be held accountable for his behavior both at school and home, you may begin to see a marked improvement in behavior.

Student Perspective

Another strategy is to gather the student's perspective on his/her progress and/or behavior.

Have the student share a written evaluation of his/her experiences during the course of the last grading period. You want her to include how she feels she has done academically and how she would rate her behavior.

Communicate Good News, Too

Some students will never have an urgent need for a parent conference. They behave perfectly and do well in your class. Does this mean that you can simply dismiss ever contacting their parents? Absolutely not! Building a relationship with the parents of these students works to your advantage. It keeps your students motivated and it builds a parent support base for you. Below is a sample letter you might send home:

Dear Mr. and Mrs. Parent,

I am pleased to inform you that Joy continues to be a well behaved and dedicated student. It certainly is a pleasure to work with her on a daily basis. Joy demonstrates a high level of effort in her class work, and shows a positive attitude toward learning.

I sincerely appreciate all of your hard work in helping Joy to become a responsible student. If you have any questions, or feel the need to communicate further regarding Joy, please do not hesitate to call or schedule a conference.

Encouraging Parent Involvement

Routinely Invite Parents to the Classroom for Special Events

Don't be afraid to invite parents into your classroom for special events such as poetry theater, reader's theater, oral reports, science project displays, etc. Parents love to see these kinds of student presentations! You may need to arrange to hold class in the library, cafeteria, or auditorium to accommodate for extra bodies. Plan ahead for these kinds of special arrangements so that there are no mix-ups or misunderstandings.

Making a Special Phone Call

For upper grades, a special phone call may make more of an impression than a handmade invitation. Take some time to call the parents personally and invite them to your class presentation, open house, or any other special event you may be doing. While your students may get embarrassed that you called, the parents will appreciate the fact that you took time out of your day to include them. Don't be afraid to leave a message on their answering machine or voice mail.

If you know that you will be calling parents who speak another language, ask for the help of a translator. There may be someone in your school who speaks that language and can help you out. A personal invitation means so much more when the teacher/school makes an effort to use the parent's native language.

Bulletin Board

Post upcoming events on a bulletin board in your classroom and on a school bulletin board (if possible). Some schools have voice mail bulletin boards where parents can phone in to find out the latest assignments and news. Use whatever resources your school has available to post events.

Web Site

Do you have a web site for your classroom? Give parents your web address at the beginning of the year so they can check for new assignments and upcoming events on their own time. You'll still need to remind them, but many computer savvy students and parents will appreciate the ease a classroom web site offers.

When posting events, make it easy for parents to find what they are looking for. Keep your site simple and easy to navigate. Most parents aren't interested in a lot of cute graphics and sound bytes.

Our website, http://www.inspiringteachers.com has free websites available to teachers to post their classroom information. We encourage all teachers to utilize this free resource.

Once we have parental support, we must determine where help is most needed. Every school and every classroom has different needs. You also need to consider the resources available to your parents. Does your school have parents with an abundance of time and money, no time or money, or something in between? When asking for help from parents, be sure not to ask more than they can give.

Supplies

Depending on the resources available to you through the school, you may need to ask parents to provide supplemental materials for the classroom. Generally the supplies needed for classroom projects are easily obtainable, such as household items. If you let parents know what you need near the beginning of the school year, they can begin collecting items such as paper towel rolls, paper sacks, plastic baggies, baby food jars, mayonnaise jars, yarn, scraps of material, and anything else you might need.

Spend some time thinking about what projects you may want to do with your students throughout the year. New teachers should ask other grade level or department members for suggestions since they may or may not know the curriculum right away. Develop a list of what you'll need so that parents can be informed in advance.

> **Teacher Talk**
>
> *"One year we did a special project with our fifth grade class that required a bale of hay - which was hard to find in April. Trying to locate the hay at the last minute was stressful and we were afraid we might have to cancel the special event! The next year we created a list of special supplies and had a parent sign up to get us that bale of hay. Since the parent signed up at the beginning of the year, she had plenty of time to locate our hay and have it in time for the project."*

One of the biggest ways a parent can help in the classroom is by volunteering. There are so many wonderful things that we'd like to do in our classrooms, but are unable because of lack of help. By encouraging parents to sign up as volunteers, you can plan to do a variety of activities for both older and younger students that will enhance their learning! Parents can volunteer to:

- Help out with class projects/events
- Be a guest speaker
- Tutor students
- Chaperone field trips

Remember, a parent who volunteers is doing so because they know it is important. However, their time is just as valuable as ours and they don't want it wasted. Have a list of duties or items you want completed ready for those parents who come ready to volunteer in the classroom.

Also, remember that no matter how often you see a parent, it is vital to refrain from chatting and sharing information about other students in the classroom. Not only is it bad form, but it can backfire and cause an extremely difficult situation for everyone.

Offering a Helping Hand

One of the ways you can ask for parents to help is with classroom projects and events. Most parents will be happy to come to your classroom as long as they are doing something meaningful. Try asking for help in monitoring lab activities, science fair projects, historical/cultural bazaars, and learning centers.

When a parent comes to help, be prepared for them. Explain the project and what you'd like for them to do with the students. Think of it as a job description. The parent is arriving with no prior knowledge and needs to be instructed as to his or her duties while in the classroom. If the parent arrives and finds himself simply hanging around because you aren't sure what you want him to do, you can kiss your volunteer good-bye. That parent will probably never volunteer in your classroom again. Create a checklist of skills and/or activities you'd like the parent to monitor.

Guest Speaker

Parents can be an excellent source of expertise that you can use to teach your students. Consider asking for volunteers to be a guest speaker or demonstrator in your classroom. You never know which parent may be a writer, artist, musician, practical mathematician (architect, construction, etc.), or scientist. Ask if they would be will to share their expertise with the class.

Be sure when hosting a guest speaker (any guest speaker) to offer a warm and welcoming environment. There are several ways you can do this:

- Greet them at the door of the school.
- Have a student greet them.
- Have a badge ready for them with their name and occupation
- Offer a drink and simple snacks in the lounge area before heading to the classroom.
- Prepare students with appropriate questions to ask the speaker.
- Have a thank you card ready to give them before they leave.
- Write a second thank you note and mail it to them the following day.
- Have students write a thank you note to them.

Idea Share

Draw from the strengths of all parents to enhance learning in the classroom. For example, you might have a Spanish speaking parent demonstrate tortilla making to enhance a discussion about life in an early Texas Mission. Their child can translate for the parent making them a team! This will help both the parent and child feel proud that they can contribute to the learning experience!

Tutoring

How many of us have thought, *If only I had the time to work with _____ one on one?* Why not use parent volunteers to help tutor students? Encourage your parents to volunteer once a week or even once a month as a tutor in your classroom. You may even be able to get working parents involved with tutoring if they work for a business that encourages community service. Some parents will not want to volunteer as a tutor because they are unsure of their own skills. You can encourage parents to become tutors in the following ways:

- Ask for help in specific areas. For example, "I need someone to read to a student one on one."

- Give a specific time amount, but be flexible as to when the parent can come. "I need someone to help for 30 minutes on Mondays."

- Give the parent tutor answers to the questions.

- Arrange for the parent and student to use a quiet corner in the library, PTA room, or conference room.

- When you see a need, make a general announcement through the newsletter, bulletin board, or by calling parents you think might be able to help.

Administrative Assistant

There are many parents who are willing to help out the teacher in any way they can. This may include stuffing weekly envelopes to go home with elementary students or copying handouts for the upcoming week. The parents who volunteer their time to help out with these necessary but time-consuming tasks are so important! They are helping you to create and maintain the learning environment through their efforts. What are some other ways you might use an Administrative Assistant?

- Laminating and cutting out materials

- Setting up bulletin boards

- Rearranging/Straightening/Organizing the Classroom Library

- Typing up the parent newsletter

- Copying administrative/management forms to use in the classroom

- Organizing classroom materials

Parent Volunteer Form

Dear Parents,

It is our firm belief that when schools and parents work together, our students are more successful. We want to establish a partnership with you this year in order to better service your child. Part of this partnership is parent involvement in the school. Research shows that when parents are actively involved in the school, students attain higher levels of success. We would like to invite you to be a part of our school in whatever way you feel you can. Please complete the following form and return it to your child's homeroom teacher so that we can better know how you would like to be involved. Thank you!

_____Class Parties

_____Field Trips

_____Tutor in:

        Reading_____   Math _____   Science_____

_____Library

_____Main Office

_____Special Classroom Events

_____Monitor stations/learning centers

_____School Fair/Bazaar

_____Guest Speaker

_____Teacher Assistant (copying, cuting, laminating, etc.)

_____Other: _____

_____

We sincerely appreciate all you do to help your child have a successful school career and look forward to working with you this year!

Sincerely,

Conclusion

In reading this chapter, we can see that parent involvement is vital to student success. Research shows us that students who have actively involved parents are higher achievers in school. They cause fewer behavior problems and are more engaged in school activities. It is vital to develop a working partnership with parents throughout the school year. This cannot occur without some time and effort on the part of the teacher.

Be sure to call parents regularly from the first week of school and throughout the year. Ask parents to offer their perspective. After all, they know the child much better at this point than you do! Keep parents informed of what is happening in the classroom. Regularly ask for volunteers to read and work with student groups, or utilize parents as guest speakers. Whatever tools you use, be sure to keep up constant communication with parents to help ensure student success.

Questions to Ponder

What is my philosophy of parent communication and parent partnerships? Why?

What are several ways I keep parents informed about classroom events and activities? Is there any way I could improve my methods?

How do I currently encourage and maintain two-way communication between myself and parents?

What parent communication systems do I already have in place? How successful is each strategy? What are some ways in which I could improve these systems?

Additional Resources

ABC's of Effective Parent Communication
by Dyan Hershman and Emma McDonald

Home-School Relations: Working Successfully with Parents and Families
By M. L. Fuller and G. Olsen

How to Deal with Parents Who are Angry, Troubled, Afraid, or Just Plain Crazy
by Elaine McEwan

Teachers' Messages for Report Cards
by M. McDonald

Developing Cross-Cultural Competence: A Guide for Working with Children and Their Families, 2nd Edition
E.W. Lynch & M.J. Hason (Editors)

The Professional
Teacher

Being a part of the teaching profession is a noble act. As teachers we have a profound impact on our society as a whole. In shaping young minds, we influence many lives and guide the learning of our future leaders. This being said, it is important for teachers to be positive role models in schools and in the community. The way we are perceived by those around us influence whether we are considered part of a profession or just glorified babysitters.

As Vivian Troen and Katherine Boles so eloquently state in their book, *Who's Teaching Your Children?:*

> "...teaching is a complex skill that requires specialized training. Once we understand that teaching is much more than simply conveying information from one person to another, certain truths begin to emerge, and persistent myths disappear." (p. 148)

Teachers can have an impact on how we are percieved by society if we all make a concerted effort to demonstrate our professionalism.

Being a professional teacher requires:

- Dedication through extra effort and time
- Professional appearance and demeanor
- Positive interpersonal skills
- Working collaboratively with other educators
- Mentoring others
- Continuing professional education throughout career
- Resourcefulness and flexibility

This chapter is designed to be a "refresher" course for being a professional each and every day. Most of these tips and ideas are common knowledge. However, there are those times when being so deeply "in the trenches" we forget about many of these basics.

Dedication

Teaching Is Not An 8 to 3 Job

Although we can get tired, stressed out, and often "brain dead," by 3:00, we must remember that while students may be dismissed, our job is not finished. As we all know, it takes time outside of school hours to organize and manage the classroom, plan lessons, develop positive relationships with parents, work collaboratively with school staff, and attend professional development sessions. We have a heavy load. After all, our mission is educating our future leaders. Just remember that other business professionals also must work late night hours and attend continuing education courses. This extra effort simply maintains our goal to be viewed as professionals.

Dedication Means:

- Participating in meetings
- Tutoring after school
- Joining committees
- Calling parents

- Attending school events
- Staying after school to plan
- And more!

Maintaining a Professional Appearance and Demeanor

Being a professional includes maintaining a certain type of appearance and demeanor. Think about other professionals in the world. Generally they are sharply dressed and use appropriate language for their field. When seeing a doctor or lawyer, you expect a certain level of speech and attire. When that does not occur, do you still feel confident in that person's abilities? Now apply that to how others in the community view you as a professional educator.

Attire

Primary and special area teachers, who are on the floor half the time, must wear practical clothes, not a 3-piece business suit. But what kind of image does baggy shirts and stretch pants present to students, parents, and other members of the local community? This is something we all must consider when trying to show our professionalism.

"Remember, everything you say and do reflects upon your professionalism."

Demeanor

The language we use with students, parents, and other educators helps to define us as professionals. Use care when talking. Be aware that others are responding to your level of dialogue. Before you get ready to say something, think through what you plan to say before you say it. This will help keep you from making serious communication mistakes.

Demeanor is also the way in which you carry yourself. Good posture (ie - standing up straight, personal grooming, etc.), all play a part in whether or not you appear professional. Below are some tips for maintaining a professional demeanor.

- Refrain from using slang
- Be aware of your body language and facial expressions
- Be diplomatic in your relations with other colleagues, students, and parents

Interpersonal Skills

Our interactions with others can be either positive or negative depending on our interpersonal skills. Look at the tips below to help you have positive relationships with your colleagues.

√ Be respectful to all school staff including office staff, maintenance staff, paraprofessionals, and others.

√ Acknowledge the enthusiasm of newer teachers and be willing to try something new, even if you don't agree with them.

√ When implementing innovative strategies, be prepared to support your ideas with appropriate background reading and research.

√ Be considerate of others.
- Inform other school staff when utilizing school resources, going on field trips, holding an assembly.
- Always ask before taking supplies or using resources.
- Don't make assumptions.

√ When working with others, be diplomatic in making suggestions or sharing ideas.

> **For example,** If another teacher leads the planning of a lesson and you want to input your ideas, you could say, "What do you think about (insert idea)?"

"Remember, approaching a situation with a humble and agreeable tone is more effective than being confrontational."

© 2004 McDonald and Hershman

Collaboration with Others

As part of the school community, you are working with other professionals. Collaboration is not only important because it makes your job easier, but it also benefits the students. You know the saying, "Two minds are better than one." Whether you are working as a mentor, with other veteran teachers, a special area instructor, or the office staff, it is beneficial for all to engage in a sharing of ideas and resources.

Become a part of the School Culture and Community

√ Team teach with other veteran teachers

Once again, we feel that Vivian Troen and Katherine Boles have accurately described the importance of team teaching in the school. Here is what they have to say:

> "Numerous studies conducted both in the United States and in other countries, notably China and Japan, have shown that teachers become more proficient by continually working on curriculum, demonstration lessons, and assessments together. Research shows that not only does working in teams improve the practice of teaching; it also eliminates the isolation inherent in most teachers' work lives." (p. 150)

√ Attend school events to show support

Being a part of the school community means being visible at school events. Students and parents want to see you actively involved. They are invested in their neighborhood school and want to know that you are part of the community. Additionally, students love it when you show up for their art shows, science fairs, sports events, carnivals, etc..

Teacher Talk

"As fifth grade teachers, there were just the two of us and both new to the grade level. In order to help our students and each other, we chose to team teach the majority of the year. Each week we planned our lessons together, and often taught together as well. We gathered the students into one room and presented the lesson as a team. One would be at the front giving information, while the other was monitoring students, providing one-on-one help and interjecting timely and insightful comments throughout the lesson. In this way, we were both teaching and students were getting the benefit of two different perspectives and experiences. Whenever we covered a topic that was my expertise, I taught the majority of the lesson. Alternatively, my partner taught the topics/concepts that were her forté. Our students really enjoyed the banter between the two of us and often told us it was more exciting to learn this way."

√ Participate in vertical planning teams

Due to the isolation often experienced by teachers, student learning can become disjointed between grade levels. Therefore, many schools have implemented Vertical Planning Teams to build consistency from one year to the next.

Example: Second grade teachers and third grade teachers meet together to determine benchmarks (where students need to be at the end of the year/ skills learned) for student progress.

Additionally, it is helpful for students when teachers agree on certain terminology to use in different subject areas.

Example: Students are exposed to the term "pre-writing" from Kindergarten as a means for brainstorming and gathering ideas. This same term is used throughout their schooling.

√ Participate in other school committees

Working with others as a team in a committee situation helps us network with other teachers in the school and build a camaraderie. There are times when we may feel that being a part of a committee is just another item added to our already large workload. Think of this as a type of "break" from the usual routine of re-tying wet shoelaces, wiping off tears, and redirecting behavior. All day you are surrounded by children or adolescents. When do you have time to be part of an adult group?

√ Working with other Special Areas teachers and para- professionals

When planning lessons, be sure to include your special area teachers such as Art, Music, PE, Special Education, and ESL. Why? Their input can be valuable for student learning as well as to make connections for students between subject areas. Additionally, these teachers are fantastic sources of expertise in their field and can provide you with ideas, support, and resources.

For example, when studying the continent of Africa, you might approach the Art teacher to do a unit on African masks. Also, the music teacher could provide different types of music from that culture.

"As the parent of a non-sighted child, I have seen the value of teachers working together for the benefit of my son. The classroom teacher plans lessons with the speech teacher and the VI (Visually Impaired) teacher to make sure that my son can take part in the fun and exciting lessons going on in the pre-school classroom.

Although the regular teacher is wonderful, the special area teachers can offer specific ideas to make the lessons more meaningful for my son. For example, the class planted seeds in a garden one day. The VI teacher knew that my son wouldn't like to touch the dirt. Although he still participated, they also did an edible garden as an extension. Pudding and oreo cookies became the dirt, with jelly beans as the seeds. He certainly didn't mind touching and using food! This really made the lesson come alive for my son, and the other kids loved it too!

As a parent, this type of collaborative effort really impresses me!"

-Dyan

√ Working as a Mentor

By being a mentor you have a profound impact, not only on the new teachers, but on the education system as a whole. Why do we say this? Because as a mentor you have the ability to shape a new educator into an effective teacher over the course of one or more years. This means that you also impact all of their students. Wow! What a legacy you can leave on the world! Just think of how many lives you can touch with each year that you act as a mentor.

This sounds like quite a daunting task, but supporting new teachers is not as challenging as you may think. The key is to take everything step-by-step rather than all at once. By offering advice and training in small spurts throughout the year, the beginning educator is better able to absorb and apply this new knowledge.

> **For example**, it is better to discuss report cards sometime during the fourth week of school rather than overwhelming the new teacher with this information right before school starts.

Your role as a mentor is an important one. Most new teachers feel overwhelmed by the reality facing them when they enter their very own classroom. They have not been trained in the practical day-to-day operations, and flounder at the first sign of trouble. As the experienced educator, you have the opportunity to create a confident successful teacher.

4 A's of Mentoring

According to the National Mentoring Partnership, most of what a mentor provides falls into the four areas mentioned below. Please keep these in mind and communicate this information to your mentee.

Source: *Carol J. Carter, The Key, Spring 2002*

Advice: Mentors can offer *advice* to help the new teacher evaluate their options and make better choices.

Access: Mentors can give new teachers *access* to a world of ideas and experiences. They can include their mentee into their own network of friends and colleagues.

Advocacy: Depending on your relationship, the mentor can work as an *advocate*. That is, the mentor can speak up for their mentee in important situations.

Accountability: Mentors help new teachers stay true to their goals by holding them *accountable*. They can check and evaluate the progress made by the new teacher and give helpful feedback.

Guidelines for Mentors

✓   Refrain from being judgmental in your actions and comments to the new teacher.

✓   Ask guiding and specific questions rather than "umbrella" questions such as "How is your week going?" or "How are you doing?"

Specific kinds of questions might include:

- •   What did you like about the first day?
- •   Have you had any contact with parents?
- •   Are your students meeting your classroom expectations?
- •   Do you feel you are maintaining control with your class?

✓   Do not be afraid to offer suggestions, but don't be offended if they are not used immediately. It may not be that the new teacher thinks your ideas are bad, but they may be too overwhelmed to make any changes at that point.

✓   Being a buddy is fine, but it shouldn't be your only goal as a mentor.

✓   Give information and ideas in small amounts and at appropriate times.

✓   When observing new teachers, be ready to provide an immediate positive comment and one area that needs improvement. Save the rest for your "debriefing" session.

✓   Allow the new teacher to listen to some of your initial parent phone calls and/ or sit in on one of your parent conferences as a "team-member." This allows them to see how you handle different situations and builds their comfort level.

✓   When going over paperwork, be ready to fill out an example with the new teacher.

✓   Offer a time for the new teacher to observe you on a regular day or class period. Talk to the principal and have them set up someone to cover the new teacher's class during that time.

✓   Take your role seriously. Use the time with your mentee in a constructive manner. Don't give in to the temptation to simply gossip.

✓   Be ready to provide constructive criticism when necessary. As with anyone, always start out with a positive comment first.

✓   Help the new teacher get acquainted and involved with other faculty members.

Additional Resource: National Mentoring Partnership - www.mentoring.org

The Practice of Reflection

The concept of journaling is something we stress to our students. We use the journal as a way to help them become better writers. But for years journals, or diaries, have been used as a way of recording daily thoughts. These diaries, while sometimes a simple recollection of what was done each day, are often a self-reflection. This is evident in those diaries of famous persons who have been published into books. They offer us a way to understand how a particular person thought. We are able to see their stream of conciousness in print. What about us? As teachers, is reflection an important part of teaching?

When you start thinking about it, you may realize that you are already reflecting each day. Do you mentally make a note of what works and what doesn't in each class? Do you try to implement a change to your plans for the next class? At the end of each class period, do you briefly think back over what worked and what didn't in that particular class as a whole? Do you then use that information to mentally adjust your attitude, plans, and approach for the next class? Informal reflecting like this is a continual process for many teachers. But what happens at the end of the day when school is over and everyone has gone home? How can we make full use of the reflections we do each day?

Catch yourself thinking. Whenever you have a thought about the way your lesson or activity is proceeding, jot them down on your lesson plan or on a separate sheet of paper. At the end of the day, label the paper for easy identification later and staple it to your original lesson plan.

If you work in a teaming situation where you and one or more teachers work together teaching the same or related lessons (interdisciplinary units, etc.), be sure to do some reflection together each day or each week. Find out how the lesson went for the other teachers. Did they approach it differently than you? Was their approach more or less successful? The purpose is not to compare teaching styles in order to judge, but to determine the most successful way to help your particular group of students. This will often change from year to year.

Keep a journal. When we write down our thoughts and feelings, we are better able to analyze them. I know that when I write about a situation or problem I face in the classroom, I am better able to think through it. Later I can go back and follow the flow of my thoughts. This especially helps when I feel frustrated but cannot identify the problem. Often I am better able to pinpoint the exact issue through my writing.

Writing can also help us clarify our thoughts and feelings on different topics. We work from nebulous thoughts to a concrete statement of what we believe. Once these ideas are solidified in our own head, then we are able to clearly communicate them to others.

If you are not in the habit of keeping a journal, start small. Try to write for five or ten minutes right after your students have left so that everything is still fresh in your mind. Make it a part of your daily schedule so that it becomes a habit. Reflection, both informal and formal, helps us to both understand and improve our teaching practice. This is vital for effective teaching and learning to take place in the classroom.

Professional Development

It is important for teachers to continually increase their knowledge about effective teaching practices to implement in the classroom. This new knowledge is often gained through staff development either within the school or from outside sources. For those of us who have been in the profession for a while, we come to think of staff development as torture equal to any medieval stretching machine. However, staff development should be a time of professional growth and continuing education. Here are some things you can do to turn a potential waste of time into a valuable learning experience.

Take the Learning into Your Own Hands

Remember that YOU are the one who needs to benefit from this information. Come to the session with an open mind and a willingness to learn. Just as our students need to be open to what we teach them, so should we be open to what others have to teach us. You never know what jewel of an idea or strategy that you may discover. Remember that this is life-long learning.

Do Not Bring Anything Else to Do

Although you run the risk of being bored, take a chance and be proactive in your learning. If you don't bring any other tasks with you to the workshop, you won't be tempted to start working on them when the presenter is speaking. It is difficult to listen and learn when your mind is focused on other tasks. While others may be grading papers, looking over lesson plans, or some other task, ask yourself, *"Are they missing out on potential ideas for their classroom?"*

"Attitude can be infectious, whether positive or negative. How do you want to influence others?"

Request Meaningful Activities and Information

Before the workshop begins, speak with the presenter and request that they give practical ways to apply and implement the information throughout their presentation rather than all at the end or only in a handout. If you let the person in charge know what you are looking for ahead of time, he/she may be able to adapt the presentation to meet your requests.

Don't Be Afraid to Ask Questions

Go ahead and speak up. If something is confusing to you, raise your hand and ask for clarification. The workshop will not do you any good if you sit through half of it confused. Most likely if you are confused, several others are too. Also, ask for examples of how strategies presented would work in the classroom. Don't wait until the end to ask your questions, but instead ask when the question is pertinent.

Go With a Positive Attitude

We are always saying this to our students and it applies to us as well. If you walk into a staff development with a poor attitude and no intention of learning anything, then you will have a wasted day. If, however, you walk in with an open mind and positive attitude, you just may get several great ideas to use during the school year. I find that sometimes I get ideas, not only from the workshop itself, but also from casual conversations or side conversations happening during the workshop.

Encourage Others Around You to Maintain a Positive Outlook

We all know teachers who prefer to sit in the back and complain about the workshop before it even begins. This negative attitude can infect everyone around that person which causes a chain reaction through the room. Instead of responding to a negative comment with a negative comment of your own, try to infect that person with your positive attitude. You might try pointing out something positive for each negative comment that is said. If all else fails, move to another seat so that you are not distracted.

Provide Specific Constructive Feedback to Presenters

If the workshop still ends up making it on your "worst" list, let those in charge know why it was a complete bust. Don't forget to start out with one or two positive comments first. Be sure to offer a couple of suggestions for correcting the problems. Sometimes those who are presenting staff development forget how to be good teachers. Your comments may help someone else have a great staff development in the future. Who knows, perhaps one day you'll find yourself presenting to a group of teachers and will appreciate helpful feedback from them.

Idea Share

If you have questions during a presentation, but don't feel it is appropriate to interrupt the speaker, write them down on an index card. Then, when the time is right, you will have not forgotten what you were planning to ask.

This strategy can also be used with comments or ideas of your own that you wish to share with others around you. Write them down, and then at a break in the presentation, feel free to share.

Resourcefulness and Flexibility

Teaching is a profession of constant change and movement. At a moment's notice a school-wide assembly may be called, interrupting an important lesson. Additionally, students are often unpredictable in their thoughts and actions which means that you need to be prepared to handle a myriad of situations. Being flexible also means being able to utilize resources on hand and go-with-the flow when necessary.

> *For example*: If the Art teacher is ten minutes late letting your kids in her room, what are you going to do with them standing out in the hallway? This calls for flexibility and resourcefulness. What quiet instructional activity can you do to keep students occupied? Also, how are you going to spend your planning period now that you have ten minutes less of it?
>
> If a Pep-rally or other type of assembly is called at the last minute, how will that affect your lesson plans? What will you require of your students to make up for this loss? Will you rearrange your plans to compensate?

Situations like the ones above (and others) can cause serious frustration and stress. A teacher's professional life is full of stressful events. In talking about stress, we recently attended a professional workshop where the presenter stated, "Stress makes you stupid." What he meant was that when you are working in stress mode, you are not performing at your optimum level. Below are some "Stress Busters" and other strategies to help you along.

Take Time Outs

We give our students time outs when they need a break to cool off and get back on task. Why not give yourself one every now and then? When you are feeling a little hot under the collar and are ready to strangle somebody for something...anything... that's the moment you need to take a time out.

"Like a tree, bend with the wind. Try not to snap."

Turn away from the situation, go out into the hallway, and collect yourself. You'll find that even with a small amount of distance, your blood pressure will lower, and you will have a fresh look at the situation.

Take Time for You

Our life is not meant to be spent inside grading papers all the time! You need to take some time for yourself. Leave those papers at school at least one night a week and treat yourself to something fun. Go see a movie, attend a happy hour, cruise the mall, or get to the gym. There is more to life than teaching and, let me tell you, there will always be more papers to grade.

Set a Goal, then Pamper Yourself

Set a goal for yourself such as, "I'll plan lessons for next week." Then, when you've reached your goal, pamper yourself! Treat yourself to a relaxing bath, a nice dinner out, or a great dessert. Although these are things you should be doing for yourself every now and again anyway, you might feel better about doing them if you know you've accomplished at least one goal.

> **Teacher Talk**
>
> *" I've always made it a priority to take one day off a week from my usual after-school, into the night, working-like-a-dog, routine. Most of the time I go to the local movie theater and watch a bargain matinee. As a movie buff, this is a real treat for me and helps me remember that there IS life in the world outside of school."*

5 Minute Exercises

If you are feeling exceptionally stressed, try some of these 5 minutes exercises:

- Count slowly to ten. Breathe deeply in on the odd numbers, and breathe out on the even numbers.

- Tighten your body from head to toe. Then, slowly relax the muscles in your body starting with the toes and working your way up the neck and shoulder muscles.

- Do a few small circular muscle stretches with your wrists, ankles, and neck.

- Close your eyes and imagine a place where you feel happy and relaxed. Keep that image in your mind when you are stressed.

- A moment of meditation goes a long way towards serenity.

Working in Difficult Situations

There may be times where you are faced with a difficult situation while working with your colleagues and administrators. This can be very stressful. Whether it is a personality conflict or differing attitudes about teaching practices, it is in your best interest to maintain a professional demeanor.

- Be diplomatic. *"You can catch more flies with honey than vinegar."*
- Work to solve problems through mediation and compromise.
- Respect the experience and knowledge of other teachers and/or the administrator even if you don't agree with their strategies.
- Be humble when approaching and working with others.
- Keep open lines of communication with that person. Don't let assumptions build to further damage the situation. In other words, don't let a spark of anger turn into a raging inferno.

Conclusion

Upon reading this chapter we can conclude that teaching is a stressful, intense, unpredictable and difficult job. Teaching carries a heavy burden. However, with the right attitude, level of dedication and coping strategies at your fingertips, teaching is also the most rewarding career in the world! For the same reasons that make it hard, it is also exciting, challenging, and fun! Teaching is never dull. It is a wonderful career made all the better with a positive attitude.

Additionally, when we act as education professionals, we change the public's view of teaching. Since the early 1900's teachers have often been viewed as nothing more than "glorified babysitters." It is time to change this perception and it is up to us to change it! Remember, the more we act like professionals, the more we will be treated as such by others.

Questions to Ponder

Do you feel you come across as a professional to others? Why or why not? What are some ways you could help others see you as a professional?

Think about the way you relate to others. What are some positive and negative reactions you've experienced when working with other people? What kinds of changes might you make to your interpersonal skills to receive more positive reactions than negative?

Do you think collaboration among teachers is important? Do you collaborate with others in the school?

What is your attitude towards professional development workshops? How does this attitude affect your ability to learn and apply new information? What are some ways you can be sure to get the most out of a professional development workshop?

Additional Resources

Who's Teaching Your Children?
by Vivian Troen and Katherine C. Boles

Making Teaching a True Profession
by J. D. Saphier

Notes/Reflection on the Chapter

REFERENCES

N. Atwell, *In the Middle: Writing, Reading, and Learning with Adolescents*, (Upper Montclair: Boynton/Cook, 1987).

D. Baumrind, *Child care practices anteceding three patterns of preschool behavior* (Genetic Psychology Monographs, 75, 43-88, 1967).

U. Bronfenbrenner, *Is early intervention effective? Facts and principles of early intervention: a summary* (in Early Experience: Myth and Evidence. London: Open Books, 1976).

P. Cunningham and R.L. Allington, *Classrooms That Work: They can ALL Read and Write*, (New York: HarperCollins, 1994).

J. Dobson, *Bringing Up Boys*, (Wheaton: Tyndale House Publishers, Inc., 2001).

H. Gardner, *Multiple Intelligences: Theory Into Practice*. (Basic Books, 1993).

H. Gardner, *The Unschooled Mind*, (Basic Books, 1993).

W. Glasser, *Choice Theory in the Classroom*, (New York: HarperCollins, 1988).

Hacker & Barden, *Living with Technology*, (Albany: Delmar, 1988).

D. Hershman and E. McDonald, *ABC's of Effective Parent Communication*, (Dallas: Inspiring Teachers Publishing, Inc., 2000).

V. Hildebrand, *Knowing and Serving Diverse Families*, (Columbus: Merrill, an imprint of Prentice Hall, 1996).

W.M. Fawcett-Hill, *Learning Thru Discussion*, (Beverly Hills: SAGE, 1986).

E. Jensen, *Teaching with the Brain in Mind*, (Washington D.C.: ASCD, 1988).

S. Kovalik, *Integrated Thematic Instruction: The Model (3rd Ed.)*, (Village of Oak Creek: Books for Educators, 1997).

R. McConkey, *Working with Parents: A Practical Guide for Teachers and Therapists*, (Cambridge: Brookline Books, 1985).

K. Olsen, *Synergy*, (Village of Oak Creek: Books for Educators, 1998).

S. Swap, *Enhancing Parent Involvement in Schools*. (New York: Teachers College Press, 1987)

V. Troen and K. Boles, *Who's Teaching Your Children?: Why the Teacher Crisis is Worse than You Think and What Can be Done about It*. (New Haven: Yale University Press, 2003)

Maps, Charts, Graphs, and Diagrams, (Teacher Created Materials, Inc., 1990).

INDEX

Inspiring Teachers Quick Order Form

Fax orders: 972-495-2702. Send this form.

Telephone orders: Call 1-877-496-7633 toll free. Have your credit card ready.

 Internet orders: http://www.inspiringteachers.com/catalog/index.html Have your credit card ready.

Postal orders: Inspiring Teachers, 2510 Meadowridge Dr., Garland, TX 75044, USA

Products Available - View our online catalog at http://www.inspiringteachers.com/catalog/index.html

BOOKS
Survival Kit for New Teachers - $36.95
Survival Kit for New Secondary Teachers - $36.95
ABC's of Effective Parent Communication - $19.95
Classroom Reflections: A Journal for Teachers - $14.95

Classroom Materials/Gifts
Yacker Tracker Traffic Light - $39.95
TAG Attention Getter - $18.95
Teacher Therapy CD - $15.00
Teacher Therapy Tape - $10.00

Please send the following products:

Quantity	Item	Unit Cost	Total

Please send more FREE information on:

☐ Staff Development Workshops

Name: _____

Address: _____

City: _____ State: _____ Zip: _____

Telephone: _____

email address: _____

Sales tax: Please add 8.25% for products shipped to Texas addresses.

Shipping
U.S.: 15% of the total order. Order 4 or more, 10% of total. Order 10 or more, 5% of total.
International: Same as above plus $15.00 to cover International shipping charges.

Payment: ☐Check   Credit Card: ☐Visa   ☐ MC   ☐Amex

Card Number:_____   Exp. Date: _____

Signature:_____   Billing Zip Code:_____

About the Authors

Emma McDonald and Dyan Hershman, experienced classroom teachers and educational consultants from Texas, are known for their unique teaching strategies and techniques that motivate both teachers and students. Going beyond theories, these educators provide proven practical strategies to help teachers improve student learning. McDonald and Hershman have worked with and educated both children and adults over the past fifteen years. Currently, both mentor new teachers and work as Consultants with the Teacher Certification & Preparation Program for the Region 10 Education Service Center. Their strategies have been featured in Instructor Magazine, Classroom Connect, and other quality education magazines, and have been widely used by both new and veteran teachers. McDonald and Hershman now share their "tools" for success with educators all across the United States. They are well-known for their motivational, positive, practical, and energetic presentation style which inspires and encourages both new and veteran teachers.

About the Publisher

We are a teacher created and owned business, dedicated to empowering and inspiring teachers, creating quality learner-centered classrooms, and improving student success!

Our mission is to empower teachers with effective teaching strategies through resources and support services.

We believe a well-prepared teacher is an effective teacher.

We believe that teachers who are given the right resources and support will stay in the classroom and make education a life-long career. This is important for our schools, our students, and our communities.

OUR SERVICES AND RESOURCES:

We provide many different services and resources to help new teachers. Learn more about these resources on our website at **www.inspiringteachers.com** .

Books

- Survival Kit for New Teachers
- Survival Kit for New Secondary Teachers
- ABC's of Effective Parent Communication
- Mr. Tim's Tips for New Teachers
- Classroom Reflections: A Journal for Teachers

Website - Free Resources - www.inspiringteachers.com

- Tips, Articles, Inspirations, Recommended books and websites - updated monthly
- Ask a Mentor
- Professional Development - Book Studies, Links to additional resources
- Classroom Resources - Links to books and websites that are content related
- Classroom ToolKit - Gradebook and communication tool for students and parents
- Classroom Websites - Create a classroom or teacher website
- Teacher Preparation - Resources and links for becoming a teacher and getting a job
- Community - Email discussion lists and message boards to network with others
- Idea Share - A place to share great lesson ideas
- Mentor and Administrator Resources - articles and tips for working with new teachers (in progress)
- Teacher Trainer Resources - articles and tips for teacher preparation (in progress)
- NABT - National Association for Beginning Teachers (partnership)

Staff Development

- New Teacher Preparation
- Tools for Classroom Success
- Reading & Writing Across the Curriculum
- Student Assessment: Strategies and Ideas that Go Beyond Testing

Notes

Notes

Notes

Fall 2006 : BBd - world outline, plot locales from lit set rdg
w/ flag containing basic info; "treasure chest" card
file w/ add. info.

Games (thinking)

p.249   ideas to tie lit. books to geo/ss skills   p.253 FunBrain.com

p.251   "mini" concept bds (tri-fold)

p.251   "story bd." drawings for pre-write "how-to" essay

p.252   "round robin" activities for writing, SS, math, etc.

p.254   The Important Book : true statements

p.257   "Cube It" - applying Bloom's Taxonomy   p.265 Modify work: cross out or highlight

p.257   Poems for S.S., etc.   p.267-269 ESL considerations

p.258   Paper Bag Activities

p.258   Uses for Quotes !!   p.100 Modified Grading Scale

p.259   Paper Bags for celebrating birthdays - do @ 1st of yr.

p.259   "Mini-research" - bbd ?? cards to post (so many per quarter or month)?

p.260   Spelling Bee Basketball + Spelling Bee Race

p.260   Sentence Strips

p.261   True/False Statements

p.261   Underlining Parts of Speech

p.262   Learning Vine

p.262   Vacation Brochure : integrated activity -
                - plot latitude/longitude
                - mileage ; gas cost ; lodging; food, etc.
        Give set location for group activity
        Indiv. act : stud. determine location

✱ p.263
   After School Possibility : Walkabout Activity

p.263   X small or X large pieces of paper for variety

p.264   Yard - Go Outside !

p.264   Zoom In - on a detail + research or expand !

p.277   "About the Author" writing activity

p.279 + 280   Websites

p.321   Classroom website - available to all teachers
              (free)